A GUIDE TO
BALTIMORE
ARCHITECTURE

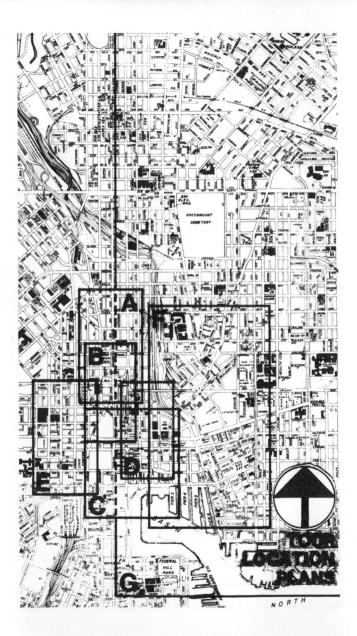

A

B

C

D

E

F

G

GREENMOUNT
CEMETERY

FEDERAL
HILL
PARK

TOUR
LOCATION
PLANS

NORTH

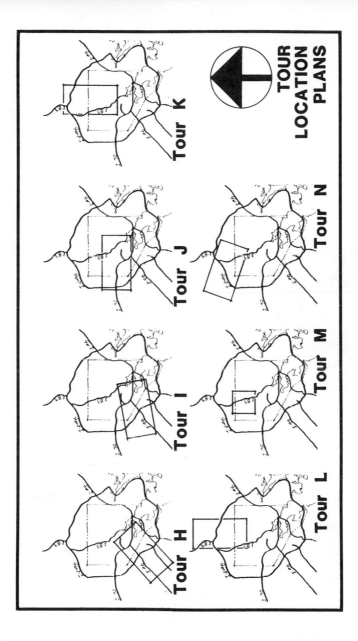

A GUIDE TO BALTIMORE ARCHITECTURE

Second Edition
Revised and Enlarged

By John Dorsey
and
James D. Dilts

Foreword by John Dos Passos
Introductions by Wilbur Harvey Hunter
and Alexander S.Cochran

 TIDEWATER PUBLISHERS

Centreville, Maryland

Copyright © 1981 by Tidewater Publishers

Cover photograph © 1981 by Marty Katz

Library of Congress Cataloging in Publication Data

Dorsey, John R   1938-
  A guide to Baltimore architecture.

  Includes index.
  1. Architecture—Maryland—Baltimore—Guide-books.
2. Baltimore—Buildings—Guide-books.   I.   Dilts,
James D., 1936-   joint author.   II.   Title.
NA735.B3D67   1981   917.52′60443   80-27243
ISBN 0-87033-272-4

Manufactured in the United States of America
First edition, 1973; Second edition, 1981

Contents

Acknowledgments

The first edition of this guide appeared in 1973. At that time, we stated that our purpose in writing it was to interest visitors and residents alike in Baltimore's architecture, and that while the book was primarily for the layman, we hoped that the expert (whether architect, critic, or scholar) might find it useful as well. In preparing this second edition our aims have remained the same, but over the past seven years Baltimore has changed considerably. The most noticeable change, as every Baltimorean knows, has taken place in the area around the inner harbor, where a vast renovation project which was just beginning to take shape a decade ago has now progressed to the point at which it is a magnet, as well as a symbol of renewal, for the whole city. But much else has happened, too: a considerable amount of building elsewhere in the city and its environs (some of it good), and some unfortunate destruction—though the city's consciousness of its heritage continues to grow, thanks in no small part to Baltimore's Commission for Historical and Architectural Preservation and its dedicated staff.

Accordingly, we felt that merely to reprint the original guide with a few additions would be a disservice both to our readers and to the city. With much expert help, we have reviewed the book from beginning to end, both to correct errors and to take advantage of recent scholarship. We added thirty-six buildings and deleted six, for a net gain of thirty. These buildings have been incorporated into the tours, and new maps have been drawn to include them. The North Charles Street tour, however, became so long that we split it into two, adding the Beltway tour for a new total of fourteen. Another new feature of the book is a section of capsule biographies of architects formerly active in the city; for obvious reasons, we decided not to include any living architects in this section.

We are indebted to many people for their aid on one or both editions of this book. The late John Dos Passos graciously contributed a foreword to the first edition which though it is by now in a few respects out of date, is reprinted here exactly as written. To tamper with it would have involved the risk of doing an injustice to the tone which Mr. Dos Passos achieved. Mr. W. Hunter's introductory essay, which deals with the history of the city's architecture down to about 1900, also stands. Mr. Cochran has reviewed and updated his essay on the city's more recent architecture.

The authors had the benefit of informed advice from an advisory board of architects and architectural historians which included Mr. Hunter (former director of the Peale Museum) and Mr.Cochran (of the architectural firm of Cochran, Stephenson, and Donkervoet), chairmen; Ian McCallum, architect and architectural historian; and architects Michael F. Trostel of Edmunds and Hyde Inc.; Orin M. Bullock, Jr.; Warren Peterson of Peterson and Brickbauer; William Boulton Kelly; Francis Jencks of Wrenn, Lewis and Jencks; and Van Fossen Schwab.

This book was published in cooperation with the Peale Museum. We are also grateful to the Peale for the use of its collections and resources. Mrs. A. Aubrey Bodine kindly gave us permission to use the A. Aubrey Bodine Photographic Collection, now at the Peale. We are also most indebted to four professional photographers, Jon-Eric Eaton, Susan T. McElhinney, Susan Iglehart, and Paul T. Raedeke, who took most of the photographs. A complete list of photo credits appears at the end of the book.

William C. Riggs drew the maps for the original edition, and the new ones for this edition. It was, to say the least, a prodigious labor in both cases, and one performed with great skill and dedication. We thank the American Automobile Association of Maryland for the use of maps upon which our maps are based.

Others who helped with the collection of materials and with advice were: the staff of the Commission for Historical and Architectural Preservation, in particular Executive Director Barbara Hoff, William J. Pencek, Jr. (now with the Maryland Historical Trust), and Fred Shoken; Christopher Weeks, of the Maryland Historical Trust; Randolph W. Chalfant, architectural historian; Morgan H. Pritchett and the staff of the Maryland Room of the Enoch Pratt Free Library; and Charles Boyles, Mrs. John Howard Eager, Mrs. Irving Neuman, Mrs. Michael E. O'Connor, Penelope Patterson and James Wollon.

We wish to thank the Baltimore chapter of the American Institute of Architects for a grant that helped underwrite the costs of photography.

Finally, we are most grateful to Richard Parsons, of the Baltimore County Public Library, who not only gave us his enthusiastic encouragement but also introduced us to our publisher.

The authors selected the buildings which are included in this guide, and needless to say are solely responsible for any errors or omissions.

J. D.
J. D. D.

Baltimore
August, 1980

The Streets of Baltimore

When I was a child, Baltimore held special eminence among the cities I knew. Baltimore, much more than Richmond or Norfolk, was the capital of the Northern Neck of Virginia, where I was more or less brought up. At our Potomac River wharf at Lynch's Point, or Cintra as my father liked to have it called, in deference to his Portuguese ancestors, we had most days a steamboat out of Baltimore and another bound for Baltimore from Washington. The stately *Three Rivers* made the round trip in two nights and a day. On the way she nosed into incredibly small creeks and tied up at a great variety of little wharves. You'd wake up in the night to hear the roustabouts laughing and singing as they unloaded guano, as we always called fertilizer in those days, or rolled bags of wheat or barley up the gangplank.

All our stores came from Baltimore and all our produce was shipped up there. It was the center of the tall tales the watermen told. To tell the truth I never saw much of the city except the dockside section as a child, because when I went through I was usually on my way to boarding school or college and was taken straight to the B&O depot. One odd little scene has stuck in my mind. My father, who was full of all sorts of curiosity, had discovered a cobbled street that still had an open sewer running down the middle of it. He exhibited it to me with some pride as an example of how people lived when he was a boy.

Up to very recent years Baltimore city was full of survivals. There was a wealth of public markets, each one with its peculiar population and lingo. Neighborhoods had a special flavor. Somehow the houses and people of Hampden didn't look the same as the houses and people around Union Square where the Mencken brothers lived. The modest calm of Govans was entirely different from the faded nineteenth-century elegance of Mount Washington with its enormous groves of trees. There was the old-time German section of Patterson Park that specialized in scrubbed white marble steps and a sort of bead curtain that I've never seen before or since in this country. These bead curtains were hung in the front doors to help keep out the flies in summer. The gaudy colored beads were strung so as to make pictures of castles on the Rhine or Niagara Falls or a lighthouse or a clipper ship in a stormy sea. Haussner's restaurant with its magnificent collection of "pompier" paintings and bronzes set the key for a whole region of East Baltimore. You may not think this sort of thing is "art" but it certainly manifests a cheering exuberance of spirit.

To this day there is still Dickeyville, a New England village encysted in a Baltimore suburb, and Castle Street where the colored hucksters stable their ponies and their spring wagons with the polished brass trim. And Little Italy. That corner of South Baltimore, in spite of the hideous false fronts that have been plastered over many of the old brick houses, still has a character of its own. Maybe it's the smell of tomato paste and garlic and parmesan cheese that filters out of the Italian restaurants. There's something special, too, about the docks in South Baltimore, particularly if there are a couple of freighters tied up with their loading lights on—vistas of the harbor through cables and anchor chains. That old-time maritime feeling is focused for me in a little restaurant on the harbor side of Pratt Street where my wife and I occasionally stop for a plate of oysters on the way to eat manicotti at Sabatino's. There are chromos of old steamships on the walls. The moment I step out of the car and sniff the sludgy harbor I feel again, just for an instant, the chill down the spine I felt as a small boy at the sight and smell of seagoing ships, the desperate urge to sail blue water.

Dundalk, way off east, with its higgledy-piggledy shacks and marinas and boatyards has a special Chesapeake Bay character—it might be Crisfield—but the culmination of the port of Baltimore, from the point of view of drama and visual excitement, is the foot of South Broadway. If you are so lucky as to see it when the bow of a large freighter towers above the street you immediately feel, as you do in some of the squares in Venice, that the stage is set for a play. Between the old market, and the Acropolis Restaurant with its bellydancers, and the steamers and the gold-splattered black lacquer of the nighttime harbor beyond, you get a concentrated impression of a seaport town. The Block might be anywhere but South Broadway is pure Baltimore.

This guide to the city won't come out a day too soon. There'll barely be time to get a look at the last vestiges of the old seaport before they are obliterated, as old-time mercantile Boston was, under concrete and speeding automobiles.

Some day the prime movers who decide our destinies may come to understand that the character of a city as a fit place for men and women to live depends on the survival of intriguing vestiges of the past. They give a city the historic dimension that, whether people are entirely conscious of it or not, imbues the inhabitants with a certain dignity they would not otherwise attain.

The ideal city would be one where, as in so many cities in Europe, samples have been preserved of all the different phases of architecture and decoration the place has gone through since the beginning. It isn't enough to do a Williamsburg on a few choice mansions. It is the modest buildings, adapted and readapted to a thousand uses, showing the special tricks of local bricklayers, peculiarities in stonework, some unusual way of setting chimneypots, that give the color of history. In the old architecture intimations of the kind of lives the citizens lived linger on.

Local and neighborhood idiosyncrasies tend to cluster about old buildings. Survivals and traditions enrich the city's life and make up somewhat for the disadvantages of overcrowding and bad air. Up to a few years ago there used to be street criers in Baltimore. Somebody probably made a recording of them but folk arts without the folk are a dreary business. Baltimore will be poorer again, when the Negro hucksters give up their spring wagons, put aside the gay harness they dress up their ponies with, and take to driving trucks.

I don't mean that Baltimore doesn't still have individuality. It has. A few years ago I drove a sharp-eyed friend around who could not ever remember having looked at the town carefully before. "Why it's a city of domes," he cried out, "a city of domes and spires."

We were looking up Mount Royal at the handsomely proportioned dome of the old synagogue of Eutaw Place. A few minutes later we stopped to look east across the Fallsway at the odd cityscape which then included the old jail at one end, the dome of Johns Hopkins Hospital in the center, and odd masses of indeterminate brick buildings, topped by an unexpected little cupola, along the ridge to the southward. The noblest of Baltimore's domes is undoubtedly Latrobe's dome which caps the original Catholic Cathedral. You see it best from a distance when you are headed west across the viaduct.

One really unique building is the Shot Tower, further south down the Jones Falls valley. Besides being an interesting reminder of an outmoded technology it is an elegant piece of brick construction. Anyone who enjoys good brickwork can study it for some time. Looking down the hill from St. Paul Street there is a marvelous view of the Shot Tower and the sparkling white semi-Palladian tower of the church of St. Vincent de Paul, framed by tall dark walls. It's the sort of thing tourists go to Bologna or San Gimignano to see. Nearby is Godefroy's Battle Monument, one of the most satisfactory pieces of urban decoration I know anywhere. From the Shot Tower, Gay Street runs obliquely towards the northeast across a dilapidated part of town. Even in decay there are inklings of the fine old mercantile street it must once have been. Up towards North Avenue on Gay Street is the American Brewery, a thoroughly entertaining example of what could be called the nineteenth-century circus style.

Mills's Washington column, given a handsome setting by the distinguished landscaping of Mount Vernon Place a good many years later, is much more than a period piece. In my opinion the combined design of the monument and the garden ranks with some of the well-planned public squares of Europe.

Roaming around Baltimore, as in most of the older American cities, you keep coming across traces of often brilliant essays at city planning. Usually the plans have been left incomplete or destroyed by the irresistible march of the commercial banal. The latest effort and the most ambitious is, of course, Charles Center. Perhaps it is too early to gauge the final effect. Hamburger's and the Mechanic Theatre seem to me all to the good, and the amusing overhead walks that take the pedestrian across the streams of traffic. There's an accomplished little square with a fountain in it near the theater; but I'm afraid the final ensemble will be irrevocably marred by a hideous new hotel and by the stolid bureaucratic bulk of the Federal Building which looks as if it had been designed by a particularly uninspired computer. "That's what you think," I hear someone saying.

Let me hasten to add that any zany notions or architecturally off-color ideas expressed in the foregoing notes are purely my own. The gentlemen who compiled this guide are in no way responsible for them. My aim was merely to whet the visitor's appetite before placing him in the hands of more competent cicerones.

John Dos Passos

December 1968

Baltimore Architecture in History

Although "Baltimore Town" was officially created by an act of the Colonial Assembly in 1729 and the original 60 acres surveyed in 1730, it was a long time before substantial buildings were erected within its precincts. In fact, the oldest surviving pre-Revolutionary War structure within the city's present boundaries is the country house Mount Clare [104], which was built without reference to the town.

In the midst of a large tobacco and wheat plantation, and facing southeast toward the Middle Branch of the Patapsco River where the farm's own wharf was situated, Mount Clare was what the Maryland country gentleman considered elegant and necessary in the l750s. Charles Carroll the Barrister, as he was called to distinguish him from other Carrolls, was familiar with the current fashions in Annapolis and undoubtedly had access to some of the many English architectural style books. We can assume that he designed the house himself, as did many another plantation owner, and it is certainly a personal variation on the standard English Georgian themes.

It is a miracle that Mount Clare should have survived two centuries when its few contemporaries in the town have vanished. After the Revolutionary War, however, Baltimore Town became an important mercantile center, specializing in the export of wheat and flour and in the kindred industries of shipbuilding and ropemaking. The population grew rapidly and the building trades prospered. Thousands of small, simple houses were put up to accommodate the artisans and merchants, and a dozen new churches were built.

Very little remains of this pre-1800 town. Architecturally we see the culmination of the earlier English Georgian, already old-fashioned in England, in such houses as St. Paul's Rectory of 1789 [30] and the somewhat earlier "Captain John Steel House" [88] at 731 Fell Street. The former is located on a substantial lot, as if it were a country house, and the latter was originally the end of an attached row of houses.

The old Otterbein United Methodist Church of 1785-1786 [101] and the 1783 Old Town Meeting House [84] stand alone as the survivors of such churches as the Christ Protestant Episcopal (1785), First Presbyterian (1791), and German Reformed (1796)—all of which might have been designed out of James Gibbs's *A Book of Architecture* (1728) or similar British building guides.

At the turn of the century a new elegance appears in the country houses of the wealthy merchant princes. Homewood [155], built in 1801-1803 by Charles Carroll (son of the famous Charles Carroll of Carrollton), is the perfect example of the fashion. Sadly, it is also the last example in existence. Others were Thoroughgood Smith's Willowbrook, whose oval parlor was salvaged for display in the Baltimore Museum of Art; General Samuel Smith's remarkable Montebello; Henry Thompson's Clifton; Robert Oliver's Greenmount; John Eager Howard's Belvidere. Their names alone remain current, although the houses have long been demolished—or, in the case of Clifton, grossly altered.

Once again, the style of these country houses was old-fashioned, being a Baltimore variation of the manner of Robert Adam, introduced to England in the 1760s. It offered a new delicacy of ornamentation, based on the decorative style shown in the wall paintings and mosaics found in the ruins of Pompeii and in Diocletian's palace at Spoleto. It compared to the earlier Georgian as the severe delicacy of the furniture designs of Hepplewhite compared to the voluptuous curves of Chippendale. In this country it is described as the Federal style because it became popular about the time of the creation of the new Constitution and federal government (1789).

If this first flowering of architectural quality in Baltimore was old-fashioned by European standards, the very newest fashion followed quickly with a force that has marked the city ever since. The avant-garde architectural style of the later eighteenth century came from a new awareness of the essential forms of Greek and Roman buildings. In England, Sir John Soane, S. P. Cockerell, and others were experimenting with the ancient motifs to express volume and scale without fussy detail. In France, Claude-Nicolas Ledoux and others went even further toward geometrical simplicity; after Napoleon's 1798 expedition to Egypt they added ancient Egyptian mannerisms to the repertoire.

It was Baltimore's fortune that highly original representatives of both the English and French schools came to practice here: Benjamin Henry Latrobe, a self-styled refugee from an England whose politics he could no longer accept; and Maximilian Godefroy, a real political refugee from Napoleonic France. Their great works, and those of their students and followers, have indelibly marked the city. They gave Baltimore its first truly creative period.

Latrobe, a pupil of S. P. Cockerell, immigrated in 1795. He became a friend of Thomas Jefferson, who soon employed him as architect of the United States Capitol. Since that project moved fitfully, Latrobe worked in Virginia, Philadelphia, and particularly Baltimore. His great opportunity came when John Carroll, Archbishop of Baltimore, desiring an appropriate Cathedral for the first Roman Catholic Diocese of the United States, was sophisticated enough to employ the best architect available. Latrobe submitted alternative designs for the Cathedral in 1805. One was Gothic, the other classical.

To Archbishop Carroll and most other Baltimoreans of the day Gothic was too radical and too unfamiliar for such an important building; he chose the classical design. It is a lesson in the changing fashions in architectural style that forty years later a Presbyterian building committee would make precisely the opposite choice for a church on Franklin Street across from the Cathedral.

The Baltimore Cathedral [22] is Latrobe's masterpiece. The design is a precise and powerful arrangement of form, space, and mass in a manner reminiscent of the best classical architecture, but entirely original as an ensemble. One of America's greatest buildings, it has even been ranked with the best European buildings of its period by such historians as Henry-Russell Hitchcock and Sir Nikolaus Pevsner.

Meanwhile, Godefroy arrived from France in 1805 and was employed as the professor of civil and military architecture at St. Mary's College. The college was operated by the Sulpician Order, who also conducted St. Mary's Roman Catholic Seminary, founded in 1795. It was natural that the Sulpician fathers would ask Godefroy to design a new chapel building. Dedicated in 1808, and Godefroy's first work in Baltimore, St. Mary's Chapel [109] is an anomaly for its

St. Mary's Seminary Chapel

time and place: it is in the Gothic manner, the first church of this architectural style to be built in America. Godefroy did not really understand Gothic architecture; the chapel is a pastiche of Gothic detail mixed with some classical motifs. The effect is pleasant, nevertheless, and the oddity of the style adds to its considerable charm.

The architect's Commercial and Farmers' Bank of 1810 showed his knowledge of the current French geometrical classicism. Although this has been destroyed, Godefroy's mastery of the style is preserved in the largest and most important of his buildings, the Unitarian Church of 1819 [20]. The interior has been greatly altered but the overall composition—literally a cube surmounted by a hemisphere and a simple arcaded porch capped with a pediment framing a sculpture of "The Angel of Truth"—is a pure expression of the architectural theories of C. N. Ledoux. It would have seemed very up to date had it been built in Paris instead of Baltimore.

Godefroy's third surviving production was the Battle Monument [49], built in memory of those who fell in the British attack on Baltimore in September 1814. The symbolism of the Roman fasces, the Egyptian tomb, and mythical griffons reflects the architect's background in Revolutionary France, where patriotic holidays and military victories were marked by great civic celebrations featuring elaborate symbolic stage settings, floats, and temporary monuments. The unique aspect of the Battle Monument is that it was a democratic monument commemorating only those who died in action—not, as was the custom, the surviving politicians and generals. Appropriately, it was adopted as the official symbol of the city of Baltimore in 1827 and appears on the city seal and flag.

Godefroy returned to France in 1819, and Latrobe left for Pittsburgh about that time, going on to New Orleans, where he died in 1820. Although the prime movers of the classical movement had left the scene, their followers continued the influence for another decade. It was one of Latrobe's students, Robert Mills, who created Baltimore's primary landmark, the Washington Monument [1]. Mills, who liked to call himself the first American-born trained architect, also worked in Philadelphia, Washington, Richmond, and Charleston.

When it was decided to erect a monument to George Washington in Baltimore, the Committee advertised for designs. Three or four were rejected, including one by Godefroy, and Mills's scheme for a giant column won the prize in 1813, with a solution almost as novel as Godefroy's Battle Monument.

It was an ancient Roman conceit to use a tall column as the base for a statue, as for example Trajan's Column in the Forum. The earliest post-Roman use seems to have been the London Monument of 1677, commemorating the Great Fire of 1666. The two other pre-Mills examples were the Colonne de La Grande Armée in Paris (1801), which was demolished in 1870 for political reasons and rebuilt later, and the Nelson Column in Dublin (1808), which was blown up in 1966. Dozens of columnar monuments of this type have been built since Baltimore's and may be found from Leningrad to London in all sizes and styles. Mills's column is easily the largest of the genre, as well as the second oldest, and it is the best proportioned.

Both begun in 1815, the Battle Monument and the Washington Monument gave Baltimore its most famous sobriquet. In 1827, when both of them were nearly finished, President John Quincy Adams at a big public dinner in Baltimore gave as his toast, "Baltimore, the monumental city." It was more than an idle comment: no other large city in America had even one substantial monument to show. And the Monumental City we have been ever since.

A local architect, Robert Cary Long, Sr., carried forward the romantic classicism of Latrobe and Godefroy with considerable versatility. Long began as a carpenter but learned quickly from association with the masters. His first major building was the Assembly Rooms of 1797, essentially in the Georgian manner. The break into classicism came with his Union Bank of 1807, which seems to have been derived from plates in Sir John Soane's *Sketches in Architecture* (1798).

The example of Latrobe is clear in Long's Medical School building for the University of Maryland (1812). Now called Davidge Hall [74] after one of the founding physicians, it is an exercise in the Pantheon design—circular domed structure with a pedimented portico. In this case the plan provided instructional theatres, one above the other. In 1817 Robert Mills used the same plan for the First Baptist Church, now demolished.

Long's other major works were the St. Paul's Protestant Episcopal Church (1812), the Holliday Street Theatre (1813) where the "Star-Spangled Banner" was first sung, and up the street, Peale's Baltimore Museum [63] (1814). Only the last of these survives, but it has a special interest: it is the oldest museum building in this country and one of the oldest in the world.

One of the few features of Long's St. Paul's Church that survived its fire in 1854 was a pair of sculptured marble reliefs of Christ and Moses, now on the facade of the present church [27]. A unique aspect of Baltimore architecture in this period was the extensive use of sculptured ornament. Some sculptors came from France, while President Jefferson imported Italian sculptors to work on the Capitol; some of these had time to spare for Baltimore. Antonio Capellano did the work on the Battle Monument, the Unitarian Church and St. Paul's Church. Enrico Causici did Washington's statue for Mills's great monument. Others who worked here were Giuseppe Cerracchi, Andrei, Franzoni, and Chevalier.

Latrobe's direct influence was continued in Baltimore in the 1820s by a young man named William F. Small, who had trained in the great architect's office for two years. He produced such important buildings as Barnum's City Hotel, the Athenaeum, several churches, and a number of town houses—all now gone. Remaining are the 1829 Archbishop's Residence [25] on Charles Street, the great country house Folly Quarter in Howard County, and in collaboration with William T. Howard, the little McKim Free School [83].

The first two are derivative of Latrobe's "stripped classicism," with their flat wall surfaces relieved by shallow recesses for the windows, and the simple decorative moldings and capitals. However, the school is quite another page in architecture.

Small died in 1832, before the building was completed; the records of the Baltimore Library Company show that Howard had borrowed a volume of the 1762 *Antiquities of Athens*, by James Stuart and Nicholas Revett, in which there are accurate plates of the Temple of Haephaestus in Athens. The McKim School is a good three-fifths scale model of one end of that building.

Robert Cary Long, Sr., died a year after the younger Small; by then, Robert Mills had finished the Washington Monument and left for Washington and other places. The direct influence of Latrobe and Godefroy was gone. The field was left open to a new generation—the next phase of Baltimore's architectural development was led by Robert Cary Long, Jr.

The young Long was not content to follow his father's practice, but went to New York for professional training in the office of architect Martin Euclid Thompson. Here he found in the midst of the continuing classical fashion a countertrend toward Gothic and even more exotic styles. It is probable that he first saw in New York *Specimens of Gothic Architecture*, (1821) by A. C. Pugin and E. J. Wilson, whose handsome illustrations of English buildings were later to be his guides in Baltimore.

Long had the opportunity to learn about the latest work of Ithiel Town and A. J. Davis, pioneers in the revival of the Gothic mode in America. In 1832 Davis had designed the Tudor Gothic country villa Glen Ellen for Baltimore's wealthy and sophisticated Robert Gilmor, Jr.

When his father died, young Long hurried back to Baltimore, but despite Gilmor's example there was no widespread demand for Gothic. Long designed the Patapsco Female Institute and the nearby house Mount Ida in Ellicott City about 1837 in a severely simple classical manner. About this time he submitted a design for the gates to Green Mount Cemetery in the Egyptian style; it was not accepted, although seemingly appropriate for the purpose. In 1836 he designed an even more elaborate Egyptian scheme for the Baltimore City and County Record Office. This was approved, but built in a very much simplified style. The new ideas were afloat.

Long's opportunity came with the sudden increase in Baltimore's population toward the end of the 1830s, largely because of the massive wave of immigration from Ireland and Germany. A good many of the Irish and some of the Germans were Roman Catholic, and some of the Germans were Jewish. There was an immediate need for more churches, and it was Long's fortune to design five churches for four different denominations within the space of two or three years. More important, he established a taste in Baltimore for the Gothic style in church building that lasted for a generation.

His first accepted design in the Gothic manner was for the gates to Green Mount Cemetery [122]—a design that was published as a lithograph in about 1837, although not built for a few years. The next was more significant—St. Alphonsus' Roman Catholic Church [32] begun in 1842.

Long's own drawing calls it the German Catholic Church, for it was built for a congregation of Bavarian immigrants. While this was under construction, he was called upon to design a church for a congregation of predominantly Irish Catholics settled near the Mt. Clare shops of the Baltimore and Ohio Railroad. A Greek Doric temple scheme was adopted for this new St. Peter's Church [112].

St. Alphonsus' Church

The ambivalence of choice was voiced formally in 1844, when Long submitted two designs to the building committee for a new Presbyterian congregation on Franklin Street. As the minutes of the committee state, he offered both a "Greek" and a "Gothic" scheme. Long argued for the latter, and the committee voted "in favor of the Gothic." This seemed to decide the issue for Baltimore—with only one or two exceptions, the numerous churches that sprang up in the next two decades were Gothic.

Franklin Street Presbyterian Church

Long provided one of the exceptions immediately. Just after the decision of the Franklin Street Presbyterian Church [21], the Baltimore Hebrew Congregation chose a classical design for its first synagogue on Lloyd Street [82]. Was this the alternate Presbyterian design? In any case, it was much less specifically Greek than St. Peter's. The Doric portico is a true porch, jutting forward from the middle of the facade, and the wing walls are pierced by round windows. Inside Long provided the usual Orthodox arrangement of a balcony for the women and ranks of pews on the main floor facing the ark at the east end.

The Lloyd Street Synagogue, for all of its classicism, is more original than the Franklin Street Church. The latter's Tudor Gothic details can be traced precisely to *Specimens of Gothic Architecture*, particularly the plates showing Hampton Court. Long's arrangement of the familiar details is skillful, however, and the general effect cannot be faulted. It must be noted that the Franklin Street Church, the synagogue, and St. Alphonsus' Church were originally painted in a color to imitate stone. The modern fondness for the natural brick is not that of the church builders.

Long decided to move to New York in the midst of this flurry of commissions, but he died suddenly; and so in the end his fame rests on his local production covering a period of only a dozen years. His experiments in eclecticism were bookish and tentative, and beneath the ornamental detail is a simple classical plan. Since he had no direct followers, it cannot be said that he was an important influence on the course of Baltimore architecture. But at least he introduced the city to the picturesque architectural ideas that supplanted the classicism of his father's generation.

The next three decades witnessed Baltimore architectural production on a scale and over a range greater than the city had ever before experienced. Immigration and economic growth in both mercantilism and manufacturing doubled the city's population and multiplied its wealth. This is the period in which Baltimore got its first comprehensive water system, its first public parks, its first public "rapid transit" system, built its first city hall, and received its first great philanthropic institutions from George Peabody and Johns Hopkins. What had been little more than an overgrown port town achieved the status of a true city.

The key factor in this era was the railroad. When Charles Carroll of Carrollton laid the first stone of the Baltimore and Ohio Railroad in a field southwest of Baltimore in 1828, he is reported to have said that it was the second most important public act of his life, the first being the signing of the Declaration of Independence.

The railroad commenced an economic revolution with results to American life every bit as far-reaching as the political revolution in 1776, and nowhere was the effect felt more deeply than in Baltimore. The B&O and the other railroads that followed linked the Baltimore port with the rich farming country of the Frederick valley and the York and Lancaster regions in Pennsylvania, and in 1852 tapped the Ohio River valley.

They also brought about the development of industrial satellite towns such as Woodberry [177] on the Jones Falls, Avalon, Oella [118] and Ellicott City [119] along the Patapsco River; industrial plants such as Cooper's Iron Works in Canton, and Winans' car and locomotive works in southwest Baltimore. The railroads were far more than transportation arteries: they ushered Baltimore into the industrial age.

Early industrialism produced little significant architecture arising out of its own needs. The development of the railroads themselves was a story of constant invention and improvisation to solve new problems, not the least of which were those relating to the right-of-way. The first sizable stream that the B&O had to cross was Baltimore's Gwynns Falls. Here was built in 1829 the first railroad bridge in this country, a simple masonry arch called the Carrollton Viaduct [105]. Much more impressive is the great Thomas Viaduct [106] over the Patapsco River at Relay, which was in use by 1835. Two other fine masonry bridges served the early railroad, the Patterson Viaduct near Oella, now mostly demolished, and the Oliver Viaduct at Ellicott City, one arch of which still supports the track and is dated 1829.

The masonry bridges were throwbacks to classical Rome, and technically obsolete when they were built. No one could fault them for permanence—the Patterson Viaduct was abandoned because the line was changed at that point, the Oliver Viaduct was altered to accommodate the highway under it, and the other two still carry the line's trains—or for the beauty of timeless design, but they were expensive and took too long to build. Construction of the railroad moved too fast to wait for stone bridges, and the age of iron was at hand.

The Baltimore and Ohio Railroad was the school for two important American iron-bridge builders, Albert Fink and Wendel Bollman. Both joined the engineering department of the railroad as young men, grew up with the industry, and then went into the bridge-building business themselves, Bollman remaining in Baltimore. His firm in Canton made bridges for Cuba, Chile, and other distant places, as well as several across Jones Falls in Baltimore, and he designed and constructed the iron City Hall dome. Unfortunately, most of his bridges have been replaced.

Another architectural by-product of the railroad was the planned industrial suburb on a large scale. The concept of a company-owned mill town was a century old in Europe and

Carrollton Viaduct

had been implemented on a small scale in early Baltimore. The Ellicotts, in developing their large flour-milling business on the Patapsco River in the late eighteenth century, had built houses for themselves and for some of their employees nearby, but the town grew in a haphazard manner. The Washington Cotton Manufactory, established in 1808 on the Jones Falls, provided some employee housing in the vicinity, although it is all gone today. The first of the new wave of industries was the Ashland Manufacturing Company, a cotton-weaving mill, which replaced an older flour mill in the vicinity of Wetheredsville (now Dickeyville), and the company built some houses for employees to supplement the existing supply.

The railroads, however, opened up stretches of the Patapsco River and Jones Falls which were eminently suitable for mills but had no prior settlements; company-built housing was essential. The Union Manufacturing Company, located at what is now Oella, is an example. Two rows of stone houses along the hillside above the mill were built for its employees. Downstream, near the Thomas Viaduct, the Avalon Rolling Mill Company was established in 1845 with a long row of company houses, of which only one house survives today.

The Jones Falls valley was the site of the most ambitious industrial suburban development. It began with the purchase of the Woodberry flour mill by Horatio N. Gambrill in 1842 and its replacement with a large cotton mill requiring many more employees. Within the next thirty years four more cotton factories went up, as well as the Poole and Hunt machinery works, and hundreds of houses were built nearby by the mill owners. The best-planned unit is on a hill above the Mount Vernon Mill, built of stone about 1850 and now known as Stone Hill. The mill owners proudly pointed out that each had a side yard so the mill operatives could grow vegetables and supplement their incomes. It was paternalism, of course, but far better than the abysmal horrors of the English mill town of the same time.

Because of the needs of the railroads, and nearby supplies of ore and fuel which the railroads could easily reach, Baltimore became a major iron-production center. The ease with which iron could be cast in complicated shapes led to its extensive manufacture in the 1850s as architectural decoration. Hayward, Bartlett and Company and others turned out large quantities of iron window cornices, roof fences, grill work for porches and balconies, and other ornamental detail.

It was James Bogardus of New York who gave Baltimore its first all-iron building in 1850, the Sun Iron Building at Baltimore and South streets. It was built entirely of cast-iron and wrought-iron pieces bolted together. His associate, architect R. G. Hatfield of New York, provided the decorative taste by styling the building like a Renaissance palazzo with columns, pilasters, arches, and cornices an exaggeration of surface details in imitation of stone and wood. It is most unfortunate that this landmark in architectural history was destroyed in the fire of 1904.

Most of the iron for the building had been fabricated by Baltimore firms, but there was no local demand for another such building. Instead, commercial builders preferred masonry bearing walls, liking the ornamental possibilities of cast-iron fronts. The material permitted larger windows and was considered the elegant way to finish a street facade in mid-century. Only a few examples of the hundreds of cast-iron fronts still remain to illustrate the skill of the Baltimore foundries of that time.

On the other hand, the Peabody Institute |2| and City Hall |61| are significant demonstrations of the first tentative uses of structural iron in conjunction with traditional building techniques.

George Peabody, merchant and financier, who had begun his business career in Baltimore but had subsequently moved to London, in 1857 proposed to give to Baltimore an endowed cultural center which would encompass art, music, and literature. It was the first philanthropy of its kind in Baltimore and among the first in the country. Peabody insisted on placing his Institute on a corner of Mount Vernon Place facing the Washington Monument, even though it was one of the most expensive building sites available. To house this magnificent gift, architect Edmund George Lind, recently arrived from London where he had been trained at the Government School of Design at Somerset House, designed an Italian Renaissance palace with marble facing. The exterior is little better than an exercise in classicism, but the extensive use of structural iron is highly original. The concert hall is spanned with iron beams and braced with iron columns, although everything is covered with plaster. There is a splendid iron spiral staircase from the cellar to the top floor, but the most exciting feature is the library reading room, a great six-story room walled with balconies and book stacks and illuminated by a skylight. All of this is supported on iron members, and iron is used extensively for balconies, floors, and shelving. It is a proto-modern construction of much sophistication.

At the same time the Peabody Institute was going forward, Baltimore put up its first large City Hall, begun in

1867 and completed in 1875. A young Baltimore architect, George A. Frederick, received the commission; for style he turned to the French Second Empire of Napoleon III as illustrated in the New Louvre of the 1850s. Popular in America at the time, it was used for such contemporary buildings as the Boston City Hall of 1862-65 and the State, War, and Navy Department building (now the Executive Office Building) adjoining the White House. Frederick capped his mansard roofs with a tall, slender dome inspired by Thomas U. Walter's recently-completed dome for the United States Capitol.

If the architectural style for the City Hall was derivative and uninspired, Frederick's use of iron was bold and modern. Although the building weight was carried on masonry walls, the floor joists, rafters, and four grand staircases are iron. The chief glory is the towering cast-iron dome and drum, designed and built by Wendel Bollman.

The exploration of the new technology of iron construction is interesting to us, but it was peripheral to the desires of the architects' clients of the mid-century. To them, superficial style was more important; the whole range of historical mannerisms from Orient to Occident was ransacked for ideas, with very little concern as to whether they were academically "correct" or not.

Where the monumental effect still seemed appropriate (the Peabody, City Hall) the designs came from the Renaissance. This elaborate and formal manner was used both for the iron-front office buildings downtown and for fine private town houses in the Mount Vernon Place area.

John Rudolph Niernsee, Austrian-born and trained, and his Baltimore partner, J. Crawford Neilson, designed a number of the great town houses. Their masterpiece is the 1851 mansion at 1 West Mount Vernon Place (Thomas-Jencks-Gladding House). Others are the Miller House, at 700 Cathedral Street, and Asbury House [7], next to the Mount Vernon Place Methodist Church, where the Italian palazzo style is rendered in brownstone. The change in fashion in only a decade is illustrated by comparing these buildings with the restrained classicism of the Mount Vernon Club (Tiffany-Fisher House [15]).

Gothic was preferred for churches, but the trend was away from the regularity and bookish quality of Long's

Franklin Street Church to the picturesque character of earlier periods such as "English Decorated" and "Norman Gothic," as contemporaries called them. Niernsee and Neilson designed three very different specimens in the early 1850s: Grace and St. Peter's Church [13] in English country-parish Gothic; Emmanuel Church [10] (originally Norman in style but remodeled in 1919 to appear more academically Gothic); and the elaborate mortuary chapel for Green Mount Cemetery [123].

Another dimension of the Gothic, figuratively and literally, was provided by Nathan G. Starkweather in the vertical lines and soaring tower of the First Presbyterian Church [12], begun in 1853 and completed in 1874. The interior is a flamboyant display of intricate plasterwork.

The freest expression of the high Victorian version of Gothic is the Mount Vernon Place Methodist Church [8] of 1870-72 by architects Thomas Dixon and Charles L. Carson. The use of green stone from the Bare Hills quarry and contrasting red sandstone trim is quite original.

Another picturesque theme competing with the Gothic in popularity was the "Italian Villa" style used for hundreds of country houses, a few city churches, and even a railroad station in Baltimore. The source was the rustic architecture of the Tuscan countryside, particularly as interpreted by the American architect Andrew Jackson Downing and published in his *Cottage Residences* of 1842, with subsequent editions. Richard Upjohn of New York was a master of this style, as well as of Gothic, and provided the Italian basilican design for the 1854 St. Paul's Protestant Episcopal Church [27], replacing the burned-out classical church of Robert Cary Long, Sr., and the elegant Wyman villa, unfortunately demolished.

Local architects followed the fashion: Niernsee and Neilson used the Italianate style for St. John the Evangelist Roman Catholic Church [87] and for the Calvert Street railroad station and the great Winans country house, Alexandroffsky. The last two are no longer standing.

Johns Hopkins "modernized" his early-nineteenth century house Clifton [96] in 1852 by adding a great tower, a broad veranda, and other features considered to be Italian. Many another villa rose through the countryside and in villages such as Catonsville and Reisterstown. A few re-

First Presbyterian Church

main: Crimea [147] in Leakin Park, Anneslie, Wood-bourne, Dumbarton. Most of the great ones are now only names for subdivisions: Guilford, Homeland, Stoneleigh, for example.

An eccentric use of Italian ideas was the 1853 tower for the Independent Fire Company house, now Number 6 Engine House [86], by architects William H. Reasin and Samuel Wetherald. The last appearance of this mode came after the Civil War in the new public high schools of Baltimore, of which only the old Eastern Female High School [85] remains.

It was in "rural architecture," as Downing called it, that the greatest inventiveness is seen. Although nominally in such styles as "Rural Gothic," "Pointed," or "Tudor," "Bracketted," "Italian," or even "Elizabethan," the rural cottages of this period were really closer to an indigenous American style than almost any other buildings. They were often sheathed in wood, or at least with heavy wooden ornamental trim, scallops, and brackets, and they usually had extensive porches or verandas, features not common in similar cottages in Europe. In particular, the board-and-batten siding technique had been invented by the American architect A. J. Davis and widely popularized by Downing and others.

Baltimore's inventory of these charming cottages is still sizable. They range from the elegant Family and Children's Society House [137] to a wide variety of wooden ornamental cottages in Mount Washington, Catonsville, Lutherville, and along the York Road corridor. The most exotic variations on the picturesque theme are the century-old pavilions in Druid Hill Park [146] that were designed by George A. Frederick.

The appearance in the 1850s and 1860s of the "rural cottage" as an extension of the city's residential area was an early symptom of a fundamental change in the structure of Baltimore brought about by improved transportation facilities. Until 1844, the only practical means of daily transportation for almost everyone in Baltimore had been walking. Few could afford carriages, cabs, or private horses.

But in that year, franchises were granted for omnibus lines, common carriers that followed regular street routes.

As the Baltimore *Sun* said: "These lines [tend] to enhance the value of property in the outskirts of the city, enabling persons to reside at a distance from their places of business, in more healthy localities, without loss of time or fatigue in walking . . ." Similar words would be repeated after every mass transit improvement: the horse-drawn street railway in 1859, the electric streetcar in the 1890s, the automobile omnibus in the 1920s, etc.

Although land use was decidedly mixed, before 1800 speculative builders were putting up short rows of identical houses in order to get the highest economies and profits. Information about such operations is scarce, but the record of one builder in 1838 shows that he built six identical two-and-a-half story houses, 12 1/2 feet wide, with two rooms on each floor and attic, on Mott Street at a cost of $400 per house. He sold them for $450-$475 each, retaining ownership of the land, which he rented separately for $11 a year for each house. Then, as ever since, the builder made little construction profit but a long-term investment gain from his "ground rent." Square miles of Baltimore speculative houses were and are being built on the same system. It is not surprising that the builders sought economy rather than architectural quality and used novelties, such as white marble steps, as sales points.

As the city's population increased swiftly in the 1820s and 1830's, residential development spread slowly away from the older core. The first planned development—and Baltimore's first planned neighborhood—was John Eager Howard's Belvidere estate, stretching north of Centre Street between Howard Street and the Jones Falls to above Monument Street.

This immense tract of high-lying ground became available for development with Howard's death in 1827. The executors of his estate decided to set it off in lots, rather than parcels. To make the most of the Washington Monument, in 1831 they established four boulevard squares about it. The north-south pair were called Washington Place, the east-west pair, Mt. Vernon Place, the name that has popularly been identified with not only the squares but an extended neighborhood.

The creation of the squares had no precedent in the United States but is an example of Baroque city planning that would not be out of place in Paris or Rome. The executors had predicted correctly: the squares around the monument became the finest residential area of Baltimore.

One or two houses had been built on Mount Vernon when the speculative building partnership of James and Samuel Canby of Wilmington, Delaware, made a proposal in 1839 for a large-scale development of middle-class housing on the outskirts of the built-up area of Baltimore. Having bought a 30-acre tract in West Baltimore, they offered the city a square of ground in the midst of the property for use as a "public square," and they pledged themselves to build substantial residences in the neighborhood for "such members of the community as may incline to retire from its more central and confined parts." The city on its part was to put up an iron fence and landscape the square.

Called Franklin Square, it was the first of the eight similar squares which encircle the heart of the city—Union, Lafayette, Harlem Park, Perkins Spring, Johnson, Madison, and Collington, to which may be added the landscaped boulevards—Eutaw Place [140], Park Avenue, and North Broadway. The purpose behind each of them was to enhance prospective residential development; in most of them, the initiative came from the owners of the adjacent ground who then built rows of identical houses about the squares, along the boulevards, and in the vicinities.

The creation of these oases in the midst of the otherwise planless and formless march of rows of houses was in itself an architectural accomplishment. Although several have been encroached upon in the name of education and recreation, some still function as they were intended, in the words of a committee of the City Council in 1839: "Ground on which the citizens and visitors may recreate themselves on summer evenings after the toils of the day are ended."

The houses themselves had little architectural distinction; their presence was all that counted, and where rows have been demolished for schools or playgrounds, or setback apartment groups, the original architectural character of the squares and boulevards is changed. The best specimens remaining are Lafayette Square, with its exciting mixture of picturesque churches and houses; Union Square, with three sides intact and the charming cast-iron Spring House in the park; and Franklin Square, the first, with the best single row of houses of any of them, Waverly Terrace [114]. The very name recalls the era of Sir Walter Scott and his romantic novels, and on Fayette Street nearby is a row called Ivanhoe Court.

The public-squares movement began in the age of the omnibus and gained momentum with the introduction of the horse-drawn street railway in 1859, but the real creation of the horse car was Druid Hill Park [146]. A syndicate sought a street-railway franchise in 1858, but Mayor Thomas Swann demanded that the franchise carry with it a tax on the railways' gross receipts which was to be applied to the establishment of "one or more large parks." By 1860, the money was rolling in, and the newly appointed Park Commission purchased the estate of Lloyd Rogers, called Druid Hill, and began the long process of landscaping and developing to achieve a properly picturesque setting for the appreciation of nature and for passive exercise.

The land was manipulated to provide scenic views, romantic pathways, lakes with swans and boats, picnic groves, rustic bridges, formal promenades, and a grand entrance gateway at Madison Avenue. Under the general superintendence of Augustus Faul, engineer, the design of the park was by Howard Daniels, "landscape gardener and engineer," and the original buildings were designed by George A. Frederick. As a specimen of romantic nineteenth-century landscape art, Druid Hill Park ranks with the best in America, as well as the oldest—New York's Central Park is only a few years older.

Howard's *Monumental City* said in 1882, "The influence of the park upon adjacent property has been wonderful. Its value has been greatly enhanced, streets have been opened, avenues created, and long lines of elegant and costly residences have been built . . ." Yet the instrument responsible for the park, the horse-drawn street railway, was also setting in motion a major change in the living habits of Baltimoreans: the garden suburb, where every house owner might have his miniature park, his own trees, garden, lawns of grass, and recreational space.

The improved transportation facilities placed a very large area within acceptable commuting distance. Speculators bought large tracts and planned subdivisions with such romantic names as Eden Terrace, Oak Forest Park, Monumental Heights, and Highland Park. The names have long since been forgotten.

The common factor of these developments was the detached house on a lot, usually rectangular and as small as the developer felt he could successfully merchandise. Streets were usually ruled off in straight lines and conventional blocks created. Although the houses were rather varied in appearance, this was mainly a matter of gables and porches—there is little of architecture and less of site planning in the late-nineteenth-century subdivisions that grew out beyond the row-house core.

The first subdivision with both architectural and planning merit was Dixon's Hill [187], in Mount Washington. The wooded hills west of Jones Falls and the old Washington Cotton Factory had all the ingredients for the setting of a picturesque cottage, and the Northern Central Railroad running along the stream valley offered fast, reliable service to Baltimore, four miles away.

Before the Civil War some substantial wooden villas had been built on the hills, and in 1856 Thomas Dixon, architect, bought Clover Hill Farm on top of one of the hills and built his own villa. After the war, he subdivided the property, laid out irregular lots and curving roads, and built about 35 large villas in a variety of the popular picturesque styles. Even Downing's favorite board-and-batten style is used for the Mount Washington Presbyterian Church [186] of 1878, which is the single most interesting building in the development.

Dixon's Hill was a true "bedroom community" from inception. By 1880, several families were in residence, and within five years almost all the houses were owned by men employed in downtown Baltimore, who had no other residential address.

The site plan was simple, a winding ring road circling the top of the hill, with several radial roads giving access to the country highway at the foot of the hill. Because of the steep terrain and exceptionally large, irregular lots, the houses are distributed freely at different elevations.

In sharp contrast to this thoughtful plan, the conventional subdivisions such as that of the Walbrook Land Company in West Baltimore or the Peabody Heights project in the vicinity of what is now Wyman Park offer nothing but a gridiron street pattern and narrow rectangular lots. No doubt the superior quality of the plan for Dixon's Hill was due to the fact that the developer was also a resident and an architect.

By the 1880s this kind of planned community was being called a garden suburb, a name coined in England, and the most distinguished designer in the new field was the landscape architect Frederick Law Olmsted, Sr. Baltimore has only one project by this pioneer city planner, the 1887 summer colony Sudbrook, near Pikesville [204]. The completion of the Western Maryland Railroad sparked the idea. A syndicate purchased an old estate to develop a family summer resort that would rely on the village of Pikesville for stores and the railroad for daily commuting by the breadwinners.

The land was essentially flat and featureless, and Olmsted laid out the development with the railroad station as the center of focus. At that place a bridge went over the tracks toward Pikesville, and space was allocated for a hotel intended to accommodate weekend guests. Gently twisting ring roads circled around the property, and large irregular lots were laid out. One large lot was set aside as Cliveden Green, a kind of common land. A number of the houses were designed by the Boston architectural firm of Langdon and Company, and the rest by local builders; there is little remarkable about the architecture.

Although the houses were originally without central heat and were later adapted to year-round living, Sudbrook has survived very well and retains its identity among acres of modern ranch houses—proof of the soundness of the original plan. The hotel is reputed to have had an interesting career during the Prohibition era; unfortunately, it burned soon after.

The plateau rising to the north of the mill town Hampden, bounded on the west by the Jones Falls valley and on the east by the valley of Stony Run, was the site of the greatest of the nineteenth-century garden suburbs, Roland Park [183]. William Edmunds owned about a hundred acres of this land, and in 1890, seeing the possibilities of a large-scale subdivision, looked for capital.

Charles H. Grasty, a newspaper publisher, put him in touch with Jarvis and Conklin of Kansas City, the agents for the Lands Trust Company of England, a syndicate of capitalists. In mid-1891 a company was formed with Samuel R. Jarvis as president, young Edward H. Bouton of Kansas City as general manager, $1 million from the Lands Trust, and a name taken from a nearby reservoir, Lake Roland.

The Roland Park Company put together a number of tracts of land aggregating 550 acres and hired George E. Kessler, a topographical and landscape engineer from Kansas City, to lay out the first plat. This was the section north of Cold Spring Lane and east of Roland Avenue, probably chosen because it was the most level part of the property, and closest to the new Baltimore and Lehigh Railroad along Stony Run (later the "Ma & Pa" of commuter fame). In June 1892, Mr. Louis Lewis bought the first lot, but sales went so poorly at first that Edward H. Bouton decided it would be wise to build some houses for ready sale. Mme. Jeanne Bret, the city's most prominent dressmaker, bought one of them and became the first resident of Roland Park.

In 1897, when less than half of the lots in Plat Number One had been sold and a dozen or more of the company-built houses were not inhabited, Bouton contracted with Olmsted, Olmsted and Eliot of Boston to plan Plat Number Two for property on the west side of Roland Avenue. Thereafter, the Olmsted firm was consistently involved in planning for the company, and Frederick Law Olmsted, Jr., was personally engaged.

In contrast with the dull uniformity and indeterminate character of most speculative real estate developments before or since, Roland Park is unusually complex in style and aspect, while also being one of the few genuine neighborhoods in Baltimore. To say that Roland Park is a state of mind is to underline the reality of the success of its planners. It has achieved in a bare 70 years the kind of historical identity we associate with much older areas in Baltimore such as the Mount Vernon Place section or Fells Point.

Roland park resulted from intensive planning of a sort almost unknown at that time and rarely applied today. It involved site design, land-use and architectural control, creation of common amenities, provision for transportation facilities, and, it must be said, selection of inhabitants.

By all accounts, one man was responsible for the formulation of the master plan: Edward H. Bouton, resident manager of the Roland Park Company from its inception until his retirement in 1935. His great contribution was the inclusion of land-use restrictions in each property deed—the so-called restrictive covenant by which the owner agreed to abide by certain regulations established by the Roland Park Company and which was intended to run permanently with the land.

The 1892 deed to Louis Lewis spelled out the basic restrictions: first the premises could be used only for a single residence; second, the house must be set back from the street 30 feet; third, no stable, outbuilding, or private sewage plant was allowed; fourth, the owner agreed to pay a proportionate share of the cost of maintaining the streets, water supply, lighting and sewer systems, supplementary fire and public service; and fifth, it must cost more than $3,000.

The first three categories are no less than land-use zoning, the first such effective restrictions to be applied in Maryland until state legislation was passed 20 years later. The fourth item reveals Bouton's equally advanced conception of providing the most modern public utilities as part of the broad plan for development, using the company's initial capital and recovering the costs out of property assessments.

Bouton's most important innovation along these lines was the founding of the Lake Roland Elevated Railway in 1893, an electric streetcar line that ran from the City Hall to Roland Park and within a few years boasted of scheduled trips every four minutes running 24 hours a day. To round out community facilities, he built a "shopping center," perhaps the first of that species in America, on Roland Avenue, and founded the Baltimore Country Club for recreational purposes; his wife helped to found the Roland Park Women's Club.

The section of the Lewis deed stipulating the minimum cost was soon transformed into a requirement that property holders must obtain the company's approval of their architectural plans. While this implies conservatism, the prevailing architectural fashion for suburban houses was quite eclectic within narrow limits.

H. H. Richardson and McKim, Mead, and White had popularized a highly picturesque version of the New England shingled cottage of the Colonial period. Most of the houses in Plat Number One, on the east side of Roland Avenue, and more than a few on the west side, belong to this genre.

No architect has been connected with these houses, but it is plain that they were built under excellent supervision and with a great deal of thought for siting. The company-built houses were deliberately scattered over Plat Number One and made an obvious standard by which to judge the "harmonious" quality of new proposals.

When the second plat, on the west side, was opened for development in 1901, Roland Park had arrived as a desirable residential neighborhood. People of considerable means and social standing bought lots and employed architects to build more impressive houses than the original cottages.

J. B. Noel Wyatt and William G. Nolting, partners in one of Baltimore's most talented architectural firms, built themselves houses in Roland Park and designed the Country Club and a good many houses for clients. The firm Ellicott and Emmart did much work, and Ellicott took up residence, too. Palmer and Lamdin were quite active in the later stages of building. The New York architect Charles A. Platt designed an entire street of houses, Goodwood Gardens.

In this phase of development can be found all the contemporary fashions in suburban architecture. Wyatt was particularly fond of the half-timbered English Tudor style which had been revived in England by Richard Norman Shaw; the shopping block is an example. Revived versions of the Georgian and the Regency styles are found, although the styles are handled quite freely and not in the later spirit of rigid copying, as seen in the "Colonial" houses in Guilford.

The steep hillsides and curious irregular lots found in the northern part of the west side called forth highly original designs which more closely identify with the British Arts and Crafts movement of William Morris, who preached the virtues of strength, sturdiness, and simplicity. Here, this was often interpreted in a new kind of Picturesque reminiscent of medieval farmhouses.

Besides these styles, we also find tile-roofed Spanish villas, Gothic churches, and in recent years, the commonplace red brick "Colonial" exemplified by the Country Club which replaced Wyatt's shingled building. It might seem that this variety would be inharmonious, but the prodigious tree cover, extensive lawns, and shrubbery unify the landscape so that even the shingle houses which have been painted white and a few white-painted clapboard houses are scarcely noticeable. Green and brown are the colors of Roland Park.

While the new suburban lifestyle was luring middle-class people out of the city, there was a great spurt of downtown private and institutional building on a scale and lavishness not seen before. It is ironic that most of these costly buildings put up in the 1870-1900 period are considered obsolete, while many have been demolished or greatly altered, since the same period saw the practice of architecture achieve a fully professional status.

The American Institute of Architects had been formed in 1857 with Thomas Ustick Walter, architect of the Capitol, as president and E. G. Lind and J. R. Niernsee representing Baltimore. The Baltimore chapter of the Institute was founded in December 1870 by 15 architects and three engineers, most of whom had been trained in the offices of such men as Lind, Frederick, and Niernsee. Within a few years there was a new influence from such men as J. B. Noel Wyatt, who studied for a year at the new course in architecture at the Massachusetts Institute of Technology and four years at the Ecole des Beaux Arts in Paris. This kind of scholastic training became the normal preparation for an architectural career.

The appearance of the *American Architect and Building News* in 1876 was most important in spreading knowledge of what the leading architects were doing, and similar English periodicals were easily available. New Baltimore architects were in close touch with the mainstream; on the other hand, these factors led to a great degree of uniformity and academicism.

The stylistic retreat from the exuberant revivalism of the Gothic First Presbyterian Church and the Mount Vernon Place Methodist Church begins in the 1870s with a group of new churches in what was often called Norman Gothic. The Eutaw Place Baptist Church, by Thomas Ustick Walter [141]; Christ Church, by Baldwin and Price; and the Brown

Memorial Church, by Hutton and Murdoch—all designed in 1869 and 1870—are severely restrained as to ornamental detail, and their character arises from the rugged walls laid up in courses of rough-hewn or quarry-faced stone. Otherwise the pointed windows, steeples, and other details are academic exercises in early Gothic.

At this point the genius of Henry Hobson Richardson began to influence architectural development. Following the trends set in England by Richard Norman Shaw, he pursued an architectural style that Professor Carroll L. V. Meeks called "creative eclecticism," in which the reminiscent forms and details are employed with great freedom rather than literally, so as to embellish the building without disguising its purpose.

A counter academic reaction was led by two of Richardson's pupils, Charles Follen McKim and Stanford White. Both architectural attitudes are well represented by Baltimore buildings, from the Richardsonian St. Michael and All Angels Church designed in 1877 by J. B. Noel Wyatt and Joseph Evans Sperry to a spate of "Colonial," "Gothic," and "classical" buildings of the 1930s and even later.

Wyatt and Sperry's Mercantile Trust and Deposit Company Building [55] of 1885 is Baltimore's finest example of one mode of "creative eclecticism." Meanwhile, in 1882, Stanford White had introduced Richardson's second major theme, the early Romanesque, in the monumental Lovely Lane Methodist Church [149] for Dr. John F. Goucher. Although by this time White was already moving away from Richardson's ideas, this church is in the master's spirit of powerful simplicity, with great rough stone walls, dramatic massing of the tower and circular auditorium, and a minimum of Romanesque detail.

Baltimore architects and their clients welcomed this manner, and over the next dozen years it was the predominant style for large institutional buildings. It was not surprising that the 1886 main building for Dr. Goucher's new Woman's College of Baltimore, adjoining the church, was an echo of White's manner by the Baltimore architect Charles L. Carson. Thereafter it was commonplace, as for example in such disparate structures as the Associated Reformed Church (now Greek Orthodox), by Charles E. Cassell, 1889 [132]; Baldwin and Pennington's Maryland

Club, 1892 [127]; Joseph Evans Sperry's Oheb Shalom Temple of 1892 [139]; and the Maryland Penitentiary of 1893 by Jackson C. Gott.

The most original evocation of Richardson's stone style was the 1895 Mount Royal Station of the Baltimore and Ohio Railroad [133]. Here Baldwin and Pennington married the Romanesque character to the needs of the railroad age as well as it could be done.

At the time Stanford White designed the Lovely Lane Church, the firm of McKim, Mead, and White had already begun the transition from Richardson's free eclecticism toward academicism. Their grand house for Ross Winans on St. Paul Street [124], begun in the same year as the church, is in the French Renaissance chateau manner, with very tightly controlled brick and stone decoration. The same tendency shows in the house built on Mount Vernon Place [16] for the Robert Garretts, with which Stanford White was closely associated. The addition in 1902 was by John Russell Pope, one of the principal continuators of the "academic reaction."

The new academicism quickly replaced free eclecticism in Baltimore as it did everywhere in the country. The tide seemed to turn just after 1900 with such formal examples as the Greek temple designed by Parker and Thomas in 1905 for the Savings Bank of Baltimore [43]; the same firm's competition-winning neo-Georgian plan for the proposed Homewood campus of the Johns Hopkins University in 1904; and Sperry's 1910 Emerson Tower [71], a hulking office building tricked out to look like the tower of the Palazzo Vecchio in Florence.

The Walters Art Gallery of 1907 [18] was intended as a copy of a Genoese palazzo by architects Delano and Aldrich in New York. By the 1920s Italian Baroque appears in the Ss. Philip and James Roman Catholic Church by Theodore W. Pietsch, and Gothic in the big City College by Buckler and Fenhagen. These re-revivals were all far more precise in historical accuracy than the first time around, although under the carefully contrived surface they were steel and concrete, the materials of the new age.

Wilbur Harvey Hunter
Director Peale Museum (Retired)

The twentieth century saw Baltimore architecture consciously grappling with the problems of industrialization. The city itself was a direct result of the industrial revolution. A railroad center with deepwater port facilities, Baltimore was a natural industrial center, attracting a growing population with all the new metropolitan problems.

The architecture of the buildings from the turn of the century is an interesting subject in itself. It is the story of coping with the esthetic and functional problems of the industrialization of building. Consciousness of urban planning and of concern for the urban individual was developing as well. This concern has become one of near desperation today.

Whereas interest in the design of individual buildings has been important throughout the entire history of architecture, it is an understanding of a larger concern about the livability of the urban complex itself that is characteristic of late twentieth-century Baltimore.

Stylism so dominated the appearance of architecture of the early twentieth century that it must be dealt with directly. The effect of industrialism on building design was of critical importance. One prevalent attitude—one still to be reckoned with—attempted to ignore industrialization and hold to the classical architectural thinking of the Renaissance, which could easily be considered continuous since that time.

A second attitude recognized industrialization but reacted to it positively by turning to the past styles of building and romantically reusing their appearances.

A third approach, differing from both of the preceding, was to accept industrialization with all its potential for new form, structure, economy, and esthetics. The interplay of these three attitudes toward architectural style must be understood in order to comprehend the appearance of twentieth-century Baltimore architecture.

The classical attitude toward architecture, unconcerned with industrialism, had real roots in the local heritage of building. The preindustrial Georgian style of building was indigenous and abundantly existent. The new Gilman Country School on Roland Avenue was done in 1906 by Parker, Thomas, and Rice in the best Georgian manner. Concurrently, the new suburban developments began to turn to classical brick design, especially in such places as Guilford and Homeland, and extending into the counties.

It was not surprising that Baltimore's memorial to its World War I dead was in the form of a Greek temple, opposite City Hall, designed in 1925 by Laurence Hall Fowler. The trustees of the new Baltimore Museum of Art [153] in Wyman Park went to New York to commission the great classicist John Russell Pope. The Johns Hopkins Homewood campus was developing in a strictly classical mode, which was picked up after World War II by the competition for Shriver Hall, won by Buckler and Fenhagen with a clean "stripped classical" auditorium.

This Homewood tradition persisted into the 1960s with the modified classicism of the Eisenhower Library by Wrenn, Lewis, and Jencks, in association with Meyer, Ayers, and Saint. The latter firm was responsible for what may be one of the final important classical buildings in the city, the 1967 addition to the Maryland Historical Society at Park Avenue and Monument Street. Thus there is a virtually unbroken adherence to Renaissance classicism in Baltimore architecture today. Adherents of this tradition are currently attempting to dictate its continuance in the state buildings in nearby Annapolis.

The second response to the industrialization of architecture was a romantic reaction, especially evident in the revival of Gothic stylism. In Baltimore, the 1920 remodeling of Emmanuel Church at Cathedral and Read streets [10] attempted to make an earlier Romanesque revival building more fashionably English Gothic, clearly illustrating this pictorial attitude toward architecture. Another example is the academically stiff procathedral for the Episcopal Diocese [159]. Less-distinguished Gothic Revival churches persisted almost up to the present, such as the Christ Lutheran Church built at Light and Hill streets by Philip H. Frohman of Washington in 1958.

The picturesque attitude toward stylism in general is no better illustrated in Baltimore than by the city's first major "skyscraper," finished as the Great Depression settled over

L

the country. The Baltimore Trust Company Building, as it was originally named, was designed in 1928 by Taylor and Fisher with Smith and May [52]. It is covered with a variety of stylistic ornament in stone and crowned by a strong mansard roof. Taylor and Fisher produced a more recent bow to eclecticism, the Boumi Temple at North Charles Street and Wyndhurst Avenue, with a proper Egyptian doorway.

The third architectural attitude toward industrialization was one of acceptance and development of its functional and esthetic potentialities. It is true that the very quality of Baltimore's classical and romantic architecture bred a self-confidence that worked against change.

But this self-confidence in turn made possible an acceptance of liberal architectural thinking not evident in comparable cities of the South. This liberalism was epitomized in Chicago at the turn of the century, under the leadership of Adler, Sullivan, and Frank Lloyd Wright. The influence of the Chicago School was to cross the Atlantic and later recross to America under the leadership of Walter Gropius, Mies van der Rohe, and Le Corbusier. The new names were "functionalism," "modern architecture," and "international style," all reflecting reactions to the traditional styles and acceptance of the new industrialism.

The direct influence of the Chicago School in Baltimore is evident in the work of Baldwin and Pennington, particularly their Mount Royal Station of 1897 [133], and the Maryland Club of 1893 [127]. The Fidelity Building of 1898 [35] at Charles and Lexington streets echoes the elevator buildings of Chicago, even in its Sullivanesque decorations.

On a smaller scale, the row houses in the 800 block of West University Parkway, constructed about 1905 of exposed poured reinforced concrete, are an example of the acceptance of a new building material. The technique was not to be seen again locally, however, until 60 years later in the Morris Mechanic Theatre [40].

Between the two world wars, important new thinking along functional lines was appearing in the work of certain Baltimore architects. In 1932, Palmer and Lamdin designed the Nurses' Home and Gateway at Baltimore City Hospitals on Eastern Avenue, with a fresh, nontraditional esthetic which stands out today. The town was startled by the facade of their new architectural offices at 1020 St. Paul Street, distinguished by the absence of decoration.

John H. Scharf's house for Judge Emory Niles [191] in Poplar Hill in 1938 represented a clean break with traditional residential design. Its skillfully articulated relationship to its site and its esthetic derived from functional plan were all but unique in Baltimore at the time.

At the turn of the century, the work of Frank Lloyd Wright came into prominence, then neglect, and finally delayed renown. Though he did a small "Usonian" house for the Euchtmans on Cross Country Boulevard [200] in the early 1940s, to this writer he later spoke of "Baltimore, that benighted city." Nonetheless, Wright's work, both directly and through his enormous influence on the development of modern architecture, was to have a great effect on the coming architecture in Baltimore.

Despite the promising beginnings, modern architecture was certainly not established in Baltimore by the onset of World War II. It is significant that the city's first postwar high-rise office building, the aluminum-paneled Commercial Credit Company Building at 300 St. Paul Street, was done by an outside firm, Harrison and Abramowitz of New York. On the Johns Hopkins Homewood campus, the first nonclassical structure, the Embryology Building [158], was done by Anderson, Beckwith, and Haible of Boston. One of the first postwar modern residences, the Albert Lion house in Stevenson, was designed by another New England architect, Walter Bogner of Cambridge, Massachusetts.

The foregoing story of the acceptance of contemporary architecture is only a part of the reason why Baltimore looks the way it does today. What has not been discussed is the twentieth-century concern for the overall urban complex. This concern was always present to some degree, as witness the earlier development of the city's park system.

A great opportunity was missed, however, after the Baltimore fire in 1904. Though this was typical of what has happened after the great city fires throughout history, it was deplorable that the city was rebuilt with no appreciable change in its plan. There were, however, subsequent efforts to improve the cityscape. The land clearance and creation of Preston Gardens in 1917 was one manifestation of the "city beautiful" movement.

The awakened social conscience about the economic and physical degradation of Baltimore led to the establishment of the city's first housing authority and first planning commission. The public housing projects built before and after World War II are typical of what was accomplished in other comparable cities. Redevelopment-enabling legislation produced significant clearance projects typical of what was being accomplished around the nation, among which should be mentioned Harlem Park, Broadway Redevelopment, and Bolton Hill.

More significant, however, in making Baltimore what it is today is the story of Charles Center and the Inner Harbor accomplishments, which make the city stand out among its peers. Behind them is the inspiration of Baltimore businessmen who faced up to the deteriorating inner core of the city with an imaginative, positive plan of private initiative. The key to the project was a Planning Council, headed by David Wallace, on leave from the University of Pennsylvania; the Council guided the renewal of 33 acres of the central business district.

The individual buildings in Charles Center form an interesting casual group, with almost no effort at monumentality. The open spaces, and especially the two major plazas, are of great importance. The separation of pedestrian and vehicular traffic, with extensive parking space under the open areas and the buildings, is also important; it is a working center, geared to bringing life back downtown. Much could be said about the financial structure of the whole operation, but here it is important only to point out Charles Center's unquestioned success in redirecting the economic development of the city; this was its fundamental purpose.

There is a general high quality among the buildings, giving the overall development a distinction among comparable ventures in other cities. The first building, One Charles Center [37], set the standard for the highest caliber of design with its clean, Miesian esthetic and open "no floor" ground level. Two Charles Center [33] has a variety of form and surface treatment that is heartwarming.

The Morris Mechanic Theatre [40] is an outstanding building in Charles Center and is recognized as one of the nation's important new legitimate theaters. It is an almost poetic expression of interior form, using rough-board concrete both inside and out. It is a foil to the adjacent Sun Life Building [41], a tour de force in clean-cut stone and metal.

The new Baltimore Gas and Electric Company Building [38], by Fisher, Nes, Campbell, and Partners, is a sensitive complement to an old stylistic office building with especially successful masonry fenestrated panels. With all its component parts, including the great spaces in between, Charles Center has set a high standard for Baltimore and other cities.

The planning process, under the same leadership, was extended almost immediately to the redevelopment of the Inner Harbor in an area approximately six times that of Charles Center. Previous activities of shipping, manufacturing, and commerce had been disappearing from this area for decades. The new facilities are of the most varied nature, including governmental, commercial, and educational architecture. Early on, the United States Fidelity and Guaranty Company's building by Vlastomil Koubek set a good example. The World Trade Center [47] by I. M. Pei with Richter Cornbrooks Matthai Hopkins local architects, is outstanding.

Charles Center South [44], by RTKL Associates, Inc., provides a transition between Charles Center and the Inner Harbor. Belluschi's IBM building is significant, and the just completed Baltimore Convention Center [46] by Naramore, Bain, Brady, and Johanson, and Cochran, Stephenson, and Donkervoet is a new centerpiece. The Rouse Company's Harbor Place by Benjamin Thompson is a fine addition, and the Cambridge Seven's Aquarium will soon be finished.

Away from the harbor, Johns Hopkins Hospital's Nelson-Harvey Tower by RTKL Associates, Inc., is important, and on the Homewood campus, Donald L. Sickler's Glass Pavilion is path-breaking. (Significantly, Sickler had been project architect for Mies on the One Charles Center.)

As a final word, something should be said about the concept of new towns within the larger urban framework. The Rouse Company's Village of Cross Keys [188] is just such a fascinating new town within the city, composed of residential, recreational, commercial, and other facilities, splendidly coordinated in a handsome site treatment. Architectural warmth is achieved almost self-consciously. The individual feels a belongingness, a relationship of scale, a kindness of environment—in all, it is a great design accomplishment. This achievement of personal identification is certainly one of the great necessities of contemporary architecture, too often overlooked by architects in the attempt to solve the tough problems of design and esthetics in Baltimore and elsewhere. Mention should also be made of Moshe Safdie's Coldspring [189] in north Baltimore.

The architecture of twentieth-century Baltimore is now clearly in the mainstream—a statement that could not have been made a few decades ago. The quality of individual buildings has improved with the realization of the potential available in the rapidly changing industrialized building process. More important, however, is the city's grasp of urban problems and the resulting physical solutions in process.

Alexander S. Cochran
Baltimore Architect

A GUIDE TO
BALTIMORE
ARCHITECTURE

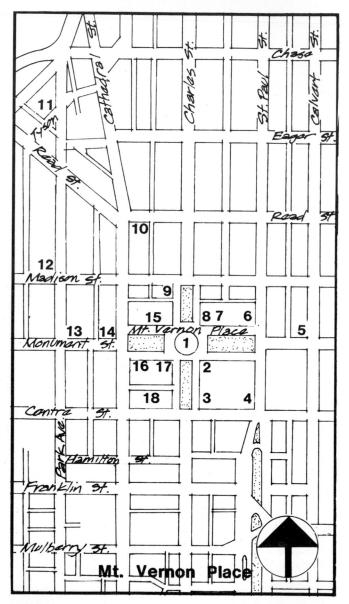

Mt. Vernon Place

Tour A   Mount Vernon Place (Walking)

Even now, this is essentially a nineteenth-century city, and Mount Vernon Place is where the elite lived in the nineteenth century; they have long since moved away, but this is still thought of as the heart of Baltimore.

The several statues (to Wallis, Lafayette, Taney, etc.) in the four squares are evidence that Baltimoreans look upon this as an historic area ("our municipal Pantheon," one resident called it), as are the efforts of numerous organizations to keep things as they are. These efforts have met with success: the only twentieth-century buildings on the squares are the addition to the Garrett-Jacobs House (1902), the Washington Apartments (1906), the Walters Art Gallery (1909), and the Peabody Conservatory's Leakin Hall (1926).

Those two institutions are not only themselves significant additions to Baltimore's life, but represent the many institutions created or largely endowed by huge gifts from the rich and philanthropic—in these cases William and Henry Walters and George Peabody. Thinking of Baltimore as a whole, one could also cite in this context Johns Hopkins, Moses Sheppard, the Garretts, Mrs. Jacobs, Enoch Pratt, and Claribel and Etta Cone.

If Henry Walters was the richest man ever to live on Mount Vernon Place, he assuredly was not the only one of that breed. Because this was the neighborhood of the rich, many of the buildings here are the work of architects prominent in their times—some of them nationally: Robert Mills, Niernsee and Neilson, Edmund G. Lind, Stanford White, Dixon and Carson, John Russell Pope.

Here too one can see several, though by no means all, of the styles that were successively popular in Baltimore: Greek Revival, Italian Renaissance, Gothic Revival, White's eclectic modernism, Pope's Roman pomp. And the fact that there is a building by Edward Durrell Stone just off the squares is indicative of the recent revival of interest in architecture—to the point of commissioning architects of international stature to work here—that has taken place in Baltimore.

But the variety of architects and the succession of styles cannot hide a certain uniformity of outlook that reflects a civic attitude. Henry James, who visited the city in 1904, later recorded his impression of the Baltimore character to be inferred from these squares:

"There . . . were the best houses, the older, the ampler, the more blandly quadrilateral; which in spite of their still faces met one's arrest, at their commodious corners and other places of vantage, with an unmistakable manner . . . . A certain vividness of high decency seemed . . . to possess them, and this suggestion of the real Southern glow, yet with no Southern looseness, was clearly something by itself . . . ."

There is another factor, as well, though it is certainly related to what James said. The blandness that he mentioned reflects in reality a quality of quiet and somewhat smug inhibition which is as close as Baltimore comes to having a tangible character. These houses built by the wealthy as personal monuments are imposing—but they make no effort to overwhelm. The sizes of the squares and of the individual pieces of land on which the houses were built prohibit grand gestures. One can sense in the mentality of those who lived here a certain reserve: for fear of being vulgar perhaps, but also as an indication of the Baltimorean's inverse pride in not being noticed—which comes, of course, from not being noticed.

Like the typical and somewhat defensive attitude of many Baltimoreans today, as they regard the world from their largely overlooked city, these houses seem to project not only what they are, but also, and as a virtue, the quality of not being something more.

Mount Vernon Place, which tells us so much about its city and the people who live in it, is actually two places. That part of Monument Street running east and west between Cathedral and St. Paul streets is named Mount Vernon Place. That part of Charles Street between Centre and Madison streets, the north and south squares, is named Washington Place. The distinction is worth noting, though most local residents group all four squares, and even the neighborhood around them, under the name Mount Vernon Place.

It all belonged, at the beginning of the last century, to John Eager Howard, a Revolutionary War hero whose statue is in the north square. From his estate he gave the land for the Washington Monument; his heirs gave land for the four parks and later sold the lots around them to private citizens who were interested in building.

The area became fashionable by 1850, when the city had expanded far enough from the harbor to make this a desirable living place. The parks themselves, subject to more than one landscaping, were most recently relandscaped in 1916 by Thomas Hastings, of the New York firm of Carrère and Hastings.

It was shortly after this landscaping, during the twenties, that the automobile made suburban living as practical as it made urban living unpleasant. During the next 20 years most of the old families moved out; many of the houses were divided into apartments and then redivided into smaller apartments—the area entered a period of decline.

But in the last decade the trend toward moving back to the city has induced some renovation. Examples include One and 3 West and 16 and 18 East Mount Vernon Place. It is possible that a renaissance is on the way.

1 WASHINGTON MONUMENT
Mount Vernon Place and Washington Place
1815-1829—Robert Mills

In 1809, a group of patriotic citizens formed a committee to commission and fund a monument to George Washington. An architectural competition was announced, and among the well-known architects submitting designs were Maximilian Godefroy and probably Benjamin H. Latrobe. Although Robert Mills entered his design after the competition's closing date, and though it was clearly the most expensive design, the judges awarded him the commission in 1815.

The cornerstone was laid on July 4, 1815, and the Washington statue was raised, virtually completing the monument, on November 25, 1829.

Mills's original design was more ornate than the present column, involving balconies at several levels, inscriptions, and other decorations. One by one these were discarded owing to lack of funds—as it was, the monument cost twice the budgeted $100,000. In its final form, the monument in its simplicity is more elegant and forceful than the proposed design.

The monument is of local Cockeysville marble. Its square base contains a room surrounding the column, which is 19 feet high as it leaves the base and tapers to the foot of the sculpture, a pedestrian statue of Washington, at Annapolis, resigning his commission as commander of the Continental Army. The sculptor was Enrico Causici, an Italian who also worked on the Capitol in Washington. The total height is 178 feet.

Between five and six diameters high, the column is a little less than classical in its proportions. This, plus the height of many modern buildings, makes it seem to modern eyes to be less tall than it is. But it was a considerable architectural achievement for its time, and it remains so.

The iron fence surrounding the base of the monument was designed by Robert Cary Long, Jr.

Visitors can climb an interior winding staircase of 228 steps to windows in the base of the statue, from which there is a fine view.

2 PEABODY INSTITUTE
One East Mount Vernon Place
1858-1878—Edmund G. Lind

The Peabody Institute's formal Renaissance Revival facade gives little indication of what lies within: a high spacious hall, completely surrounded by stacks of books that rise, supported by cast-iron columns and railings, six floors to the ceiling. The room is one of the finest interiors in the city.

The library, opened to the public in 1866 with 20,000 volumes (it now contains roughly 300,000), was originally on the second floor of the west wing, consisting of the three bays to the right of the present main entrance. This section was built of Beaver Dam marble as a separate building in 1861. The west wing contains the Peabody Concert Hall on the first floor; on the second and third, reached by a circular staircase of cast and wrought iron, are an art gallery and the classrooms and music rooms of the conservatory.

The east wing, also of Beaver Dam marble and new fireproof construction, was begun in 1875 and finished three years later. Successive elevation studies by Lind show that he carefully considered the best way of integrating the two sections into one building.

The engineers and founders of the ironwork were Bartlett-Robbins and Company. This firm and its successor, Bartlett-Hayward and Company, designed and manufactured iron-front buildings, verandas, balconies, and complete summer and light houses that appeared in cities throughout the country, including Richmond, New Orleans, and Portland, Oregon.

3   SCHAPIRO HOUSE
609 Washington Place
ca. 1848—Architect unknown

Formerly known as the Abell House, this is especially interesting by virtue of the cast-iron balconies that decorate it. In the nineteenth century such cast iron was more in evidence in Baltimore than now, though it is still to be seen on occasion. The balconies were probably added some years after the house was built.

The next four houses, reaching to the corner of Centre Street, were probably built as a group in the 1840s.

4   PEABODY DORMITORY
St. Paul and Centre streets
1969—Edward Durrell Stone

The addition to the Peabody Institute combines several uses. The wedge of space created by the sloping site is a parking lot, its walls decorated with Stone's characteristic grilles. On the roof of the parking lot the architect has created a landscaped plaza and on the south end he has put two dormitory pavilions.

The perimeter of the terrazzo-paved plaza is defined by a row of 101 arches. Those on the southeast corner, enclosed with gray-tinted glass, form the outside walls of the student lounge; around the rest of the building they form an arcade. The dormitory sections are identical in form, but one is turned a quarter with respect to the other. The first floor of the west, the men's dormitory, houses a kitchen. The sections are linked by a one-story common dining room lighted by conical skylights.

Although neither the materials nor the architectural style, which has been called Romantic Classicism, is indigenous, the complex fits surprisingly well in its more traditional surroundings. A drawback is the formidable wall formed by the parking enclosure, but the view from the plaza at night, with the lights of the city shining through the arches, more than compensates for any minor deficiencies.

5 ST. IGNATIUS—CENTER STAGE BUILDING
700 North Calvert Street
1856—Louis L. Long; 1899—James W. O'Connor and James F. Delany; 1975—James R. Grieves Associates

The exterior of this block-long building, completed in two stages in the latter half of the nineteenth century, reveals little of what is inside. First constructed, to a design by Louis L. Long, were the church on the northern end and the porticoed central section next to it; finished in 1856, they would doubtless look more Italianate than they do if two projected 180-foot towers had been completed. The rest of the complex, from the present Center Stage entrance section to the southern end, was added in 1899 to a design by architects O'Connor and Delany of New York. Aside from the church, these buildings were the home of Loyola College and High School.

The principal delights of the building are to be found inside. The elegant white Baroque interior of the church, only open during services, is a revelation. And the glass and metal Center Stage canopy only begins to reveal that the southern portion of the building has become one of the finest examples of adaptive reuse in the city.

In 1974, Center Stage's previous home on North Avenue burned. A little over a year later came the announcement that the Jesuits, who owned the St. Ignatius complex, had in effect given two-thirds of it, vacant for some years, to the local professional theater for a new home. Architect James R. Grieves, working with theater consultant Roger Morgan, conceived a masterful plan for this space; construction of the first half was completed in 11 months.

Using half of the 90,000 square feet of available space, Grieves designed a broad, shallow, 500-seat auditorium with moderate thrust stage, two-level lobby, offices and workrooms above the theater, and provision for a café and restaurant off the first and second levels of the lobby. The rest of the plan, including two more theaters, rehearsal space, offices, classrooms, and apartments, will be undertaken when funds are available.

Grieves's achievement is most noticeable in the theater itself, which is extremely flexible, technically modern, and has a seating plan in which no seat is more than 35 feet from the stage. The extensive use of found space and found materials, less evident to the visitor, was a factor that kept the cost to $1.7 million and the conversion time to less than a year. It is additionally important to note that according to estimates published at the time of the conversion, if Center Stage had built its own building it would have taken two to three times as long, cost close to $1 million more, and provided less space.

In 1978 the conversion received a national American Institute of Architects Honor Award.

6 BROWNSTONE ROW
22-32 East Mount Vernon Place
1853—Louis L. Long

Brownstone facades became popular in many American cities in the second half of the nineteenth century. This row is contemporary with Long's design of the original St. Ignatius buildings down the street.

7   ASBURY HOUSE
10 East Mount Vernon Place
ca. 1855—Niernsee and Neilson

Now owned by the Mount Vernon Place Methodist Church,
this house is somewhat typical of the Italianate Renaissance design patterned after houses by the English architect Sir John Barry and first appearing in this country in
the Philadelphia Atheneum. The richly decorated interior
is the result of an 1890s renovation.

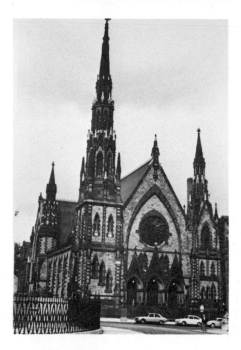

8 MOUNT VERNON PLACE METHODIST CHURCH
Mount Vernon Place and Washington Place
1873—Dixon and Carson

"No picture, unless carefully colored, and no mere description, can give the reader a notion of its appearance," said the author of an 1888 guide to Baltimore about this Victorian Gothic church, one of the best examples of its type in the city. The polychromatic effect is achieved by green serpentine marble from Baltimore County, which is complemented by buff and red sandstone trim. (Neither stone wears well; in 1932, 5,000 individual pieces had to be replaced.) The main exterior features are the three sandstone spires and the large relieving arch that encloses the rose window.

In the interior, metal columns support six pointed arches on either side separating nave from side aisles. Above are plaster fan vaulting and low clerestory windows.

9   GRAHAM-HUGHES HOUSE
718 Washington Place
ca. 1895—Charles E. Cassell

At the corner of Washington Place and Madison Street
stands one of the French-chateaulike houses popular
among the wealthy toward the close of the last century,
although this example is considerably less grand than
those found in New York and other major cities. It is remarkably well squeezed into its lot, however, and gives an
impression of being larger than it is. Cassell was also the
architect of the Stafford Hotel next door.

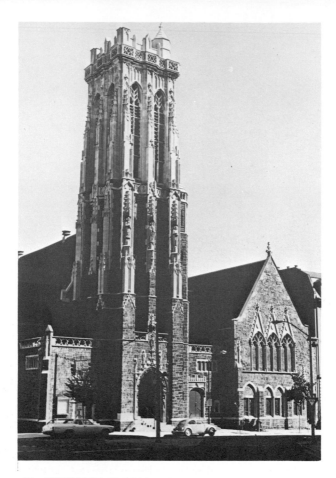

10 EMMANUEL EPISCOPAL CHURCH
Cathedral and Read streets
1854—Niernsee and Neilson

The facade of this church was considerably changed in 1920, when Niernsee and Neilson's simple church and J. Appleton Wilson's parish house to the south got a facelift designed by Waldemar H. Ritter of Boston, who clothed the

simple stone tower in Flemish Gothic finery. John Kirch-
mayer provided the sculpture representing the Christmas
story, hence the sobriquet "Christmas Tower." A look at the
stone work on the Read Street side will show where the
original stops and the newer facade begins.

11   TYSON STREET
Off Read Street between Park Avenue and Howard Street
ca. 1830

Originally built for Irish immigrants, the little houses
along Tyson Street are interesting not so much for their
architecture as for the fact that this is a highly successful
private urban renewal effort. Most of the houses had fallen
into disrepair when, one by one, beginning in the early
1950s, they were bought and renovated by people wanting
to live near the center of town. Real estate values have risen
sharply since then, and Tyson Street has become a highly
desirable place to live.

12 FIRST PRESBYTERIAN CHURCH
Park Avenue and Madison Street
1854-1874—Nathan G. Starkweather

Starkweather's Gothic church, with its brownstone facade, is notable for the truss construction of its roof, similar to that used in St. George's Chapel at Windsor, England. The trusses eliminate the need for interior pillars, satisfying a requirement of the church's building committee. Whether this is an advantage, however, is doubtful; the interior plaster vaulting looks a little silly terminating in mid-air.

The 273-foot steeple, the tallest in Baltimore and the principal attraction of the church, was a remarkable structural accomplishment. Solid stone piers 8 feet thick and 14 feet deep form the base and penetrate the ground to a depth of 8 feet. Atop these are granite blocks 6 1/2 feet square from which clusters of cast-iron columns, each 21 inches thick, rise 35 feet. Above these are iron shafts 23 feet high reaching to the pediment and formed into a frame by wrought-iron ties.

The spire is a core of brick, reinforced with wrought-iron I-beams placed on the iron pillars, and the whole is faced with the same New Brunswick freestone that faces the body of the church. The height of the spire is emphasized by its smaller companion to the east, which is 125 feet high. Much of the ironwork was fabricated by Wendel Bollman's Patapsco Bridge and Ironworks.

According to architectural historian Phoebe Stanton, much of the building of the church was supervised by Edmund G. Lind, who also may have been partly responsible for its design.

The manse, or rectory, to the west was finished after the church and is compatible with it. Reid Memorial Chapel to the north of the church, a former lecture room, was redesigned in 1940 by Ralph Adams Cram.

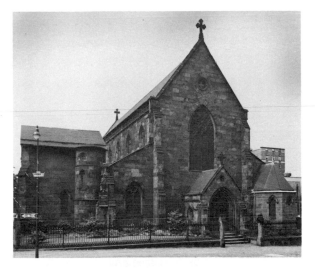

13   GRACE AND ST. PETER'S CHURCH
Park Avenue and Monument Street
1852—Niernsee and Neilson

A nineteenth-century rendition of English rural parish Gothic architecture, this brownstone church consists of nave and clerestory, transepts, and a chancel that was enlarged in 1903. There are a chapel and sacristy on the west side, where a planned tower was never completed above the first story.

The nave is defined by seven pointed arches of stone on each side, supported by stone columns each with a different capital. The interior is distinguished by black walnut furniture, wrought-iron gates on either side of the chancel, and the hammerbeam construction of the roof.

14   CAST-IRON WORK
Monument and Cathedral streets
1853—Niernsee and Neilson

The three houses at 700, 702, and 704 Cathedral Street, the southernmost (designed by Niernsee and Neilson) having an attractive cast-iron balcony on the side, are examples of the Italian Renaissance style popular in the mid-nineteenth century. The center house was originally similar in appearance to the others until its brownstone facade was replaced with limestone. It contains an elaborate library that may have been the work of Stanford White.

15 MOUNT VERNON CLUB
8 West Mount Vernon Place
ca. 1842—Architect unknown

The exterior of this house remains a fine example of the Greek Revival town house built in the first half of the nineteenth century. The three-story painted brick facade, topped by a balustrade, is divided into five bays. Two pairs of Doric columns support the small stone portico.

Built on the English basement plan, the entrance floor contains a central hall (a feature repeated on the floors above) and several small rooms. To the left is a graceful winding staircase leading up to the principal floor on the second level. About the turn of the century, the interior of the house was considerably altered to give it a Georgian appearance. In the back of the house is an enclosed brick-paved courtyard.

Formerly known as the Tiffany-Fisher House, the building has been a private women's club since 1942.

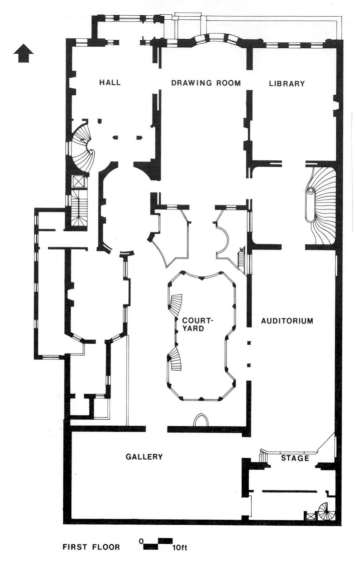

HALL

DRAWING ROOM

LIBRARY

COURT-
YARD

AUDITORIUM

GALLERY

STAGE

FIRST FLOOR   0 ▆▆ 10ft

Floor plan of Engineering Society building.

24

16   THE ENGINEERING CENTER
7-11 West Mount Vernon Place
1884-1916—Stanford White and John Russell Pope

Originally the Garrett-Jacobs mansion, this was the largest, most costly town house ever built in Baltimore. Mr. and Mrs. Robert Garrett (he was president of the Baltimore and Ohio Railroad) commissioned Stanford White of the New York firm of McKim, Mead, and White to design the first part of the house. The western two-thirds of the facade reflect White's design. It almost immediately became a subject of controversy.

Critics felt that the size and modern style of the house did not reflect the conservative character of Mount Vernon Place. One of them, Harry P. Janes, a neighbor, objected to the "monstrous vestibule" of the house, which he said cut off his light and air and deprived him of his first-floor view of the Washington Monument. He took his case to court, claiming the vestibule extended beyond the building line. The court ruled in favor of Mr. Janes, but the decision was reversed in an appeal and work continued. (Mrs. Garrett later had her revenge; in 1915, she acquired the offending neighbor's house at 13 West and promptly demolished the back of it for "light and air" for her stairway.)

The carved wooden spiral staircase and the grand hall and vestibule, with windows of Tiffany glass, are perhaps White's most distinctive contributions to the building. The hall, surrounded by a gallery and wooden balustrade on three sides, rises two full stories to a coffered ceiling. The

original dining room behind it, now the Engineering Society's board room, has a wealth of carved wood decoration in its Baroque fireplace and sideboard.

The house was the creation of Mrs. Garrett, the former Mary Sloane Frick, who was the grande dame of Baltimore society at the time. In 1902, after the death of Mr. Garrett and her marriage to Dr. Henry Barton Jacobs, she acquired and demolished 7 West Mount Vernon Place and hired John Russell Pope to design the last great extension of the house, equal in size to the original. Pope designed a facade in harmony with White's and created a library in front, a theater and art gallery in the rear, and, in between, a grand marble staircase leading down to the "supper room," now used as a dining room by the Engineering Society.

The principal architectural feature of the house, which is shaped like a hollow rectangle, was the great central roofed conservatory, which once enclosed doves, palm trees, and a trickling stream. It was later converted into an open court with terraces.

The facade, swelling out in the center, is embellished with marble columns and stone cartouches; it is 60 feet high. A balustrade once ran the length of the house.

The 40-room building, with its furnishings and appointments—including gold-plated bathroom fixtures—reportedly cost $1.5 million to construct. The walls are load-bearing brick, faced with brownstone in front. The art gallery is of steel and concrete construction. Since 1939, when Dr. Jacobs died, the house has had a series of owners. The Engineering Society of Baltimore took over the building in 1961 and has been slowly restoring it. It is occasionally open to the public.

17 THOMAS-JENCKS-GLADDING HOUSE
One West Mount Vernon Place
1851—Niernsee and Neilson

Constructed of brick and originally painted, the house is three and a half stories high, with a portico containing outer columns and steps of Beaver Dam marble. The columns behind, however, like those in the entrance hall, are of wood, described in a contemporary account as being "marbelized" by expert foreign craftsmen. The graceful free-standing curved staircase and the hall are lighted by an eye at the top of the dome above, which contains a Tiffany glass window added by William A. Delano, the architect of the original Walters Art Gallery down the street. Some of the cornices and other details are of cast iron. In 1961, after a period of neglect, the house was bought and subsequently restored by a local automobile merchant, Harry N. Gladding.

18 WALTERS ART GALLERY
Washington Place and Centre Street
1909—Delano and Aldrich; 1974—Shepley, Bulfinch, Richardson, and Abbott, with Meyer, Ayers, and Saint

William and Henry Walters were a father-son combination who, during the late 1800s and early 1900s, collected art on a massive scale and eventually amassed one of the largest private art collections in the country. In 1907, Henry Walters, who lived at 5 West Mount Vernon Place, commissioned Delano to build him a large gallery building which was in effect to be a private museum. When Mr. Walters died in 1931, he left the gallery and collection to the city of Baltimore.

The Walters Art Gallery was the first commission for its young architect. It reflects both his brilliance and his immaturity. Delano, a relative of the Walters family, later designed the Japanese Embassy in Washington, the United State Embassy in Paris, and the new Post Office Building in Washington.

The interior of the Walters was modeled on the University of Genoa's University Palace. The two-story interior arcade surrounding a square courtyard is at once exciting and intimate. Light and airy, the space is an appropriate setting for pieces of classical art and at the same time, small enough to avoid a feeling of monumentality. The stairway leading up to the court, however, is awkwardly placed.

The exterior, if less successful than the court, is a dignified addition to Washington Place, with its rusticated first story surmounted by a plain wall punctuated with pilasters and smallish windows, the wall in turn topped by a delicate frieze.

The new Walters wing, opened in 1974, manages to be both a completely modern structure and an appropriate partner for the older building. The scale is essentially the same, and the colors of the pink granite base and the pre-cast concrete slabs that stand out from the glass walls of the building are compatible. Those slabs, an ingenious design feature, permit natural light to come through from above and at corners, yet keep out the heat and damaging rays of direct sunlight.

The interior of the new wing, which contains almost twice as much gallery space as the original building (50,000 square feet compared to 28,000), was designed around the collections it holds. It was not created in the traditional manner of galleries, with a series of square rooms; rather, each floor has a central core of galleries and a passage around them, with one part leading to another in a free-flowing manner, so that visitors are constantly drawn on by being able to see what they are coming to. The galleries are of varying size and height, each designed for the scale of the pieces to be put into it.

There are, it must be admitted, certain minor drawbacks to this design. The exterior has an austere appearance which can be forbidding rather than inviting at first; and the plan of the interior can be confusing on an initial visit. But on the whole, both the old and the new gallery buildings work admirably for the collections they contain, and that is the most important point.

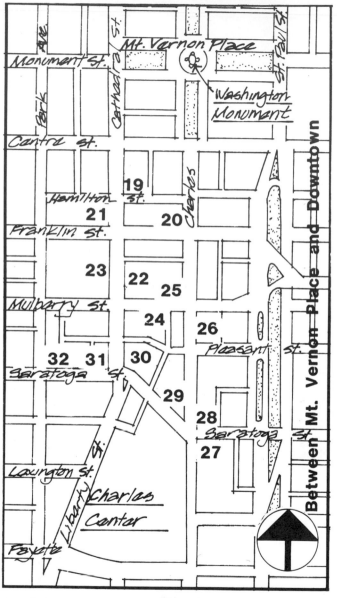

Tour B Between Mount Vernon Place and Downtown (Walking)

Curiously, Centre Street seems to have become a sort of unofficial boundary in central Baltimore. South of Centre is the downtown commercial, office, government, and financial section of town. North of Centre, the city has remained basically residential, for all the changes that have taken place.

But it was not always so. The area bounded by Centre and Lexington, Howard, and Calvert streets was largely residential through most of the nineteenth century. When it began to change toward the end of the century, Baltimore was in a period when growth was more important than beauty. As a result, the commercial buildings that replaced the residential ones are, with a few exceptions, of little note. Only what has survived from the precommercial age is significant, and that is almost exclusively ecclesiastical in nature.

Yet the area contains some of the most important architecture in the city. Three of the most famous architects to work in Baltimore—Maximilian Godefroy, Benjamin H. Latrobe, and Robert Cary Long, Jr.—are represented by their most important local work. One of the few surviving eighteenth-century houses in the city is here, as is the only Richard Upjohn building in Baltimore. Much of what Baltimore is proudest of is contained in these few blocks. Also located here is what is left of the Charles Street shopping district, at one time the most fashionable in town and still the focus of the small smart shops.

31

19 HAMILTON STREET ROW HOUSES
Hamilton Street between Charles and Cathedral streets
Early 1800s—Robert Cary Long, Sr.?

Of the seven row houses, three—numbers 12, 16, and 18—are unaltered. Their wide single windows on the upper stories are unusual. Robert Cary Long, Sr., owned the entire row of houses about 1815 and lived in one of them. He is believed to have designed them as well.

20 FIRST UNITARIAN CHURCH
Charles and Franklin streets
1818—Maximilian Godefroy

The geometry of Godefroy's major structure in Baltimore is eminently simple—a cube surmounted by a hemisphere. So is its design; the exterior of the church is an excellent example of Romantic Classicism.

An arcade encloses a vaulted porch and five doors. Above it is a plain frieze and cornice that extends around the

building, and above that is an attic story. The pediment contains a terra-cotta sculpture representing the angel of truth. The original, by Antonio Capellano, who executed the Battle Monument sculpture, deteriorated; in 1954 it was replaced with a replica by Henry Berge. The sides and back of the church have arched recesses, some containing windows. The structure is brick covered with stucco.

Originally, the church nave was formed by four arches, each 53 1/2 feet in diameter, supporting a dome of equal diameter and 80 feet above the floor at its center. The acoustics, however, were never good, and in 1893 the church was remodeled by Joseph E. Sperry, who added the barrel vault.

As it stands now, the interior consists of a large, square nave and shallow side aisles, separated by three arches on each side. They are divided by 12-inch-square posts which carry the four Howe trusses of heavy timber, each eight feet deep, that support the vault. The sanctuary in front contains the original pulpit designed by Godefroy, but a new organ, replacing the one he had designed in the shape of a lyre, was added during the renovations. The original dome, patterned on the Pantheon, lurks overhead.

21 FRANKLIN STREET PRESBYTERIAN CHURCH
Franklin and Cathedral streets
1847—Robert Cary Long, Jr.

One of Long's famous buildings of the 1840s, this resembles
an English Tudor building in its exterior style but is essentially a simple classical rectangle. The facade, which probably came to Long via A. C. Pugin, contains five nicely
balanced masses, with twin towers flanking a central door.
It is surmounted by a Gothic window filled with Perpendicular tracery. Stone is used functionally in the crenellated
towers and buttress offsets of the brick building, and aesthetically around the door. The building was originally
painted to resemble stone.

The interior consists of a small, low vestibule and an
almost square hall with a gallery at the rear over the
vestibule. There is no chancel. The flat, paneled roof is
supported on corbels. The church was lengthened in 1865,
and the pulpit furnishings and screen are additions of about
1915. The building is now the New Psalmist Baptist
Church.

It was not long after designing this church and the Lloyd
Street Synagogue that Long moved to New York and died,
leaving his most significant contributions to architecture
in Baltimore.

22 BASILICA OF THE ASSUMPTION
Cathedral Street between Franklin and Mulberry streets
1806-1821—Benjamin H. Latrobe; with later additions and alterations

Among students of architecture, the Basilica is Baltimore's best-known and, many would say, finest building. Architectural historian Nikolaus Pevsner calls it "North America's most beautiful church."

In 1805 Archbishop John Carroll asked Latrobe, an English-born architect of German and English training, to design a cathedral for Baltimore, the primary See of the Catholic Church in America. Latrobe submitted two designs, one Gothic and one classical, and the latter was chosen.

The main part of the church was finished in 1818, after numerous delays and difficulties. Latrobe designed a porch, but the one added in 1863, though appropriate, may not be exactly to his design. The architect's son, John H. B. Latrobe, has been credited with the porch. The church was lengthened on the eastern end in alterations of 1879 and 1890, attributed to John R. Niernsee and E. Francis Baldwin respectively. Latrobe had originally pleaded for the longer version and had been denied it, so the church as it now stands is, with one exception, close to his design. The exception: the curious "onion domes" on the belfry towers. Latrobe's drawings show simple rounded dome tops to the towers, surely a better treatment.

The massive walls of the cathedral, of porphyritic granite, are relieved only by a few judiciously placed windows of subtly varying sizes, set in recessed arched panels. Parts of the building project or recede slightly, "so that," writes architectural historian Henry Russell Hitchcock, "one is conscious of a well-proportioned group of geometric shapes that are carefully interrelated. These same fortunate relationships have been carried on in the new extensions of the building to the east. The handsome principal dome, which rests on an octagonal drum, is somewhat overshadowed from the west by the unfortunate towers. The best view of it is from the Orleans Street viaduct several blocks to the east."

The highest praise has been reserved for the interior. "As one enters the great west door," writes Talbot Hamlin, Latrobe's biographer, "the beautiful openness of the space envelops one, and the way in which part leads to part and the little to the big. The plan is basically a Greek cross, but there is an added short bay in the nave to transform it into a Latin cross. The central dome is supported by segmental vaults and without pendentives. To the east and west are low saucer domes on pendentives. Around the apse to the east and under the transsept galleries are Ionic columns echoing the much larger columns of the porch."

The effect of the whole, "all so simply detailed with just the right amount of ornament in the dome coffers and on the . . . capitals," writes Hamlin, "makes for one of America's truly distinguished interiors."

23 ENOCH PRATT FREE LIBRARY
Cathedral Street between Franklin and Mulberry streets
1933—Clyde N. Friz, with Tilton and Githens

Departing from the older tradition of building public libraries with monumental entrances at the end of long flights of stairs (for example, New York and Boston), Friz designed a building with an entrance on street level. This allowed for a row of display windows whose exhibits the passing public can see at a glance. It also allowed for easy access to the library's main floor, a particular boon to the handicapped. The Pratt's design has been borrowed for library buildings in several other cities.

24 7-9 WEST MULBERRY STREET
1833 and later—Architect unknown

The history of this double building is curious. The western
portion, Number 9, was erected in 1833; it contains a classical portico and much interior classical decoration. The eastern half, Number 7, was built later, but when is not known.
In 1891 the Roman Catholic archdiocese bought the two
buildings, and they became the Cathedral School. Later,
they were the home of the Maryland Academy of Sciences
before it moved to its present building at the Inner Harbor.
Now they have been turned into an office building. When
the loggia on the eastern end (earlier open at the top of a
flight of steps but now glassed in) was first added to the
house is a mystery. It may have been in 1929, or it may have
been earlier; most authorities do not think that it was part
of the original. The little cupola was added by the
archdiocese.

25 ARCHBISHOP'S RESIDENCE
408 North Charles Street
1829—William F. Small

Built specifically to house the Archbishop of Baltimore and connected to Latrobe's Cathedral, this Greek Revival house now reflects a five-part plan usually reserved for country houses. Originally it had only the center section and may even have lacked the third floor of that. The door, fanlight, windows in shallow recesses, and entrance arch are original.

The design is clean-cut and pure, with cool colors and fine proportions. The hyphens and wings, and possibly the third floor of the main building, were added in 1865. Originally stucco scored to resemble cut stone, the house was covered with a concrete veneer also resembling cut stone in the 1950s.

26 LOGGIA STORES
343 and 345 North Charles Street
Facades ca. 1925

In the 1920s there was a movement by Charles Street merchants to add marble facades to their buildings. It was done most successfully here, where the arches of the second floor "loggia" of 343 complement the Palladian window of 345 and give the pair an Italian look.

27 ST. PAUL'S CHURCH
Charles and Saratoga streets
1856—Richard Upjohn

In 1854 the previous St. Paul's, the third church on the site, burned. Upjohn, whose most famous work is the Gothic Trinity Church in New York, was commissioned to design one to replace it. Thus the location and size of the present church were prescribed by those of the 1814 church, a Robert Cary Long, Sr., design.

Upjohn designed an Italian Romanesque basilica with a high tower (never completed) on the northwest corner. The building is constructed of red brick with sandstone trim. The well-proportioned west front is distinguished by its three large arches. Above are two bas-relief stone panels, carved by Antonio Capellano for the 1814 church.

Inside, there is the same sense of restraint and effective proportion one finds on the exterior. Four arches on each side divide the church into nave and side aisles, but so open is the design that one has the feeling of a single large, rectangular space. Above the nave is a clerestory with stained-glass windows. The roof is supported by wooden trusses. Several of the stained-glass windows in the church, including the one under the coffered barrel vault of the chancel, are by Louis Comfort Tiffany.

28   COMMERCIAL CREDIT COMPANY ANNEX
301 North Charles Street
1930—Mottu and White

This nine-story building, with partial tenth and eleventh floors, was built for the Baltimore Life Insurance Company. It is the best high-rise example in the city of the then popular modernistic style. It is a steel-frame structure with a granite and brick exterior. Restrained Art Deco ornamentation is visible in the cast- and wrought-iron balconies, the inset marble and bronze panels, the piers, and the roof-top parapet. One of the exterior mezzanines at the top of the building (designated "roof garden" on the original drawings) has shrubbery and a pond; the other is open.

More spirited Art Deco devices appear at ground level: fans, chevrons, and zigzags; reed, cable, and leaf moldings; bronze gates, doors, and screens with a vine motif. The lobby is more lavish still, with bronze and marble decor, grilles, and chandeliers.

The Commercial Credit Company bought the building in 1971 for expansion, renovated it, and built a low-level walkway connecting it to its headquarters on St. Paul Place.

29 OLD YMCA BUILDING
Charles and Saratoga streets (northwest corner)
1873—Niernsee and Neilson

Diagonally across the street from St. Paul's is the former Morris Building, originally the YMCA. As designed by Niernsee and Neilson in 1873, it was in the heavily decorated Romanesque style, the brick relieved with stone columns and arches decorating the windows. The dormered mansard roof above the cornice is distinctive and was even more so when the building sprouted towers and turrets; these were removed and the entrance changed in a 1907 alteration by Joseph E. Sperry. The building has passed through several hands. The interior has been renovated, and the building was recently sold to Washington investors.

30 ST. PAUL'S RECTORY
Cathedral and Saratoga streets
1791, later altered—Architect unknown

Since 1792, all but one of the St. Paul's rectors have lived in this building. It is basically a Federal house, with some alterations.

The house was originally of five-part design. A long dependency, destroyed before 1829, connected to the east wing, or hyphen. The west dependency was never built, and the west wing was an addition of the 1830s. At the same time a second story was added to the east wing.

The main bay of the central wing is slightly projected and contains a Palladian window. The pediment of the simple door below echoes the gable above. The front windows are surmounted by pink, flat-arch headers; the string course across the front above the first story and the water table below show a restrained but careful attention to detail.

The house is only one room deep, in the manner of earlier eighteenth-century houses, but has a polygonal projection at the rear housing a staircase. The rear extension to the north of the house and other additions are from the 1830s.

31 CATHEDRAL PLACE (Odd Fellows Hall)
Cathedral and Saratoga streets
1891—Frank E. Davis

The architect of the State Normal School on Lafayette
Square, recently demolished, and the Pine Street Police
Station [111] was also responsible for this Richardson Romanesque design, with its large-arched entranceways, its
hipped roofs punctuated by long dormers, and its beautiful
brickwork. The interior was remodeled in 1931 in the Art
Deco mode, and the entire building was restored and renovated for office use, 1976-1978, this last the careful and
admirable work of Joseph R. Azola and Son, with Warren
Peterson as architect. Baltimore's Historical and Architectural Preservation Commission calls it "one of Baltimore's
best examples of an adaptive reuse project."

32 ST. ALPHONSUS' CHURCH
Park Avenue and Saratoga Street
1845—Robert Cary Long, Jr.

In 1841 a group of German and Austrian Roman Catholic
Redemptorist fathers who had settled in Baltimore to help
minister to the city's large Catholic population commissioned Robert Cary Long, Jr., to design a church for them.
The result, St. Alphonsus', was the first major Gothic Revival church in Baltimore; it was also the first important
commission for its designer, who was to become nationally
known.

The plan is simple: a rectangular room, divided into nave
and side aisles, with a rounded apse at one end and a
vestibule at the other. The latter supports a tiered tower
200 feet tall (50 feet taller than the church is long), whose
stages rise from one another "like the joints of a telescope,"
as Long described them. The church is of brick, but iron was
used in the spire, the interior columns, and the window
tracery.

The exterior, with its buttresses set flat against the front of the church, its pointed-arch windows, its battlemented walls and tower sections, and the light buttresses (which indicate that the interior vaulting is plaster, not stone), is simple, sedate, and somewhat severe. The effect is lightened by the stonework, which contrasts with the main color of the walls.

Until recently, the walls were painted putty color to resemble stone, with the buttresses slightly darker and the details painted rose. In 1968, however, the church was stripped of its paint, and the brick now appears in its natural tone, with the stonework gray. Whether it is more attractive painted or unpainted is a matter of personal taste, but it may be said to have been more authentic before, for Long had it painted originally.

The interior is ornately decorated; the columns are painted brown and marbleized; the ribbing is elaborate, 16 ribs rising from each pier toward the ridge ribs down the central and side aisles. The roof is painted in delicate patterns, and the altar and original pulpit add to the richness of the overall impression.

While the Redemptorist fathers desired a church designed after the German models, and were apparently satisfied with Long's work, the architect described St. Alphonsus' as English Perpendicular. In truth, both influences are present: German, for the most part, in the overall pattern; English in much of the detail and decoration. The residence and office building adjacent to the church on the east and St. Alphonsus' "Halle" across the street were added later. Both are in harmony with, but subordinate to, the church itself.

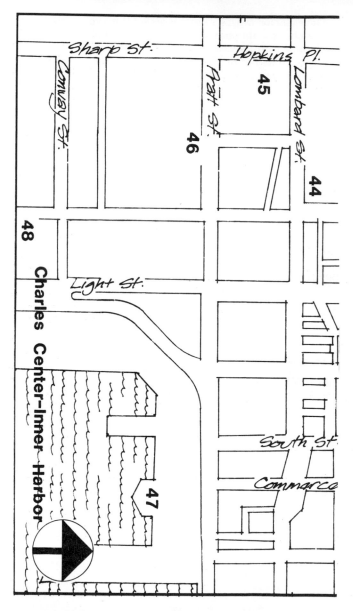

Sharp St.

Hopkins Pl.

Conway St.

Pratt St.

Lombard St.

45

46

44

48

Light St.

Charles Center-Inner Harbor

South St

Commerce

47

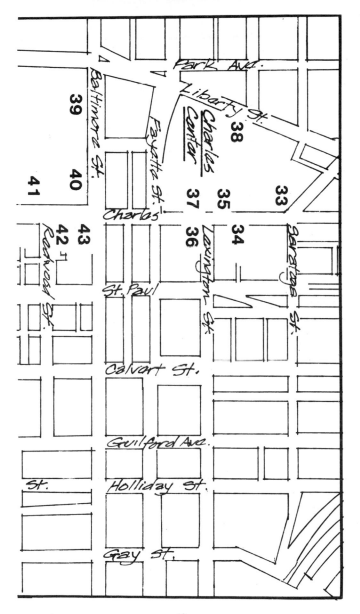

Park Ave.

Liberty St.

Charles Center

Fayette St.

A

V

Baltimore St.

39

40

41

33

35

37

34

36

38

Charles

St. Paul

42

43

Redwood St.

Saratoga St.

Lexington St.

Calvert St.

Guilford Ave.

Holliday St.

St.

Gay St.

49

Tour C   Charles Center-Inner Harbor (Walking)

Just as Mount Vernon Place, with its monument, art museum, music school, and fine old houses has come to represent the history and culture of old Baltimore, Charles Center, with its modern office buildings, stores, and theaters, has become a symbol of the new city.

Although it was but one of many downtown renewal projects launched throughout the country in the late 1950s, urban experts agree that Charles Center is one of the most successful.

Like similar projects elsewhere, Charles Center sprang from an attempt to find a solution to the decline of downtown property values, the general deterioration of the heart of the city, and the flight of development capital to the suburbs.

The idea for Charles Center started in 1954, when the Committee for Downtown, a group of merchants, organized and began to hold meetings. The late J. Jefferson Miller, a former department store executive and later chairman of the board of Charles Center-Inner Harbor Management, Inc., was its first president. The group raised $150,000 to pay for a master plan for downtown.

The Greater Baltimore Committee, composed of about 100 of the metropolitan area's financial, industrial, and professional leaders, was organized the following year. Mortgage banker James W. Rouse, the builder of the new town of Columbia, was one of its most active members. The GBC added $75,000 to the money raised by the Committee for Downtown, and in 1956 established an independent, nonprofit planning council with a highly qualified staff, headed by David A. Wallace, to produce the actual plan.

Having decided what to do, the next job was to decide where to do it. The first step "was to make a sketch plan," wrote Mr. Wallace in *Baltimore's Charles Center*, published by the Urban Land Institute.

"The result was fascinating. Charles Center simply appeared: not in its final form, but in embryo . . . . What appeared was an area of economic instability lying between the financial center on the east and the shopping district—

which was economically weakened, but still a strong anchor—on the west."

The final form of Charles Center, which is now virtually complete, is due to the excellence of the plan developed by Wallace and the Planning Council, the diligence of an architectural review board, made up of Wallace and several distinguished architects, and the close working relationship between the businessmen who envisioned the plan and the city government officials who helped them put it into effect.

In 1958, the voters approved a $25 million bond issue for Charles Center. In March 1959, the City Council adopted the urban renewal plan. So convinced were the planners of the success of the project that they went ahead even though it was not eligible for federal subsidy; six months later, through a change in federal law, it did become eligible.

The main principles of the plan were: to incorporate public open space (Charles Center is organized around three parks, all of which hide underground parking garages); to separate pedestrian and vehicular traffic (it is possible to walk from one end to the other without encountering a car, at least on the same level); and to create a focus for downtown. This the Center does admirably.

Rather than bulldoze the 33 acres and create an island of commercial towers surrounded by concrete, as other cities have done, Baltimore's plan saved five of the original buildings on the site. It also incorporated a felicitous mixture of new ones, all connected by a system of walkways (designed, as were the parks, by RTKL Associates, Inc.) that wind through the project and lead the pedestrian—on several levels because of a 68-foot drop in topography from north to south—through a succession of pleasantly scaled urban spaces.

Even before it was executed, the Charles Center plan had an effect. The Civic Center, after a long battle over whether to build it downtown or in the suburbs, was constructed in its present location largely because of the Charles Center plan. It continues to have an effect: a pedestrian mall has been built from the western border of Charles Center along Lexington Street to Howard Street. Several new buildings, including some of excellent design, have appeared to the south of the project, bridging the space between Charles

Center and the new development lining the Inner Harbor, which was to a large extent inspired by Charles Center's success. The plan itself has changed somewhat over the years, mostly for the better.

Though its planning is hard to fault, Charles Center has its share of mediocre buildings. An outstanding example in this category is the Federal Office Building, which forms the southern boundary of the project and has been described, in an admirable bit of vernacular criticism, as resembling "an IBM card with all the holes punched." But at least such buildings serve to set off Charles Center's architectural gems, which include two of the nation's best buildings of the sixties: Mies van der Rohe's One Charles Center and John Johansen's Mechanic Theatre.

Instead of isolating itself from the rest of Baltimore, Charles Center has already become an integral part of the city. In 1970, it was the site of the first Baltimore City Fair. "It looks," *Fortune* magazine observed prophetically in 1958, "as if it were designed by people who like the city."

Plans to rejuvenate Baltimore's Inner Harbor area also began in the 1950s and gained impetus from the success of Charles Center. Following the removal of the area's traditional shipping activity to deeper water and greater available land farther down the harbor, Baltimore's downtown waterfront entered a period of decline. The renaissance officially began in 1964 with the announcement of a plan to redevelop the land immediately surrounding the Inner Harbor on three sides with cultural and recreational facilities, apartment and office buildings, and hotels and restaurants. The group that guided the Charles Center project—led by J. Jefferson Miller, James W. Rouse, and David A. Wallace—also initiated the plans for the Inner Harbor.

In 1966 the city's voters passed a $14 million bond issue, and the following year the federal government approved $17.7 million in grants for the first phase of the project. The ground-breaking took place in 1971, and other local bond issues and federal grants have been subsequently approved.

The total project involves about 168 acres; the first phase, comprising 95 acres and roughly $270 million in new investment, is now complete or under construction. It includes some excellent architecture, most notably I. M. Pei's handsome, pentagonal World Trade Center. Like Charles Center, the Inner Harbor redevelopment has inspired new construction nearby. The Convention Center to the west and to the east, the new Aquarium now being built, and the proposed rehabilitation by Moshe Safdie of an old power house into a 300-room hotel, are outstanding examples.

The most recent additions to the waterfront are the two store and restaurant pavilions of James W. Rouse's Harborplace. They hold the promise of adding year-round life and spirit to a section of the city that has long lacked them.

33   TWO CHARLES CENTER
Charles and Saratoga streets
1969—Conklin and Rossant

The Two Charles Center complex, consisting of the north and south apartment towers (27 and 30 stories respectively) and adjoining stores and offices, occupies a 1.9-acre plot at the northern tip of Charles Center. The plan originally called for square apartment towers and a third, lower building, which was to house a department store. But the New York architectural firm of Conklin and Rossant, the master planners for the new town of Reston, Virginia, altered the plan somewhat.

Their changes have been for the better. The architects divided what was to have been the third commercial building into two nicely scaled areas of two-story offices, stores, restaurants, and a movie theater. At the western end they placed a small park which will serve as the termination of the major north-south pedestrian route through Charles Center. The eastern end was broadened to become a plaza, opening onto Charles Street and creating a vista of old St. Paul's Church, a landmark on the opposite corner.

The structure of the apartment towers and the adjacent buildings is reinforced concrete faced with a specially made dark brown brick. The exterior columns dividing the bays are structural and give the towers a strong feeling of verticality.

The towers are basically square, but the corners have been carved out in an irregular fashion and the resulting facades have been broken into irregular planes, some stepped back, some thrust forward. The design of the complex is clean, simple, and forceful.

34 MASONIC TEMPLE
223-225 North Charles Street
1869—Architect unknown; 1893—Carson and Sperry; 1909—Joseph E. Sperry

Fires in 1890 and 1908 almost totally destroyed this building, but pictorial evidence suggests that the facade, up to the lower cornice, remains from the 1869 structure. Sperry added the new roof in the Second Empire style in 1909, and probably the new entrance.

35 FIDELITY BUILDING
Charles and Lexington streets (northwest corner)
1893—Baldwin and Pennington

This building offers a striking contrast to One Charles
Center. Its first eight floors are solid granite. The upper
stories (added 1912-1915), with the support of steel framing, are faced with terra-cotta to match the stone.

36 CENTRAL SAVINGS BANK
Charles and Lexington streets (southeast corner)
1890—George A. Frederick

Frederick effectively combined some of Baltimore's traditional materials—granite, brownstone, and brick—with the new Commercial style to produce a handsome building that fortunately was spared by the Baltimore fire of 1904.

37   ONE CHARLES CENTER
Charles and Lexington streets
1962—Mies van der Rohe

This somber, elegantly proportioned 24-story tower, designed by one of the giants of twentieth-century architecture, was the first new office building in Charles Center.

The architect was chosen as a result of a design competition that included an entry by Marcel Breuer. The unusual eight-sided form of the building, with its T-shaped south wall, follows the building zone established by the Baltimore Urban Renewal and Housing Agency.

The tower rises from a landscaped plaza. The three levels beneath the plaza are used for parking, servicing, and retail stores. The level above it, framed by the columns supporting the building, is occupied by the relatively small lobby surrounding the elevator cores. To the west, the tower overhangs the plaza; a handsome stairway leads down to the shops and park below.

The structure of the building is reinforced concrete. The exterior curtain wall is of aluminum with a dark brown finish, and gray-tinted plate glass. The plaza is paved with travertine, the lobby walls with green Tinos marble.

The building took just 13 months to complete, and at $20 a square foot construction cost—about $10,350,000 altogether—was fairly economical for a Mies van der Rohe office building.

38   BALTIMORE GAS AND ELECTRIC COMPANY BUILDING
Lexington and Liberty streets
1916—Parker and Thomas; 1966—Fisher, Nes, Campbell, and Associates

Across Center Plaza, with its Francisco Somaini sculpture representing "Energy," is the Gas and Electric Company. The building is decorated at the fourth-floor level with a row of eight-foot figures representing "knowledge, light, heat and power." From a distance, the top of the shaft, illuminated at night, looks like a row of Greek columns. The lower addition to the building was erected in 1966.

The Hamburger's store that bridges Fayette Street on the other side of the plaza is built on air rights and supported by Vierendeel trusses.

39 MERCANTILE SAFE DEPOSIT AND TRUST COMPANY BUILDING
Baltimore Street and Hopkins Place
1969—Peterson and Brickbauer and Emery Roth and Sons

"The structure of the building is the architecture of the building," according to the designers of this 24-story office tower. The structure, in reinforced concrete, is simply yet forcefully expressed by the exterior load-bearing columns. They divide each long facade into seven bays, and the bays in turn are divided visually by vertical stainless steel tracks for window-washing equipment.

The exterior concrete finish is continued inside the lobby, where the floor is granite and the ceiling is coffered. There are three levels of the building below the lobby, two for parking and the third for vaults.

40   MECHANIC THEATRE
Baltimore and Charles streets
1967—John M. Johansen

"Functional Expressionism" is the term Mr. Johansen has used to describe the architectural style of his theater, whose outside form reflects its interior functions.

The concept is most easily understood after a visit inside the building; the stage is at the east end below a tower capable of supporting 34 tons of scenery; two stair towers are at the west end; balcony seating is in the projecting compartments, etc.

The theater was envisioned in the Charles Center plan as a relatively small sculptural form in a setting of tall neutral facades, such as the Federal Office Building to the south. The theater rests on a platform containing stores and restaurants, below which are two levels of parking and delivery docks.

One entrance is at the level of the plaza, but the lobby is carried up two stories, separated from the outside by a glass

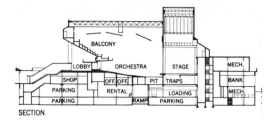

SECTION

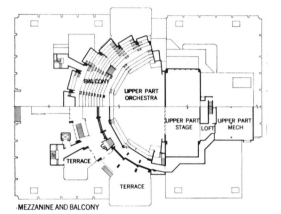

MEZZANINE AND BALCONY

ORCHESTRA LEVEL

wall, and there are entrances at the level of the pedestrian walkways, as well.

The roof of the building is supported by steel trusses. The exterior surfaces are of poured-in-place concrete, cast in forms of rough-sawn oak boards.

Some 1,600 seats, none of them obstructed by piers, fan out from the stage.

41   SUN LIFE BUILDING
South Charles Street and Hopkins Place
1966—Peterson and Brickbauer and Emery Roth and Sons

The Sun Life Building combines solidity and grace. Faced with nonreflective black Canadian granite, the 12-story building (with two sublevels) has a concrete substructure and a separate steel superstructure carried on four large steel columns anchored in bedrock. The columns are visible on the east and west sides.

According to the architects' descriptions, "These four columns, in turn, support two welded steel trusses 143 feet long and 14 1/2 feet deep. The mechanical equipment in the penthouse is supported by another system of trusses which is carried again by the four major columns. This permits the remainder of the columns around the periphery and in the core to be reduced to a minimum dimension," thereby providing wide open areas inside, flexibility of office space, and floor-to-ceiling windows.

The first-floor plaza is devoted to an open terrace and lobby whose materials—stone floors, red marble-encased elevator cores, glass, and steel—are complemented by the Dimitri Hadzi sculpture that hangs from the ceiling.

42   HANSA HAUS
2 East Redwood Street
1907—Parker, Thomas, and Rice

This neo-Hanseatic building was designed for the North German Lloyd Steamship Company after German buildings at the 1900 Paris Exposition and other buildings done in Germany at the time. It is now owned by the Savings Bank of Baltimore.

43 SAVINGS BANK OF BALTIMORE
Baltimore and Charles streets
1907—Parker, Thomas, and Rice

The architects of this "Temple of Thrift," as it was called when it opened, were inspired by the Erechtheum, which stands on the Acropolis in Athens. Their two-story building of white Beaver Dam marble is set on a low platform approached by steps. The pediment in front is supported by four massive but graceful Ionic columns; six similar columns line the side of the building. The ornamentation around the bases of the columns and the lion heads that decorate the cornice are reproduced from casts that came from Athens.

The interior, originally an impressive open banking room with Italian marble wainscoting, huge windows covered with bronze gratings, and a high, coffered ceiling, was changed in 1953 when a second floor was added. The usable banking area was increased but the grandeur of the place was lost.

44 CHARLES CENTER SOUTH
Charles and Lombard streets
1975—RTKL Associates, Inc.

This building's unusual hexagonal shape and its skin of glass are the most obvious elements in its felicitous design by RTKL (the four letters are the official title of this firm, a successor to Rogers, Taliaferro, Kostritsky, and Lamb). Poised at the southeast corner of Charles Center, the building acts, as architectural scholar and critic Phoebe Stanton has pointed out, as a kind of hinge between the city's first major downtown renewal effort and the newer Inner Harbor development. The use of dark gray glass panels fastened to the tower structure with stainless steel buttons and sealed together edge to edge with silicone caulking was a masterful idea, for it manages to accomplish several tasks at once. Dr. Stanton has noted that the shape of the building acts as a foil for the cubical Sun Life Building to the north and the slablike Federal Building to the west; in addition, the feeling of lightness achieved by Charles Center South plays well against the solidity of both those buildings. The smooth, reflective surface, reminiscent of water, is especially appropriate considering its proximity to the harbor. And in an area almost entirely populated with recent buildings, there is always the danger of a boring monotony of similar shapes, colors, and facades; Charles Center South is refreshing simply because it is unlike everything around it. Its only drawback is one of height; the architect's original rendering suggested a taller building, which could have made for an even more elegant appearance, especially in relation to its two closest neighbors.

45   EDWARD A. GARMATZ FEDERAL COURTHOUSE
101 West Lombard Street
1976—RTKL Associates, Inc.

The architects avoided what might have been just another massive federal building in this case by varying the fenestration and giving a sculptural treatment to the structures housing the mechanical equipment. The L-shape was chosen to create a pronounced border on Hopkins Place and Pratt Street (the latter is supposed to become a boulevard) and to provide an internal courtyard with a well-defined entrance. It is enhanced by George Sugarman's playful sculpture.

The building is framed in structural steel with a precast concrete exterior. An important feature of the design is the dual circulation system, which segregates judges and court personnel on the south side of the building from the general public on the north side. They meet in the 16 courtrooms located in the center. The wing facing Hopkins Place contains offices for federal agencies.

Different functions are expressed by the varying treatment of the windows: continuous glass denotes the public walkways, mullioned glass the federal offices. The deeply modeled facade with louvers planned for the Pratt Street side was unfortunately eliminated for economic reasons. However, the sculptural roof forms and the bold entrance and elevator tower, thrust forward from the rest of the building, are decided bonuses. The construction cost of the building was $22 million.

Across Hopkins Place, at 200-202 West Pratt Street, is the Moses Sheppard House, one of the few remaining eighteenth-century houses in the city.

46   BALTIMORE CONVENTION CENTER
One West Pratt Street
1979—Naramore, Bain, Brady and Johanson; Cochran, Stephenson and Donkervoet

The opposite of the box type of exhibit hall, the Baltimore Convention Center is notable for being light, airy, and spacious. Site conditions and difficult project requirements, combined with the talents of the architects and engineers, resulted in the building's highly sophisticated design.

Kept low to reduce its impact on the surrounding structures, the Center's three levels step back in successive tiers from the main entrance on Pratt Street and enclose an impressive amount of space. The first level contains a two-story lobby, four large exhibition halls, kitchens, truck docks, and other service facilities. The main lobby is connected at the mezzanine level to a secondary one facing Sharp Street (made possible by the site's upward slope to the west), with a windowed walkway that allows visitors to see down on either side into the exhibit halls. The third level has 23 meeting rooms (the largest with a capacity of 2,000), indoor lounges, and an outdoor plaza.

The roofs of the various levels, supported by 90-foot steel trusses are linked by sloping skylights, most of them running the entire length of the building. These, held in turn by angled steel beams, allow at the eastern end a well-lighted, unobstructed view from the top level down to the fountains in the main lobby. From the outside at night, they appear as narrow bands of light. The lobby, enclosed by eight-foot-square panels of suspended glass, is also highly visible from the street. The base of the building is covered in gray granite.

The major difficulty overcome by the designers was in the four 140-by-180-foot interconnected exhibit halls. Each was to have a 35-foot ceiling, 25,000 square feet of column-free space, and be able to support meeting rooms or plazas on its roof. To maintain the building's low profile, the normal deep roof trusses could not be used.

Instead, the architects and structural engineers, Skilling, Helle, Christiansen, Robertson, Inc., of Seattle, produced a radical post-tensioned reinforced concrete system whose outlines are clearly visible both inside and outside the building. The structure of each exhibit hall might be likened to four suspension bridges, angled toward each other at 37 degrees, with a roof on top. The system, developed with the aid of models and computer diagrams, consists essentially of steel cables four inches in diameter (one-quarter the size of those supporting the Brooklyn Bridge) slung between the corner posts and embedded in concrete.

The load, rather than being suspended from the cable, as in a bridge, descends from above, transmitted by angled beams. The cable structure picks up the roof load and transfers it to four corner columns, each three and a half feet in diameter. These columns rest on concrete caissons, extended to bedrock. The largest caisson is 9 feet in diameter, spreads to 16 feet at its base, and is about 70 feet deep. The corner columns, subject to outward pressure like that exerted by a masonry dome, are tied together at the bend with heavy reinforced concrete beams, also post-tensioned. The builder was the Whiting-Turner Contracting Company.

With over 400,000 square feet of space, and room for 7,500 delegates, the Center is capable of accommodating all but the largest conventions and trade shows. It cost $50 million.

47   WORLD TRADE CENTER
401 East Pratt Street
1968-1977—I. M. Pei and Partners

Several elements contribute to the success of this distinguished design: its pentagonal shape, which keeps it from looking like a bulky up-ended box and which allows two sides to come to a point on the harbor front, suggesting the prow of a ship; the proportions of the long, uninterrupted windows and the notches in the concrete between them, which provide elegant horizontals to balance the verticality of the building; the five structural piers at the corners (a sixth supports the core), with their deep recesses, which are lighted at night. These are the most obvious to the viewer, and they work functionally as well as visually. The 65-foot-long windows define the interior spaces on each floor around the service core and provide remarkable views for the office workers inside. The pentagonal shape allows "more usable office space in less visible mass to interrupt the view of the harbor," as critic Phoebe Stanton has noted. The corner piers allow long uninterrupted interior spaces for flexible design of offices.

The building, of reinforced concrete construction, was completed at a cost of $22 million for the Maryland Department of Transportation and the Port Administration, which own it, occupy several floors, and lease out the rest as offices. The 28-story tower has a public observation deck at the twenty-seventh level, with exhibits on the city's history and its port.

The principal architects were Henry Cobb and Pershing Wong of the Pei firm; the local architect was H. Parker Matthai of the firm of Richter Cornbrooks Matthai Hopkins.

48 MARBURG TOBACCO WAREHOUSE
429 South Charles Street
1887—Charles L. Carson

Warehouses can be wonderful buildings. Relieved of the obligation to present an imposing facade appropriate to a company's front offices, they can instead possess a simple strength and dignity that far surpasses the effect of any amount of embellishment. Such is certainly the case with this building. Solid, massive, understated, it possesses the attributes of a man of unimpeachable honesty.

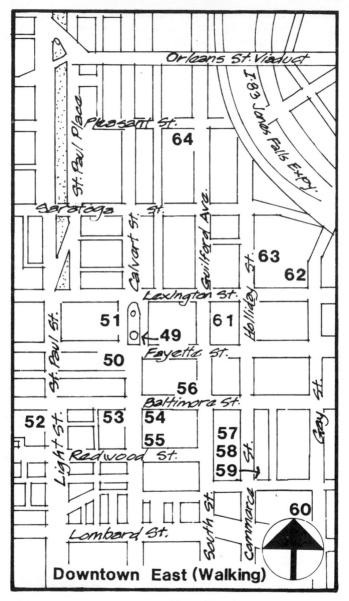

Downtown East (Walking)

This has long been the financial and governmental section of the city, as its architecture shows. As early as 1814 what is now known as Court Square was important enough to be chosen as the site of the Battle Monument, which subsequently became the symbol of Baltimore. Within a few blocks are most of the major banks and stockbrokerage houses, City Hall, and the city's municipal offices. In 1904 a disastrous fire swept through Baltimore. This area, in which many of the newly-constructed, high-rise buildings "burned like torches," sustained heavy damage.

49   BATTLE MONUMENT
Court Square
1815—Maximilian Godefroy

The Battle Monument was one of the structures (the other was the Washington Monument) that gave Baltimore the name Monumental City. It was erected 1814-1815 to commemorate the defense of Baltimore and the memory of those who died in that defense in September 1814, during the War of 1812. It is unusual for two reasons: it is a democratic monument to all who died, regardless of rank; and it was probably the first Egyptian-inspired architecture in Baltimore.

Godefroy, a Frenchman, was influenced by the popularity of Egyptian architecture in France after Napoleon's

1798-1799 expedition to Egypt. When he was selected as architect of the Monument, he used Egyptian and other ancient devices, that he combined in a heavily symbolic plan. This was also a result of his nationality, for he had lived in a France in which national heroes and holidays were lavishly commemorated with parades of symbolic floats.

The Monument, built entirely of marble, is about 39 feet high. Its base is an Egyptian cenotaph, with black stone doors in the faces suggesting entrances to a tomb. The 18 layers of marble used in the base symbolized the 18 states of the union at the time of the erection of the monument.

The four corners of the cenotaph are decorated with griffons, mythical beasts that guarded the doors to ancient tombs. From the base rises a shaft, the bottom of which is decorated with friezes depicting the two actions of the defense—the battle of North Point and the bombardment of Fort McHenry.

The column is carved in the form of a fasces, or bundle of staves, the Roman symbol of unity. It is bound with cords upon which are written the names of the 36 soldiers who died in the engagements, suggesting the sacrifice of their lives to preserve the Union. Above them are engraved the names of three officers who lost their lives in the defense, in a band below the statue.

The female statue, in this case symbolic of Baltimore, wears a mural crown of victory and carries a laurel wreath, symbol of glory. Her other hand grasps a rudder, symbolizing either stability or navigation, depending upon which account you read. The statue is of Italian marble and was executed by Antonio Capellano.

The little plaza to the north of the Monument was added in the 1960s.

50 EQUITABLE BUILDING
Calvert and Fayette streets
1894—Carson and Sperry

The Equitable, one of downtown's largest and handsomest
Commercial-style buildings, has Sullivanesque touches in
its ornamentation. Ten stories high, with an interior frame
of cast-iron columns and steel beams, and exterior self-
supporting walls, the building was regarded as "thoroughly
fire proof" when built. The walls are of granite on the lower
three stories, with buff brick above and terra-cotta trim.
The Equitable originally had Turkish baths in the basement, a restaurant on the top floor, and a roof garden.

The Equitable Building was heavily damaged during the
1904 fire when the floor arches failed and heavy safes fell
from the upper floors all the way through to the basement.
In the analysis that followed the fire, the architects were
criticized for the lightness of the construction and the poor
use of materials. Said Sperry, "The Baltimore fire has
greatly modified my views regarding the best materials
and construction for so-called fire-proof buildings."

Later rebuilt, the Equitable has recently been acquired
by new owners who have sandblasted and painted the
outside.

51 BALTIMORE COURT HOUSE
Calvert and Fayette streets
1900—Wyatt and Nolting

An imposing building in the Renaissance Revival style, the Baltimore Court House stands on almost exactly the same site as two previous ones, the first built in 1767. The present building was the result of a design competition in which some of the country's leading architects, such as McKim, Mead, and White, Burnham and Atwood, and Carrère and Hastings, were asked to participate.

It is a steel-frame structure faced with Beaver Dam marble on the upper floors and Woodstock granite on the lower. Covering an entire city block, it has three main stories, plus a fourth (due to the slope of the land) on the Calvert Street side, which is the main facade. The primary exterior feature is a massive loggia with eight huge monoliths, some of the largest in the world, that weighed 90 tons each when quarried.

Inside the Calvert Street entrance is a forest of piers supporting a series of vaults. Marble stairways on either side lead up to the first floor gallery of the Criminal Court and continue up to landings. Balustrades overlook the room, which is one of the most distinctive in the building. The floors are laid out with a ring of offices around the perimeter, then a corridor, and, in the center, the courtrooms.

The Court House was remodeled in the 1950s at a cost greater than the $2,250,000 paid for the entire building in 1900. New elevators, lighting, and air conditioning were installed. Light courts were filled in with offices and additional floors were added, making a total of six.

In the remodeling process, the stained-glass skylights and some of the other features of the building were lost. A few treasures survive: the old Orphan's Court on the first floor, with parquet floors and ornate wall and ceiling decorations; and, at opposite ends of the sixth floor, the rotunda occupied by the Supreme Bench and the barrel-vaulted bar library. Throughout the building are rich marbles, mahogany woodwork, and murals by John La Farge and Edwin H. Blashfield, among others. All in all, a "noble pile" as the chief judge described it at the dedication.

52   MARYLAND NATIONAL BANK BUILDING
Baltimore and Light streets
1929—Taylor and Fisher; Smith and May

The tallest building in Baltimore when it opened (as the Baltimore Trust Building), the Maryland National Bank Building is most notable for the exuberance of its Art Deco decorations.

The carved granite around the upper-story windows and the elaborately intricate designs in the bronze of doorways and windows on the first floor contain stylized "modernistic" designs of the twenties. Zigzags, sunbursts, and cloud and fountain motifs are all typical of the period.

The enormous banking room is of principal interest. Rising two stories from a bold stone mosaic floor to an ornate painted ceiling, it has multicolored marble columns on the upper level. This is one of the more dramatic interior spaces the city has to offer.

Thirty-four stories and 780 feet tall, the building is capped by a bold mansard roof. The disfiguring signs are an addition of the present owner.

53 ALEX. BROWN AND SONS BUILDING
Calvert and Baltimore streets
1900—Parker and Thomas

This building, which reveals an unexpected dome as one enters the door, survived the Baltimore fire of 1904. One can still see marks of the damage on the exterior.

54 ONE SOUTH CALVERT BUILDING
201-207 East Baltimore Street
1901—D. H. Burnham and Company

The Continental Trust Building, as it was known originally, is the only building in Baltimore by a major practitioner of the Commercial or Chicago style which forms the historical basis of modern high-rise construction. It was developed in the Midwest primarily through the work of H. H. Richardson, William Le Baron Jenney, Louis Sullivan, and John Wellborn Root. Daniel H. Burnham was actually more of an organizer than an original creator of architecture, but he worked with the best designers, and around the turn of the century, his firm produced a large number of buildings throughout the East and Midwest.

His 16-story, steel-frame building in Baltimore is faced with stone, brick, and terra-cotta (which was also used for the floor arches and partitions). In the building's design, Burnham made a bow to local classical tradition by adding Renaissance Revival pediments over some of the windows and a row of columns at the top under an elaborate terra-cotta frieze and cornice. The arches, raised several stories in height, and the triple windows in each bay are characteristic of the Chicago style. Burnham confined his use of the Chicago bay (a bay window repeated for several stories) to a single example at the rear.

The Continental Trust, in a location where the 1904 Baltimore fire was the hottest (an estimated 2,500 degrees Fahrenheit), was completely burned out. During the following weeks, architects and engineers from several cities came here to observe the effects of the first real test of the modern fireproof construction methods developed over the previous 20 years. For the most part, the new methods and materials, especially terra-cotta, were vindicated. Burnham himself arrived to reassure the owners of the Continental Trust, writing them later: "I have minutely examined the steel structure of your building on the corner of Baltimore and Calvert streets from the basement to the roof, and find the same intact and good as the day it was put up. . . . I advise you to at once proceed to repair this building."

They did, and the structure, now owned by the One Calvert Company, is occupied mainly by state agencies. The cornice, which once completely hid the top floor (the piece that remains is missing its topmost section) was not replaced after being damaged by the fire, and there have been some disfiguring changes at the roofline.

55 OLD MERCANTILE SAFE DEPOSIT AND TRUST COMPANY BUILDING
Calvert and Redwood streets
1886—Wyatt and Sperry

The strong, solid, castlelike forms of Richardsonian Romanesque architecture were admirably suited to banks. This one has a "Burglar Proof Money Vault" (as it was called in 1885) on the first floor. But it is the exterior, with its dramatic windows, fine brickwork, and wealth of carved stone detail that make it outstanding for its period in Baltimore. It was designed by a local firm but bears comparison with similar works by H. H. Richardson and Stanford White.

The walls of the building, brick with light red freestone trim, are load-bearing; there is structural iron in the roof and basement. (An interesting feature of the walls is the placement of "spy steps" which allowed watchful policemen to peer in the windows.)

The interior has been much changed since being damaged by the Baltimore fire of 1904. Although new buildings on all sides of the bank were gutted, the exterior of the Mercantile Trust Building was not greatly damaged. It is likely the interior would have survived as well if bricks from the Continental Trust Building to the north had not crashed through the skylight and set fire to it.

Since the Mercantile Bank moved to its new headquarters in Charles Center [39], this building has become a branch bank.

56 TOWER BUILDING
222 East Baltimore Street
1905-1912—Parker and Thomas; Otto B. Simonson

Built in three stages for the Maryland Casualty Company, the Tower Building, at 365 feet, was the tallest in Baltimore when completed (Parker and Thomas were the original architects; Simonson is credited with the tower). A five-story main building with a tower reaching 18 stories, it originally had a commercial arcade running from Baltimore to Fayette streets, and was described at the time as "one of the finest Beaux-Arts compositions standing in Baltimore." Though the elaborate ornamentation of the main entrance and other embellishments do show Beaux Arts influence, the building as a whole can be taken as less Beaux Arts than an example of the early-twentieth-century fashion of festooning office buildings, against which the Chicago school and the International style were such strong reactions.

57   SAFE DEPOSIT AND TRUST COMPANY BUILDING
13 South Street
1876—E. Francis Baldwin;   1903—Baldwin and Pennington; 1929—Laurence Hall Fowler

This intriguing building is a puzzle. The *American Architect and Building News* for January 15, 1876, reports on a new building by Baldwin for the Safe Deposit Company and shows a rendering of a Frank-Furness-like High Victorian building (but with rounded instead of pointed arches) in brick and granite; it is obviously the existing building, except that it is only three bays wide. The next evidence we have is from blueprints that still exist and give a date of 1903 and a firm name of Baldwin and Pennington. It is not clear whether in 1903 the building was enlarged from three bays to five and the entrance was altered with the addition of the pairs of columns, or whether the building was originally built in five-bay form and only the double columns, a Beaux Arts touch entirely out of keeping with the rest, were added in 1903. The latter would seem more probable, for why would an architect faithfully and scrupulously reproduce an older building in his enlargement and then stick a totally inappropriate entrance onto it? At any rate, the building survived the Baltimore fire of 1904 with, a contemporary account says, little damage. The south bay was added by Laurence Hall Fowler in 1929 and is typical of him: highly competent, ultimately dull.

58   FURNESS HOUSE
19 South Street
1917—Edward H. Glidden

This little Adam-style building, with its double orders of columns, Palladianesque windows, and delicate decorations, is a breath of fresh air among the more massive structures that surround it.

59   CHAMBER OF COMMERCE BUILDING
Water and Commerce streets
1880—J. R. Niernsee; 1904—Charles E. Cassell

Built by the members of the Corn and Flour Exchange, with an open hall at the top floor where they did their trading, the original 1880 Chamber of Commerce Building by

Niernsee was of red brick ornamented with white granite. It looked something like the Safe Deposit and Trust Company nearby [57]. It burned in the Baltimore fire of 1904 but was speedily rebuilt by Cassell, who gave it a modified Renaissance look in warm ocher brick.

60 UNITED STATES CUSTOM HOUSE
Gay and Lombard streets
1907—Hornblower and Marshall

The Custom House was constructed on the site of Benjamin H. Latrobe's domed Merchants' Exchange, a city landmark opened in 1820 and demolished about 1900. (Latrobe's building also housed a Custom House.)

Perhaps inspired by their predecessor, the architects here created a landmark of the Beaux Arts style. The main features of the facade are the three-story engaged columns, segmental and triangular pediments over the windows, and rooftop balustrade. The six-story building is actually U-shaped, its rear wings flanking a lower pavilion and courtyard. The structure is steel-frame, but with load-bearing exterior walls of granite.

The lobby inside, which once rose through four floors, and its marble and iron stairways, have been enclosed. The huge, lofty call room, where ship captains once conducted their business and which more recently housed draft boards, has been renovated and its main attraction restored. That attraction is *Entering Port*, a 30-by-63-foot ceiling canvas depicting a fleet of ships, and the surrounding smaller paintings illustrating *The History of Naviga-tion.* They are the work of Francis Davis Millet, American journalist and mural painter, whose works hang in major museums in New York and London. The paintings reflect the complementary nature of art and architecture at the turn of the century and have been called by experts "the finest decorative art in any public building in the country."

61 CITY HALL
Holliday Street between Fayette and Lexington streets
1875—George A. Frederick

The city's prime example of post-Civil War, Grant-era ele-gance, this building in the French Baroque Revival style was Frederick's first commission. He was less than 20 years old when he submitted the winning design.

The four-story building has two connected lateral wings three stories high with mansard roofs. These, the arched windows, bullet-hole dormers, and other decorations show French influence applied with a certain amount of Ameri-can flamboyance.

The roof was believed to be the largest iron-structured roof of its kind. Much iron was also used in the interior structure, but the building has brick bearing walls 5.5 feet thick faced with local Beaver Dam marble.

The interior rotunda rises 119 feet through three stories surrounded by Doric, Ionic, and Corinthian columns to an interior dome. Above this the exterior dome rises to 227 feet. The segmental dome design was by Wendel Bollman (see Introduction), with iron by Bartlett-Robbins and Company.

In 1975 the building was thoroughly renovated, with an attempt made to save the best of the old while making as much use of space as possible. The ceremonial chambers were carefully restored, the dome repaired, and two courtyards opened up and roofed with glass to make public areas suitable for exhibitions. The rotunda was beautifully restored. In addition, two new floors were infilled, to create six out of four. The renovation architects were Architectural Heritage with Meyers and D'Aleo. The building was rededicated in January 1977. Its original cost had been $2.3 million, $250,000 less than the appropriation, plus $104,000 for furnishings. The cost of the renovation was $10.5 million, plus $850,000 for furnishings.

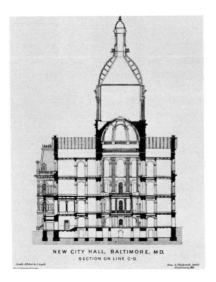

NEW CITY HALL, BALTIMORE, MD.
SECTION ON LINE C-D.

The plaza in front of City Hall and the Greek classical War Memorial Building which faces City Hall on the other side of the plaza were both designed by Laurence Hall Fowler (1925).

62 ZION LUTHERAN CHURCH
Holliday and Lexington streets
1807—Rohrback and Machenheimer, builders

The two builders responsible for this church had worked with Maximilian Godefroy on his St. Mary's Seminary chapel [109]. That is probably where they got their idea for the pointed windows and crenellations of Zion Lutheran, built two years later.

63 PEALE MUSEUM
225 Holliday Street
1814—Robert Cary Long, Sr.

This simple, early Classical Revival building was commissioned by Rembrandt Peale and was the first structure in the United States built specifically as a public museum.

Containing three stories of brick with basement and attic and a square gallery appended to the rear, the museum has a facade graced with restrained decoration. An early sketch of this museum suggests that the original facade differed from the present one in having a loggia with four double columns over the first-floor porch.

The interior has been renovated several times to serve the various uses of the building: from 1830 to 1875 it was the City Hall; later it was a school. In 1930, the front wall was rebuilt and the interior was renovated. The latest renovation began in 1979.

64 TERMINAL WAREHOUSE
Pleasant and Davis streets
1893—Architect unknown; 1912—Owens and Sisco

A fine turn-of-the-century commercial building, the Terminal Warehouse was built as a "flour house": that is, it was originally designed to handle only that commodity. The older building (the section facing Davis Street) was constructed in 1893 with pine posts and beams. Steel was used in the newer part, built in 1912, which consists of the three bays at the southern end. The total cost of the two buildings, including the land, was about $200,000.

The architects were careful to match the new work to the old, with the result that the two buildings look like one. Besides the brick string course, the only other decorations are strictly functional: steel-covered wooden shutters protect the windows, and a distinctive octagonal redwood water tank stands atop the structure. It was probably part of the 1912 addition.

The warehouse, brick with a stone foundation and Port Deposit granite door and windowsills, has six floors and a basement. The first floor was built to accommodate eight rail cars and twelve trucks (or horses and wagons in the old days). The City Archives are now housed in the building.

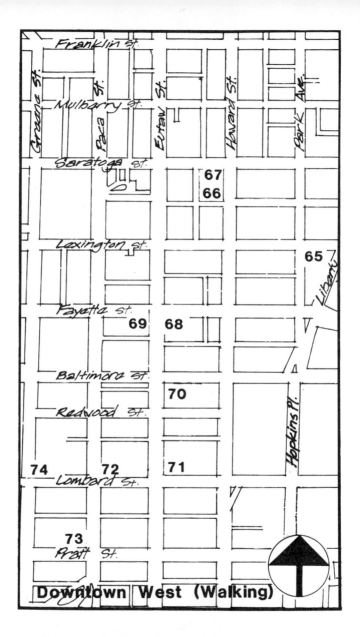

Downtown West (Walking)

Most of these buildings are commercial, for this is still a commercial section of town. Except for the Hutzler Building, all were built before 1912. Another generation may appreciate newer structures than the Emerson Tower or the Strouse Company Building, but Davidge Hall is sufficiently distant in time and style for its claim on our affections to be firmly established.

65   KRESGE'S
119 West Lexington Street
1908, 1937—Architect unknown

Little is known about this schlocky but amusing late Art Deco or "Moderne" building except the belief that it was first erected in 1908 and received a thorough face lifting in 1937. That was the heyday of what was then called the Moderne style, a successor or late manifestation of the Art Deco style of the twenties. With the streamlining of airplanes and automobiles, the rounded form supplanted the rectilinear of classic Art Deco and often resulted in such bulbous creations as the store windows here. It is fitting that what is to be seen of the Kresge Building is no more than a facade pasted on an older building, for Art Deco was, as its name implies, never more than a decorative rather than an architectural style.

66   HUTZLER BROTHERS COMPLEX
210-234 North Howard Street
1888-1941—Baldwin and Pennington; James R. Edmunds

The oldest department store in Baltimore, Hutzler Bros.
has occupied space on the west side of the 200 block of
Howard Street since 1858. None of its original buildings
remains. They were demolished for the erection in 1888 of
the oldest part of the present complex, the five-story, three-
bay, largely Romanesque building at 212 to 218. Designed
by Baldwin and Pennington, it had two four-story arches
infilled with thrust polygonal bays flanking a central entrance with a Moorish arch that can still be seen over the
altered first-floor entrance. Originally, this building was
surmounted by a turret at the north corner, at Clay Street.
It was enlarged one bay to the south (Number 210) at the
turn of the century; the addition had a similar stone facade,
but without arch or thrust bay.

The two northernmost buildings of the complex, 228 to 234, were four-story commercial buildings redeveloped as part of the Hutzler group from 1913 to 1916. In 1931 the first five stories of the central building, including four stories of air rights above Clay Street, were constructed to a design by the firm of James R. Edmunds. The Art Deco-inspired design was carried across the facade at the first level. Notable aspects of this facade include the brass grillwork over the display windows; the two large vertical windows above the first-floor level and below stylized lettering; the fluted quarter columns of the windows and their forestanding urns; the color gradations of the brickwork, growing lighter from bottom to top; and the treatment of the first-level entrances. An additional five stories were added to the central building in 1941. An interesting engineering note is that when the 1931 building went up the structural steel was welded rather than riveted; it is said to be the first field-welded (i.e., on-site welded) job in Baltimore's business district.

67 PROVIDENT SAVINGS BANK
Howard and Saratoga streets
1903—Joseph E. Sperry and York and Sawyer

This rusticated mass of granite, with walls seven feet thick at the base, was designed to simulate an old treasure chest.

It also resembles Italian Renaissance palaces such as the Strozzi in Florence.

Originally the building had an arched dome that rose 83 feet from the floor, but 1949 and 1953 renovations created third and fourth stories that blocked the view of the dome. James R. Edmunds, Jr., was the architect of the 1949 and 1953 alterations. His firm was the continuation of Sperry's.

68 BALTIMORE EQUITABLE SOCIETY BUILDING
21 North Eutaw Street
1857—Joseph F. Kemp

A handsome brick Italian Renaissance Revival building with a brownstone front, this was built as the headquarters of the Eutaw Savings Bank, which 30 years later moved across the street. The Baltimore Equitable Society acquired it in 1889.

Except for the removal of the bars over the windows, the building remains substantially as it was built. Inside is a large room with a high coffered ceiling, tile floor, dark woodwork, and clerks toiling behind the wire mesh above the old bank counter.

The Baltimore Equitable Society is the third oldest fire insurance firm in the United States. The building features a second-floor museum filled with old firefighting equipment, models, and photographs, but the society's most prized collection consists of hundreds of old fire marks (company emblems displayed on buildings to indicate they were insured) lining the walls of the treasurer's office.

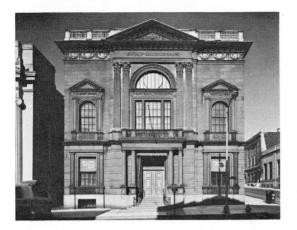

69   EUTAW SAVINGS BANK BUILDING
Eutaw and Fayette streets
1887—Charles L. Carson; 1911—Baldwin and Pennington

This Renaissance-styled brownstone banking building, with its wealth of carved material, its pediment, frieze, and Corinthian columns, and its Palladian windows, is especially interesting when compared to the Equitable Society Building across the street. The latter was the bank's first building. In moving to larger quarters, the bank obviously wished to erect a building which, though grander, would be in keeping with the style of the older structure. The later building, however, shows a scholastic attention to the correct use of Renaissance elements, while its older neighbor shows a Victorian influence, especially in its hooded windows. The last three bays on the Fayette Street side of the newer building, added when it was enlarged in 1911, although of a darker stone, show a careful effort to reproduce elements of the 1887 portion. The building is now a branch of the Maryland National Bank.

70 ABELL BUILDING
329-335 West Baltimore Street
ca. 1878—George A. Frederick

The finest Victorian warehouse in Baltimore, this five-floor store and loft building with its exuberant decoration was built by A. S. Abell, then owner of the *Baltimore Sun.* Clothing firms occupy the building now, as they did in its earliest days. The structure is mainly Baltimore brick, with bluestone, white marble, and terra-cotta trim. This gives the Eutaw Street facade a rich, varicolored appearance, enhanced by a profusion of crockets, rosettes, and other details. The three ground-level store-fronts, now mainly covered over, are framed in cast iron by Bartlett-Robbins and Company.

At 322 West Baltimore Street is a particularly fine partially iron-fronted building (top four floors only), built in 1866 and one of a dozen or so that remain in the general area.

71   EMERSON TOWER (BALTIMORE ARTS TOWER)
Eutaw and Lombard streets
1911—Joseph E. Sperry

This has been one of the most distinctive ornaments on Baltimore's skyline, particularly visible to those entering the city from the Baltimore-Washington Parkway. The adjacent six-story building has been demolished, but the tower was considered so much a part of Baltimore that it was saved.

The building once housed the offices and factory of Captain Isaac E. Emerson, developer of Bromo-Seltzer, who made a grand tour of Europe shortly after the turn of the century and was so fascinated with the tower of the Palazzo Vecchio in Florence that on his return he commissioned Sperry to design one like it.

The palazzo after which the tower is modeled is a thirteenth-century stone building with a battlemented watchtower rising above a fortified facade. The palace tower is 308 feet tall, built of rough stone, and has few windows, although it does have a clock. Despite the differences, the Baltimore tower bears a noticeable resemblance to its Florentine exemplar. It is 288 feet high, and at one time was topped with a 51-foot, 17-ton reproduction of the blue Bromo-Seltzer bottle, which revolved, and was crowned with lights.

The battlements were added to the top of the tower when the bottle was removed in 1930. In 1967, the Bromo-Seltzer business was moved to Pennsylvania by the company that bought the Emerson Drug Company. The building was left to the city with the stipulation that the tower, at least, be retained. The city now uses it for an arts and crafts center. A fire house has replaced the old Bromo-Seltzer factory.

The tower is of steel-frame construction, faced with yellow brick. It contains two elevators, with office space on most of its 16 floors.

72   STROUSE BROTHERS COMPANY BUILDING
410 West Lombard Street
1890—George A. Frederick; later addition

Frederick, a prolific architect, was nothing if not adaptable. Only three blocks and 12 years separate his Victorian Abell Building [70], from this, the first warehouse built in Baltimore in the Commercial style. It is contemporaneous with Frederick's Central Savings Bank [36]. The Strouse Brothers Company Building is a rendering, in brick (with stone at the lower level), of H. H. Richardson's Marshall Field Wholesale Store in Chicago, finished three years earlier.

It was built as a clothing factory and is still used, for the most part, for the manufacture of clothing. Inside are six open loft floors supported with wooden columns and beams. The first floor, which was the office, has iron columns and the original wood paneling in the ceiling.

Strouse Brothers began business in Baltimore in 1868. It was headed by Leopold Strouse, who was a leading philanthropist of the time. Among other things, he served as chairman of the building committee for the Eutaw Place Temple. City directories show that the company was located in the Abell Building in 1890 but by the following year had moved to their new quarters.

In 1906, an addition to the building was built to the east, on Lombard Street. Except for the use of structural iron rather than wood, it is the same inside (the floors are connected), but its undistinguished exterior makes Frederick's talents all the more obvious.

73   PACA-PRATT BUILDING
Paca and Pratt streets
ca. 1905—Otto Simonson and Theodore Wells Peitsch, with Lucius R. White

This is reported to have been one of the earliest steel-and-concrete buildings in the city, and the most modern structure of its kind in Baltimore when it was built. Two of its hydraulic elevators are still in use.

74 DAVIDGE HALL
Lombard Street near Greene Street
1812—Robert Cary Long, Sr.

One of the earliest buildings of its type in the United States, predating Jefferson's Rotunda at Charlottesville, Davidge Hall is also the oldest medical school building in the United States. It was designed after a similar though smaller building by Benjamin H. Latrobe for the University of Pennsylvania.

The low dome, which sits upon a round drum, is behind a plain, simple facade with a Doric porch. The partially rounded side walls are slightly less severe than the front, each having a fan window.

The circular anatomical theater is roofed by an interior wooden dome. The room below was a chemistry hall with the same diameter as the theater. Between the hall and the porch is a section with offices.

In 1979 a complete restoration of the building was begun by the firm of Edmunds and Hyde, with Michael F. Trostel the architect in charge.

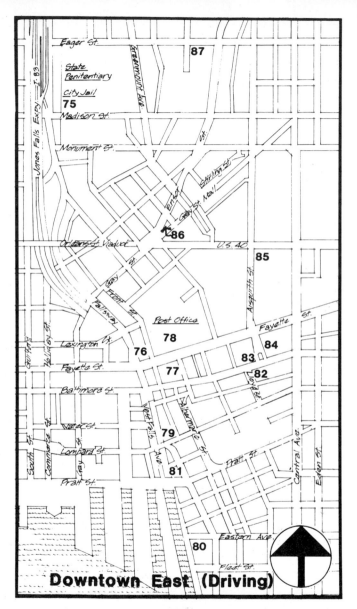

Downtown East (Driving)

Tour F   Downtown East (Driving)

This tour is through the section known as Old Town, which the Peale Museum's Historical Guide to Baltimore describes: "In 1732 the Assembly authorized the surveying of 'Jones-Town,' to be located east of the falls 'on the land whereon Edward Fell keeps store'." The original bounds included Front, High and Exeter Streets between Hillen and Lexington. David Jones and Jonathan Manson had lived here years before, and Fell was already in residence. Jones-Town was annexed to Baltimore Town in 1745 when a bridge was put across the Falls at Gay Street, but the memory that this was actually the oldest settlement has survived in the popular name of 'Old Town' for the neighborhood." Appropriately, most of the buildings on this tour date from well before the Civil War.

75   OLD BALTIMORE CITY JAIL GATEHOUSE
Buren and Madison streets
1859—Thomas and James M. Dixon

Thomas and James Dixon designed a new jailhouse for Baltimore; only the gatehouse remains. The jail was one of the major public buildings of the period, a Gothic structure that at the time was criticized as a "palace for felons." It was a brilliant design nevertheless, incorporating security with maximum light and air for the inmates.

The power and dignity of the jail design are suggested by the stone gatehouse with its octagonal towers and the Gothic portal and windows. A drawing in Gobright's *The Monumental City*, a guidebook of 1858, shows a tall cupola atop the gatehouse building. Either it was not built or was subsequently removed.

76   ST. VINCENT DE PAUL CHURCH
Front Street near Fayette Street
1841—The Reverend John B. Gildea

The distinguishing feature of St. Vincent's, an example of Classical Revival church architecture, is its three-tiered tower, topped by a dome and cross. The church and tower are of brick, painted to resemble wood; there is a stone foundation.

Inside is a vestibule, with winding staircases on either side leading up to the balcony. The nave is a single large room, open and light, with simple wooden pews and an ornate altar.

St. Vincent's was once the center of Old Town, where many of the fashionable residences of the city were maintained. The Reverend Mr. Gildea, its designer, was also its founder and first minister.

77   SHOT TOWER
Fallsway and Fayette Street
1828—Jacob Wolfe, builder

This Baltimore landmark is an architectural relic. Once there were three such towers in Baltimore; now there are only a few left in the world. In shot towers, molten lead was poured in drops from the top. It formed into balls as it fell, and solidified upon hitting cold water at the bottom, forming shot.

Charles Carroll of Carrollton laid the cornerstone for the 234-foot tower, originally known as the Phoenix Shot Tower, in 1828. Its stone foundation walls are 17 feet deep and rest on rock. The tower's outside diameter is 40 1/2 feet at the base and tapers to 20 feet at the top. The weight on the base is estimated at 6.5 tons per square foot.

From the ground, the walls of the circular brick structure, which has an incline of about half an inch to the foot, are 4.5 feet thick for about 50 feet, then drop off 4 inches at each story until at the top they are 21 inches thick. The whole is crowned with an 18-inch parapet wall.

The first 12 of the 14 floors inside are of wood construction, the thirteenth and fourteenth of iron; the building has a twentieth-century concrete roof. There are an estimated 1.1 million handmade, wood-burned bricks in the tower.

In 1976, after a restoration, the tower was reopened to the public for the first time in 84 years, and it is now open several days a week for tours and a film detailing the building's history. The neighboring eighteenth-century house, known as 9 Front Street, was recently renovated.

78   UNITED STATES POST OFFICE
800 East Fayette Street (corner Front)
1971—Cochran, Stephenson, and Donkervoet; Tatar and Kelly

This is the largest public building in the city. However, the architects attempted to scale it to its surroundings, and the result was a distinctly nongovernmental-looking structure.

Built of concrete, the Post Office contains six stories and 883,000 square feet of space (about 16 football fields). It cost about $24.1 million. The building houses mail-handling equipment, offices, and a sixth-floor gallery from which there is a fine view of the city.

79   CARROLL MANSION
800 East Lombard Street
ca. 1812—Architect unknown

Henry Wilson, Baltimore merchant, originally built a house on this property about 1808. In 1811, he sold it to Christopher Deshon, who greatly enlarged it. In 1818, it was bought by Richard Caton, son-in-law of Charles Carroll of Carrollton, who bought out Caton's interest in 1824 and lived in the house part of each year until he died there in 1832.

The house is somewhat typical of London houses of the middle to late eighteenth century. The Flemish-bond brick-work of the exterior is excellent. The first floor of the house was reserved for business and informal family use; a graceful stairway winds to the second floor, where the formal entertaining rooms are located.

The house was bought by the city of Baltimore in 1915 and served a number of purposes for the next 40 years. Almost demolished in the fifties, it was lovingly restored in the sixties and seventies, with Empire-style decorations of the kind that were in fashion when Charles Carroll lived there. It is now open to the public several days a week.

80   SEWAGE PUMPING STATION
701 Eastern Avenue
1912—Henry Brauns

The pumping station, part of Baltimore's original sewage system, is an essay in free eclecticism. It includes Classical and Renaissance Revival details at the first level, and as if that weren't enough, the architect then begins again with squat towers, dormers, and a mansard roof topped by a clerestory. Inside is a single large space where the pumps, on a lower level, go about their business, while pilasters and pediments, rendered in brick, stare down from either end of the room.

The result is a late-Victorian building that is handsome in spite of its pedestrian function. It is built of brick; the roof is copper trimmed. In 1960, electric turbine pumps replaced the original machinery installed by the Bethlehem Steel Company, and the 205-foot chimney was shortened considerably.

81 STAR-SPANGLED BANNER FLAG HOUSE
844 East Pratt Street
1793—Architect unknown

The Flag House is the best-preserved local example of a small residence of its period. It is a Federal-style house, distinguished by its hipped roof, dormers, heavily molded cornice, brick laid in Flemish bond, and wooden trim. It was originally part of a group of four. The exterior has been restored to its original appearance, and its interior has also been renovated. A museum building has been added to the rear, on the site of the original kitchen.

The Flag House still stands primarily because of its occupant in the early 1800s, Mary Pickersgill, who sewed the huge flag that flew over Fort McHenry during the British bombardment of 1814. The flag, the sight of which inspired Francis Scott Key to write *The Star-Spangled Banner*, now hangs in the Smithsonian Institution in Washington.

82   LLOYD STREET SYNAGOGUE
Lloyd and Watson streets
1845—Robert Cary Long, Jr.

The oldest synagogue in Baltimore and the third oldest in the United States, the Lloyd Steet Synagogue has a strong Greek classical spirit. It was a style in which Long seemed to be as comfortable as he was in Gothic. This, taken with the other buildings he designed in the same period [21 and 32], shows the architect's versatility. The building was erected at a time when the Classical Revival style was dying in Baltimore.

It has a stone foundation with brick walls in common bond. The interior is a rectangle, lengthened 30 feet in 1860. A niche in the far wall contained the ark. The stained-glass window above the ark is by Long; this and the other two windows in the east wall are original but greatly restored.

The building was restored, 1962-1964, by the Jewish Historical Society of Maryland and is now a Jewish historical museum.

83 McKIM FREE SCHOOL
Baltimore and Aisquith streets
1833—William F. Small and William Howard

William F. Small was the first Baltimorean professionally trained as an architect. His teacher was Benjamin H. Latrobe, and his training was to enable him to complete Latrobe's Cathedral [22]. He was also the architect of the archbishop's residence [25]. William Howard was a physician who designed several buildings in the city, all of which, with the exception of this one, have disappeared.

The building was for Isaac McKim's school. It is purportedly a scale model of a Greek temple, and several have been mentioned as the original, including the Haephaestion, the Theseum, and the Propylaea at Athens. Whatever the case may be, it is probable that Howard and Small took it from Stuart and Revett's *Antiquities of Athens*.

The building is of stone, with an original copper roof that was covered with tin some years ago. The interior has been altered several times, including the addition of a ceiling about 12 feet above the floor and about 19 feet below the apex of the roof. A wooden floor was also added over the original brick floor.

84   OLD TOWN MEETING HOUSE
Fayette and Aisquith streets
1781—George Matthews, builder

Originally erected by the Society of Friends, and restored by the city in 1967, this simple structure is the oldest religious building in the city.

85 EASTERN FEMALE HIGH SCHOOL
Orleans and Aisquith streets
1869—R. Snowden Andrews

There was a great expansion of secondary public education after the Civil War, and this school is one of the buildings erected as part of it. It is the oldest surviving public school building in Baltimore and one of the city's few surviving relics of the Italian Villa style of architecture which flourished here about the middle of the nineteenth century. It is too symmetrical to be entirely typical of the style, but its two stunted towers and ornamental woodwork give some of the Italianate flavor.

After a long period of neglect and decline, this old high school building, along with several other abandoned school buildings in the city, have been rescued and are being converted to apartments. The developers of the six schools are the Crowninshield Corporation of Peabody, Massachusetts, and the Jolly Company, together known as Baltimore Schools Associates.

86   NUMBER 6 ENGINE HOUSE
Gay and Ensor streets
1853—Reasin and Wetherald

The Venetian Gothic bell tower of the Number 6 Engine House is a landmark in Old Town. It was added to an existing engine house, there having been one on the site since 1819.

The wedge-shaped brick firehouse with its six-story tower (a wooden stairway leads up among the pointed arches to the bell) is one of the few remaining examples in Baltimore of the old volunteer company firehouses. This one was owned by the Independent Fire Company. The volunteer companies, which used to fight pitched battles with rivals over who would have the honor of putting out a blaze, were consolidated in 1858 when the city's fire department was organized.

Except for the rusticated concrete reinforcement at the base of the tower added in 1874, and the four-face clock installed near the top sometime before the turn of the century, the tower stands as it was built.

In 1960, the Fire Board recommended razing the tower because it had "outlived its usefulness." But several citizens, including the mayor, responded to the alarm and the building was saved. It is now a museum exhibiting old fire engines and relics.

87 ST. JOHN THE EVANGELIST CHURCH
901 East Eager Street at Valley Street
1856—Niernsee and Neilson; 1882—E. Francis Baldwin

This Italianate church, though now empty and forlorn-looking, is of interest for a number of reasons. Its twin-towered style, closely resembling the Niernsee and Neilson earlier Calvert Station (since destroyed), managed at once to be fashionable in its time and to accommodate a church interior resembling an early Christian basilica. Its five-part exterior facade expresses the components of the interior, which has a high-ceilinged nave, separated from lower side aisles by two five-part arches supported on cast-iron columns. The roof of the nave reaches almost to the height of the two towers, which are capped by pyramidal roofs. The plan of the church has been called strikingly similar to that of San Apollinare in Classe at Ravenna. In 1882 Baldwin added the apse and two side rooms or pavilions at the southern end without violating the original composition. The building is of brick covered with stucco and has a rubble stone foundation.

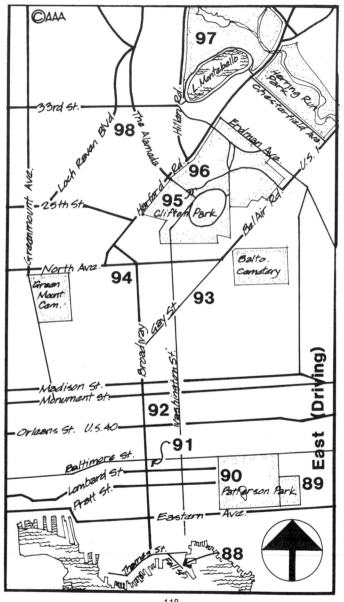

©AAA

97

33rd St.

L. Montebello

Herring Run Park

Chesterfield Ave.

98

The Alameda

Loch Raven Blvd.

Hillen Rd.

Erdman Ave.

U.S. 1

96

Greenmount Ave.

25th St.

Harford Rd.

95

Clifton Park

Bel Air Rd.

North Ave.

94

Green Mount Cem.

Balto. Cemetery

93

Broadway

Gay St.

Madison St.

Monument St.

92

Washington St.

Orleans St. U.S. 40

91

East (Driving)

Baltimore St.

Lombard St.

Pratt St.

90

Patterson Park

89

Eastern Ave.

Thames St.

Fell St.

88

118

The harbor was—and still is—one of the main reasons for the existence of Baltimore as a city.

Fells Point maintains some of the aspects of the seaport community it became after being founded in the early eighteenth century by shipbuilder William Fell. It was the birthplace of the Baltimore clipper; the *Constellation*, the first ship of the United States Navy, was launched nearby in 1797. A foreign visitor to the area in the early 1800s described an English schooner anchored among the racier Baltimore-built craft as "a hog amid a herd of antelopes."

Many of the remaining structures once housed the shipbuilding trades and places of entertainment for the sailors. The Broadway Market, at the center of the community, was established in 1783 and is one of the city's oldest.

Fells Point later became one of the main points of disembarkation for thousands of immigrants from Europe. The area retains its early cosmopolitan flavor, and though currently threatened by a proposed expressway, it exists today as one of the few remaining downtown waterfront residential communities on the East Coast.

This tour includes Canton, another early seaport section, and Highlandtown, the epitome of Baltimore's row-house communities. The tour also takes in some of the structures associated with Baltimore's water supply.

88 CAPTAIN STEEL HOUSE
931 Fell Street
ca. 1784—Architect unknown

This is one of the last remaining virtually intact eighteenth-century town houses in Baltimore (see Introduction). It was built for John Steel, a shipbuilder of some wealth.

The house is three stories high, with a basement and attic. The foundation is stone and the walls are Flemish-bond brick. There are three bays, two dormers in the roof, and a double chimney on the north side.

The door, surmounted by a fanlight, leads to an inside hall where an archway divider, characteristic of the period, separates the doorway from the staircase. The two rooms downstairs were originally used as the captain's counting rooms. (An addition to the back of the house around 1850 created more rooms.) On the second floor are the dining and drawing rooms; on the third, the bedrooms; on the fourth, two small rooms.

Most of the original mahogany, poplar, and pine woodwork on the staircase (which is suspended from the walls without interior posts) and the baseboards, chair rails, and elaborate mantelpieces remain.

In 1968, the house, after it had been used as slum housing for many years, was bought by new owners who have done much restoration.

89 OLD PATTERSON PARK HIGH SCHOOL
Pratt and Ellwood streets
1933—Wyatt and Nolting

This is faintly reminiscent of the work of the Bauhaus architects in the 1930s. It represents the first break with traditional eclectic school design in Baltimore. It is now the Hampstead Hill Junior High School.

90 PATTERSON PARK OBSERVATORY
Patterson Park
1891—Charles H. Latrobe

Known for generations as "The Pagoda," the observatory today usefully serves its original purpose: the views from the top of it are magnificent. The 60-foot octagonal tower is essentially a steel skeleton wrapped with glass and wood. Observation decks both inside and out are supported on exposed cantilevers. A spiral stairway in the core of the building ascends the four stories to the top.

Light and airy in appearance, and one of the most enjoyable architectural phenomena on the Baltimore scene, the tower was restored in 1965 after extensive vandalism had left it an empty shell. It is painted for the most part in its original colors.

91 CAST-IRON DECORATION

On the southeast corner of Broadway and Baltimore Street is one of the many examples of the way cast-iron decoration has been used on houses in the city.

92 JOHNS HOPKINS HOSPITAL
Broadway and Monument Street
1877-1889—J. R. Niernsee, Cabot and Chandler

When Johns Hopkins died in 1873, he left $3.4 million to create a medical school and hospital "for the indigent sick of this city and its environs, without regard to sex, age or color, who may require surgical or medical treatment."

Plans were solicited from five doctors who were experts in hospital design. The resultant elaborate essays were published, and one of the doctors, John S. Billings of the Army Medical Corps, was chosen as medical adviser.

Billings then studied the best hospitals in the United States and Europe before producing the overall plan for the Johns Hopkins Hospital. Niernsee was selected as architect, and Cabot and Chandler of Boston also had a hand in the design of the buildings.

Construction began in 1877 on a high point of land in East Baltimore. The 14-acre site covered four city blocks. Billings's plan called for three-story buildings fronting on Broadway, with a series of one-story pavilions, linked by covered corridors, in the rear, the whole forming a U-shape. In the middle there was to be a "central garden." A great deal of attention was given to how the wards were to be heated and ventilated to check the spread of communicable disease; some were arranged so that it was impossible to pass between them without going outside. There were heated areas in each ward where the patients could sit facing the lawn, shrubbery, and flowers. (In contrast, the plans for disposal of waste water were primitive in a city that lacked sewers—it flowed into open gutters or cesspools.)

The buildings were constructed of Baltimore brick (20 million of them), terra-cotta, and Cheat River bluestone; the roofs were slate. When the $2,050,000 hospital opened in 1889, a contemporary critic in the *American Architect and Building News* called the Victorian design "not impressive," but that was not the point. The point was that the Johns Hopkins Hospital represented the latest scientific knowledge and medical planning at the time.

Billings's plan lasted exactly 100 years. In 1977, the hospital dedicated a new high-rise tower and officially abandoned the low-pavilion and corridor scheme. The architecture of the new buildings is for the most part institutional but some are less institutional than others: Reed Hall by Gaudreau, Inc., to the west across Broadway from the administration building; the postdoctoral research center to the north, a reinforced concrete structure by Fisher, Nes, Campbell, and Partners (Charles H. Richter); and to the east, the 11-story Nelson-Harvey Building, by RTKL Associates, Inc., master planners for the $135 million hospital redevelopment.

93   AMERICAN BREWERY
1700 block Gay Street
1887—Architect unknown

Architecture is too seldom just good fun. But it is at the
American Brewery, a marvel of asymmetrical design in red
brick that stands on a hill in East Baltimore and is visible
for blocks around.

The brewery was founded in 1863 by John Frederick
Wiessner, a Bavarian, who built a three-story brew house
on the site. By 1887, the business had outgrown the building, and a new five-story brewery was erected. (Whether
the old was incorporated in the new is not known.) It has
three wooden towers, an assortment of windows—some of
them stained glass—and a delightfully unbalanced yet
carefully ordered facade.

Since 1887, a complex of buildings has grown up on the
site. In 1892, a brownstone building was built across the
street from the brew house; it served as the offices of the
Allegheny Beverage Corporation, which produced American Beer and was the last to operate the brewery. In 1896, a
brick building was added next door, and about the same
time, on the other side of a garden, the Wiessner house
(1636 North Gay Street), a three-story brick structure with
brownstone trim, was built. The house is large, because like

other brewers, Wiessner followed the custom of providing board and lodging for his workers, many of them immigrants from Germany.

Other buildings were added later. Warehouses and stables were built in 1889, and there were numerous changes and additions to the plant in the mid-1930s. A completely modern brewery was created behind the old facade, and a number of owners have, to their credit, respected the unique building that John Wiessner created.

The brewery was closed in 1973. The site is now leased by the East Baltimore Community Corporation, which has renovation plans for the city-owned property.

94   BAUERNSCHMIDT HOUSE
Broadway and North Avenue
ca. 1889-1890—George A. Frederick

The architect of the City Hall designed this house for a Baltimore beer baron. Its late Victorian grandeur is notable for the controlled but extensive use of brownstone and such detail as the decorative iron rail at the top of the mansard roof, the stylized Corinthian pilasters, and the nicely curved brickwork under a window on the Broadway side. The building is now a funeral home.

95 VALVE HOUSE
Clifton Park at the bend in St. Lo Drive
1887

A substantial Victorian Gothic structure with an interesting series of arches, the valve house was built as part of the city's water system. It is now badly deteriorated.

96 CLIFTON
Clifton Park
1802; 1852, additions with tower—Architect unknown

Johns Hopkins lived here; he bought the property at auction in 1836 from the original owner, Henry Thompson, another Baltimore merchant. In 1852, he enlarged the north wing of the house and added the third floor and tower.

The remodeled farmhouse was converted into an Italian villa; the 500 acres of grounds once included an artificial lake, islands, rustic bridges, ornamental structures, an orangery, and 100 pieces of marble statuary and sculpture. Here Johns Hopkins conducted his business, pursued his hobby—horticulture—and entertained visiting celebrities, including King Edward VII when he was Prince of Wales. In his will, Hopkins requested that the university and hospital he established be built here, but the trustees decided otherwise.

The house, which rests on a stone foundation, is built of brick covered with plaster. The walls are more than a foot thick in some places. A massive arcade runs around three sides, and at the side is an Italianate tower built over a vaulted porte-cochere. The side entrance led, according to an 1852 newspaper account, "through an arched way into the principal hall, 23 feet high, paved with marble, lighted by four richly-stained arched windows and wainscoted with black walnut, of which the doors and massive stairway are formed."

The hall and stairway are still visible and the tower still offers a fine view of the city; but the drawing room, the library, dining room, 1850 saloon, and billiard room have long since been converted to other uses.

Johns Hopkins died in 1873 and the property went into decline. In 1895 the city purchased the land and buildings for about $722,000. Today Clifton is a city park with an 18-hole golf course and clay tennis courts. The mansion is used for park offices and also houses a pro shop, locker room, and snack bar for the golfers.

97 MONTEBELLO FILTRATION PLANT
Hillen Road south of Argonne Drive
1915; 1928—Various engineers for the city of Baltimore

The design of these buildings, with their long, low, horizontal planes and projecting eaves, is faintly reminiscent of the work of Wright.

The buildings rest on groined vaults that cover reinforced concrete filter tanks beneath the ground. (The low buildings house valves; the towers provide storage space for chemicals used in the filtration process.) Reinforced concrete forms the structure of the above-ground buildings as well; they are faced with local red brick. The string courses are buff-colored terra-cotta, and the roofs, carried on steel trusses, are covered with dark green tiles.

The eastern group, (shown here), completed in 1915, marked the beginning of Baltimore's modern water supply system. It is also the more successful architecturally. The western group was built in 1928; both of its square towers are overly massive.

98 CITY COLLEGE
Thirty-third Street and the Alameda
1928—Buckler and Fenhagen

When this edifice was erected in the then popular Collegiate Gothic style, it cost $2.5 million and was considered wildly extravagant for a school building. Forty years later it was threatened with destruction; fortunately it was saved and thoroughly renovated by the Leon Bridges company for $8 million.

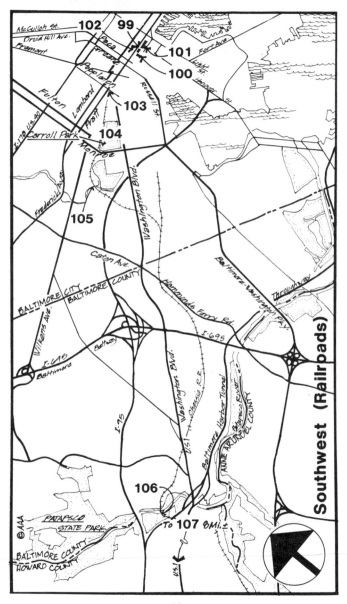

Southwest (Railroads)

McCulloh St.
Druid Hill Ave.
Fremont
102 **99**
101
100
Paca
Greene
Poppleton
Light St.
Fort Ave.
Hanover St.
Russell St.
103
Fulton
Lombard
Pratt
Carroll Park
I-170 US 40
104
Monroe
Washington Blvd.
Frederick Ave.
105
Caton Ave.
BALTIMORE CITY
BALTIMORE COUNTY
Wilkens Ave.
Baltimore
Hammonds Ferry Rd.
Baltimore-Washington Pky.
Throughway
I-695
Beltway
I-695
Baltimore
I-95
Washington Blvd.
Chessie R.R.
Baltimore Harbor Tunnel
Patapsco River
ANNE ARUNDEL COUNTY
US 1
©AAA
PATAPSCO
STATE PARK
106
BALTIMORE COUNTY
HOWARD COUNTY
To **107** 8 Mi.±
US 1

132

Tour H   Southwest-Railroads (Driving)

The Baltimore and Ohio was the first railroad to begin operations in the United States. The Baltimore area, therefore, boasts a number of railroad firsts, among them the first railroad bridge in the country—the Carrollton Viaduct in West Baltimore. It is still standing and still in use. A few miles outside the city is the majestic Thomas Viaduct, the first multispan railroad bridge in the nation; it is also still in use.

In 1825 a group of delegates from all parts of Maryland met and decided to construct a canal from Baltimore to intersect with the planned Chesapeake and Ohio Canal, which was to run from Washington to Pittsburgh and the Ohio River via the Potomac valley and Cumberland Gap. They even induced the Maryland Legislature to subscribe $500,000 to the stock of the Chesapeake and Ohio Canal Company. But Philip E. Thomas, the commissioner representing Maryland, soon became convinced of the futility of the project and began looking for another means of reaching the west.

At a dinner in the fall of 1826, Thomas and other leading citizens first began discussing the possibility of building a railroad. Although railroads had been used for nearly 200 years to haul coal from mines, they had not until 1825 (the Stockton and Darlington Railroad in England) been linked with steam power and used to carry general traffic.

Some of the early participants in the venture in Baltimore had been to England to see the Stockton and Darlington, and gradually the merchants and bankers who met during the next few months became convinced of the possibility of building a similar railroad line from Baltimore to the Ohio River.

On July 4, 1828, Charles Carroll of Carrollton, the last living signer of the Declaration of Independence, turned a spade of earth to lay the first stone for the railroad at a spot near the Mount Clare Station. July 4 seemed the appropriate date for such occasions; practically the only dignitary not present for the ceremonies in Baltimore was President John Quincy Adams, who was at Georgetown officiating at similar ceremonies marking the beginning of the Chesapeake and Ohio Canal.

The Baltimore and Ohio's first board of directors included Philip E. Thomas as president, Charles Carroll of Carrollton, and Alexander Brown, the banker. To locate and design the new railroad they hired Colonel Stephen H. Long from the Army Corps of Engineers, Jonathan Knight, a mathematician who had done work on the National Road, and Caspar W. Wever, his superintendent of construction. Other important engineers on the project were Benjamin H. Latrobe the younger, son of the designer of Baltimore's old Catholic Cathedral, and later Wendel Bollman.

In October 1829 the laying of the permanent track began, and on January 1, 1830, the first passengers traveled from Mount Clare Station to the Carrollton Viaduct. The fare was nine cents one way. On May 24, the line was opened to Ellicott's Mills. The fare was 75 cents for a 26-mile round trip.

The railroad pushed on to Frederick in 1831. Although there were furious disputes in the 1820s and 1830s between the backers of the railroad and those who favored the canal, the Baltimoreans had chosen wisely. In 1850, the canal finally staggered into Cumberland, to go no further. Two years later the railroad reached the Ohio River at Wheeling.

99   CAMDEN STATION
Howard and Camden streets
1855-1867—Niernsee and Neilson, Joseph F. Kemp (?)

This old station, which looks distinctly Italianate with its truncated towers and heavily corniced windows, was originally considerably different in appearance. The chief mystery about it is the architectural attribution, which, as one local architectural historian has put it, is a mess.

In 1855, Niernsee and Neilson, who had been employed by the B&O, submitted a plan for the station, but the firm's board of trustees decided not to accept any plan at that time. An 1858 guidebook shows a plan for an elaborate station with a tall tower in the center and two smaller towers at the ends; this plan is signed "J. [Joseph] F. Kemp, Archt." Kemp may have been employed by Niernsee and Neilson. It is thought that Kemp, at any rate, completed the central section of the station in 1857. Then, between 1865 and 1867, Niernsee and Neilson added the towered wings. Whether the central tower, originally 180 feet tall, was added by them at that time is a matter of conjecture.

The end towers were originally 80 feet tall. Eventually the towers were vastly reduced; a 1902 photograph shows what looks like the original cupolas of the towers resting on the tower bases at each end and on the central block. They, too, were later removed, leaving the building about as it is now in general appearance. The interior has also been vastly altered over the years.

100   B & O WAREHOUSE
Southwest of Camden Station
1898-1905—Baldwin and Pennington (and possibly others)

Actually an office building at the northern end, with six
adjoining and communicating warehouse buildings, this
four-block brick and stone complex is over one-fifth of a
mile long (1,116 feet by 51 feet wide) and contains 430,000
square feet of storage space. The bulk of the building is
lightened somewhat by the cadences of its windows and
recessed arches. Its great length and the repetition of its
parts, which suggest a huge railroad train, achieve a rhyth-
mic power which, as has been noted, "attest to the power of
the railroad in shaping Baltimore."

   The use of the complex for warehousing was discontinued
in 1974; more recently, a plan was put forward for its
possible development as part of an office/residential/com-
mercial complex planned for the area.

101 OTTERBEIN CHURCH
Conway Street near Sharp Street
1785—Jacob Small, Sr.

This is the oldest church building in Baltimore. Its proper
name is the Old Otterbein United Methodist Church, but it
is popularly called the Otterbein Church after one of its
first pastors, Philip Wilhelm Otterbein. According to
church records, it was designed and built for $5,000 by
Small, a local carpenter-builder.

The small (48 feet by 65 feet), two-story church in the
Georgian style is constructed of brick. Each story has sev-

eral round-arched windows. The other distinguishing feature is a squat, provincial version of a Wren tower, built in 1789 with the proceeds of a lottery. Legend has it that when Small completed the tower, some of the church members complained about the incongruous proportions. "Maybe when you see the bill you will find it high enough," he supposedly replied.

Inside, drastic changes have been made over the years. The pulpit, originally on the north wall and reached by a winding staircase, has been moved to the east end, where a modern apse has replaced a large window. The gallery formerly extended around three sides, but only the portion at the west end, containing the organ and choir space, remains. The interior is plain, with painted plaster walls.

In 1977, the sagging roof was replaced and the church rededicated. The Otterbein Homestead Area to the south received an award for restoration design in 1980 from the local chapter of the American Institute of Architects.

102   ROBINS PAPER COMPANY BUILDING
310 West Pratt Street
ca. 1870—Architect unknown

One of the city's more prominent cast-iron fronts, the facade of the Robins Building was fabricated by Bartlett-Robbins and Company. Its future is cloudy.

103   B & O PASSENGER CAR SHOP
Pratt and Poppleton streets
1883—E. Francis Baldwin

Robert M. Vogel, in his 1975 *Some Industrial Archaeology of the Monumental City and Environs*, gave an excellent description of this fascinating building: "A unique structure, undoubtedly the largest circular (actually 22-sided polygonal) industrial building in the world, commonly misidentified as a 'roundhouse.' Erected to build and repair passenger cars [it so served] to about 1953 when it was converted to the B & O Museum's principal building, housing the collection of full-size locomotives, cars and other large exhibits. The sloping lower roof is supported by radial trusses carried at their outer ends by brick exterior walls and at their inner by 22 wrought-iron columns that also

139

support the lantern and cupola, and surround the 60-foot turntable. Diameter: 235 feet; height to top of cupola: 123 feet."

104 MOUNT CLARE
Carroll Park
1753-1787, with later alterations

The only surviving colonial plantation house within the city limits, Mount Clare is a fascinating Georgian complex which shows the changing styles of the period in which it was built.

Charles Carroll, barrister (not to be confused with Charles Carroll of Carrollton), returned from England in 1754 upon the death of his younger brother to carry on the family plantation and business. The brother had built a modest one-and-a-half story house on the site of the present building (1753-1754). Between 1757 and 1760 the barrister tore down this house and built, partly upon its foundations, a two-and-a-half story house—the present main block— retained the older kitchen and constructed a wash house and orangery on either end of the complex. The two-story pilasters on the garden front are an unusual and interesting feature of the main house.

The next major addition occurred in 1768. The main house was altered by the addition of a Palladian front, including the portico and the chamber above containing a Palladian window. At this time also the kitchen was enlarged and an office wing was built complementary to it on the other side of the main block; both were given polygonal fronts, and attached to the main house with hyphens. The rectangular forecourt was replaced by a semicircular one, and an icehouse was added between the laundry and kitchen, matched by a small building, purpose unknown, on the other side between the office and the orangery. Counting the hyphens, the complex now had nine parts, and was symmetrical.

The barrister died in 1783. Shortly thereafter, his widow made further alterations and additions. These included a pantry, passages connecting some of the outbuildings, and two more buildings at the far ends of the complex: a greenhouse beyond the orangery and a service building beyond the laundry. At this time, the complex reached its greatest extent, about 360 feet from one end to the other.

Mrs. Carroll also changed a round window on the southeast facade to a semicircular lunette, and installed several new mantelpieces. Before these latest alterations and additions, the house had been in the Georgian style characteristic of Annapolis, the capital of fashion before the Revolutionary War. As architect Michael F. Trostel, author of a book on Mount Clare, points out, the changes of 1783 "are more in the Federal style of which Baltimore was a leader than in the Georgian style of Annapolis, indicating that as early as 1787 Baltimore was supplanting Annapolis as the leader of style."

Over the years all but the main block of the house disappeared at various times. After the Civil War the original hyphens and wings were removed; the present replacements date from 1906. The present chimneys are Victorian.

A notable feature of the interior of the house is the stair hall to the left of the entrance, a more sophisticated plan than the center hall, as it permitted a larger drawing room, but rare in colonial country houses. The house was paneled throughout in plaster that imitated wood.

The city purchased the mansion and the land around it for use as a city park in 1890. Mount Clare was designated a National Historic Landmark by the National Park Service in 1970. It has been excellently restored and is operated by the Maryland chapter of the Colonial Dames of America.

105 CARROLLTON VIADUCT
Carroll Park
1829—Caspar W. Wever, engineer; James Lloyd, contractor

The Carrollton Viaduct, the oldest railroad bridge in the United States, is still in use. It consists of a single 80-foot Roman arch spanning the Gwynns Falls, and a 20-foot arch on the western bank, built for the passage of a wagon road. The bridge is 297 feet long, 26 1/2 feet wide, and 62 feet high from the crown to the stream bed. It is built of gray granite, primarily from the Ellicott's Mills quarries. The viaduct is named for Charles Carroll of Carrollton, who participated in the official opening ceremonies.

106 THOMAS VIADUCT
Relay
1835—Benjamin H. Latrobe, the younger, engineer; John McCartney, contractor

The Baltimore and Ohio Railroad pioneered a second time by constructing the first multispan masonry railroad bridge in the country and the first built on a curving alignment. Named for the first president of the railroad and designed by the son of the renowned Greek Revival architect, the bridge is "an architectural as well as a functional masterpiece," according to Carl W. Condit in *American Building Art, The Nineteenth Century*. It is divided into eight granite arches, each spanning about 58 feet. The viaduct extends 612 feet overall and the double-track rail line it carries is 60 feet above mean water level.

The main problem to be overcome was in building on a curve and avoiding variations in span and pier width on opposite sides of the structure. This problem was solved by laying out the lateral pier faces on radial lines to fit the four-degree curve of the track alignment; the piers are therefore wedge-shaped. They are faced with half-columns and capitals. The two-year construction period was particularly arduous, and so proud was builder McCartney of his achievement that he erected the granite obelisk on the far side of the bridge. Its inscriptions are now barely legible.

The bridge gives the impression of great power and dignity. Built to carry horse-drawn coaches and engines that weighed only a few tons, the Thomas Viaduct has proved strong enough to support the 300-ton diesel locomotives used to haul freight and passengers on the railroad's line between Baltimore and Washington.

107 BOLLMAN TRUSS BRIDGE
Savage, Maryland
1869—Wendel Bollman

Bollman was a self-taught engineer and the pioneer builder of iron truss bridges in America. Hired by Benjamin H. Latrobe, the younger, to work on the B & O Railroad, he began his career as a carpenter and patented the Bollman truss in 1852 (see Introduction).

The Bollman truss was a highly original arrangement: the bottom chord was not functional, and the load, transmitted by wrought-iron diagonals, was suspended from the end posts. These were kept from inclining toward each other by a cast-iron member that Bollman called a stretcher.

"Bollman's intention in this highly redundant and bewildering array of separate pieces was undoubtedly to combine the truss with a mode of support comparable to that of the suspension bridge," according to Carl Condit. Its only drawback was that the diagonals, being of different lengths, distorted unequally during temperature changes, making the bridge difficult to keep in alignment.

144

The bridge at Savage is a two-span structure on a branch line of the B & O. It was moved to its present location in the late 1880s. Bollman also engineered a seven-span bridge for the B & O across the Potomac River and the Chesapeake and Ohio Canal at Harpers Ferry and a 14-span, one-and-a-half mile bridge for the railroad across the Ohio River at Bellaire, Ohio, both using his truss invention. The bridge at Savage, an ancient mill town dating from about 1815, is the only Bollman truss bridge now in existence, however.

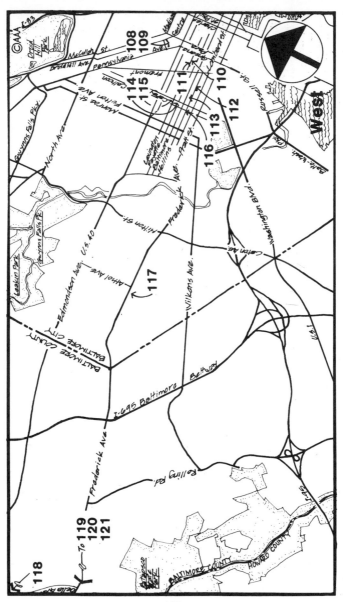

Seton Hill is one of the city's important historic sections. Attracted by St. Mary's Seminary, French-speaking students settled in the area in the early nineteenth century.

The section bounded by Franklin, Eutaw, McCulloh, and Orchard streets is now one of the best examples of private redevelopment in the city. The houses on Jasper and George streets were among the first to be renovated, but the movement has spread to include about half the buildings in the district.

The tour includes several of Baltimore's more distinctive rows of houses and public squares and the great eighteenth-century estate, Doughoregan.

108   MOTHER SETON HOUSE
600 North Paca Street
ca. 1805—Architect unknown

It has been speculated that this charming Federal-style house was designed by Maximilian Godefroy, who was working on the nearby St. Mary's Seminary Chapel about the same time. But there is no proof.

The two-and-a-half story house has casement windows and a typically Federal entrance to one side of the center. Notice the detailed brickwork around the windows, as well as the way in which the exterior brick curves up to meet the roof instead of adjoining at right angles.

The house is not large (26 feet by 42 feet), but for its size it has an unusually large entrance hall. Another interesting interior feature is the inclusion of small windows between rooms to facilitate cross-ventilation.

Restored in 1963 by John H. Scharf and also by William C. Harris of Meyer, Ayers, and Saint, the house is open to the public by appointment. A visit is rewarding not only for the architecture but also for the interesting story of Mother Seton, founder of the American Sisters of Charity, who was canonized in 1975 as St. Elizabeth Ann Seton, the first native-born American saint.

109   ST. MARY'S SEMINARY CHAPEL
600 North Paca Street
1808—Maximilian Godefroy

Godefroy's small, elegant chapel is regarded as the first significant Gothic Revival church in the United States.

The Sulpicians established St. Mary's Seminary in 1791, and in 1805, Godefroy arrived in Baltimore to teach there. By the following year, he had designed the chapel. However, as a result of the Sulpicians' desire to build economically, his original plans, which included a tower, "suffered drastic alterations," according to Robert L. Alexander, Godefroy's biographer. The church cost about $35,000.

As the church stands now, the brick, sandstone, and stucco facade is topped by a parapet wall. Godefroy originally planned this level to contain six rectangular windows, with a rose window in the middle, opening into the church itself. But because the barrel vault was lowered as an economy measure, the windows ended up above the roof—the result was the parapet wall, with 12 niches replacing the rectangular windows. They were to be occupied by statues, but the statues, a pair of stained-glass windows flanking the main entrance, and the tower were all eliminated. Nevertheless, the main elements of the Gothic Re-

vival—pointed arches, groined vaults (here suggested in plaster), and flying buttresses—are all present. The dramatically proportioned interior is distinguished by rows of columns with tall pedestals and acanthus-leaf capitals.

The chapel's first major period of change came during the 1830s and 1840s, when Robert Cary Long, Jr., added a tower, spire, and interior decoration. In 1916, Long's tower fell down. Some of Godefroy's original wooden arches, screens, and plaster vaulting were removed about the same time, and heavy oak seating with overhead canopies was added, obscuring the bases of the columns.

The chapel was renovated and altered again in 1967 by Cochran, Stephenson, and Donkervoet. The seating was removed and separate chairs took its place. The floor was replaced and carpeted, a new altar and new lighting were installed, and the interior was painted in white and gold with reddish candy-striping on the arches. There were two reasons for the alterations—to restore the chapel as much as possible to Godefroy's original design, and at the same time make it more suitable to the new liturgy of the Catholic church.

110 PASCAULT ROW
600 block West Lexington Street
ca. 1816—Attributed to Christopher Deshon

Supposedly designed by the man responsible for the Carroll Mansion, this is an especially fine row of eight three-story houses, named for their developer, Louis Pascault, who lived nearby. Most of the first floors have been altered to accommodate store-fronts, but the house at 655, with its Doric columns flanking the entrance, remains essentially unchanged.

Current plans call for the University of Maryland to acquire the buildings and renovate them as student housing.

111 PINE STREET POLICE STATION
Pine Street, between Lexington and Saratoga streets
ca. 1871—Frank E. Davis

The pointed arches and alternating patterns of brick and stone trim make this building a fine example of High Victorian Gothic. Scheduled to be torn down for an interstate highway, the police station was saved in the mid-1970s through the efforts of the Commission for Historical and Architectural Preservation. The interior has been renovated, and the building is now used as a community center.

112   ST. PETER THE APOSTLE CHURCH
Hollins and South Poppleton streets
1845—Robert Cary Long, Jr.

In the early 1840s the versatile Robert Cary Long, Jr., designed three major Baltimore churches and a synagogue. The Greek temple design of St .Peter's closely resembles that of the Lloyd Street Synagogue [82]. Its six-columned double portico with pediment introduces a simple brick rectangle, originally painted, with a gently sloping peaked roof. The foundation is of hammered granite from Ellicott City quarries. The interior is an open and unobstructed space with a basilica-style ceiling bearing on outer walls adorned with Corinthian pilasters. The building and its interior have been altered several times. The eastern end, containing the chancel, originally square, was extended in 1849 and again in 1868 when the present circular apse was added. At that time various windows were also added in the west, north, and south walls, though the stained glass in them was installed during alterations carried out between 1898 and 1912; frescoes added to the walls at that time were covered in the most recent renovation in 1968, when side altars were removed and a sanctuary table facing the congregation was installed. The high altar of Vermont marble is from 1914.

Long is also responsible for the rectory behind the church on Hollins Street. It is a three-story, three-bay brick town house with a flat roof. Architectural scholar Phoebe Stanton has remarked that when the house was built, "the flat roof was clearly the last word in modernity."

Other parts of the church complex were the Convent of the Immaculate Conception at 11 South Poppleton Street, built from 1865 to 1880 in a style in keeping with the church, and the House of Mercy around the corner on Callendar Street, incorporating two houses purchased by Emily McTavish, granddaughter of Charles Carroll of Carrollton, who presented them to the Sisters of Mercy.

113   HOLLINS MARKET
Hollins Street and South Carrollton Avenue
1865—Architect unknown

Baltimore has always been a market town. The earliest attempts to establish a public market began in 1751, when there were no more than 25 houses in the community. By 1796, when the city was incorporated, it had three market houses. These municipally owned but sometimes privately operated markets continued to grow in popularity until at one time there were at least 12 in the city. There are still half a dozen, the best known of which is the Lexington Market.

A *market* in the Baltimore sense is typically a building (or buildings) and the area around it, filled with stalls of vendors selling meat, fish, produce, and other goods, mostly foods. Here is an early-twentieth-century description of a typical market: "A large, low-roofed open area with a . . . centre aisle running throughout the length, bordered on either side by 8- or 10-foot-front stalls or booths, with crossing aisles at regular intervals for two or three or more city blocks, and in addition stalls known as movable stalls located back against the outer sides of the markets. In addition at either extreme of the market trailing along the curb for several squares . . . may be seen on market days numerous street stalls which the vendors, farmers, truck raisers and Italian fruit dealers carry to and from the market." Such is an accurate description of Hollins Market in the late nineteenth and early twentieth centuries, when it consisted of the building now standing, a long, shedlike building in the rear with more stalls in it, and more stalls along the streets.

Most of the Baltimore markets were owned and run by the city, at least at first, with stalls rented to the vendors. Gradually this gave way to a system whereby the vendors bought their stalls, the more ambitious of them buying several stalls and in turn leasing all but their own out to others. The city, which still maintained the buildings, ended up losing money on such a proposition in the long run, and some of the markets fell into disrepair. They were further hurt by the post-World War II era of supermarkets and suburban shopping centers, but in the last decade or so there has been something of a revival of interest in them, and the city has renovated several.

The story of the Hollins Market is fairly typical. It was organized in 1836; apparently some sort of building was erected immediately, for it promptly blew down in a windstorm of 1838. Another structure went up in 1839. The Italianate style of the present main market building proclaims it a product of the 1860s, but whether it replaced the 1839 structure or was added to it is not known. The form of this building, with its low first floor and high hall above, is typical of early markets. They served not only as markets; the halls were used for traveling entertainment and as community centers. Market buildings erected later, when theaters, schools, and other public buildings had taken over the functions of the second stories, generally had one story or contained a lower second story with offices.

Hollins Market's upper story continued to be used for community purposes until it was declared unsafe in 1968. By that time the market was in something of a decline. But in 1977 it was renovated by the city and is again popular. Market days are Fridays and Saturdays.

114   WAVERLY TERRACE
100 block North Carey Street
ca. 1850—David Carson

What the steel-frame high-rise is to Chicago, the lowly row house is to Baltimore. It provides the city's architectural ambiance, its character, and—with the legendary white marble steps—its claim to fame.

Row houses are found in other cities, of course, but their proliferation and distinctive style in Baltimore are largely due to two factors: a system of financing through ground rents that enabled many people to become homeowners who could not otherwise have afforded it; and the availability of marble in quantity from local quarries. The ground rents, by which an owner rented rather than bought the ground under his house, enabled him to reduce his costs about 20 percent. The marble gave a touch of elegance to otherwise ordinary rows.

Row houses come in a variety of shapes and styles, from early wooden cottages like those in the 600 block of South Wolfe Street in Fells Point to handsome structures such as Waverly Terrace, which forms the eastern border of Franklin Square, one of several public squares in the city (see Introduction). The Waverly Terrace houses were built on the English basement plan by the father of architect Charles L. Carson. They are enhanced by their cast-iron balconies. Rehabilitated in 1979 under a federal program, they have been made into cooperative apartments. Canby Place, another handsome group of brownstone fronts, also with cast-iron balconies, borders the square to the south.

A contemporary variation on the theme is the award-winning group of houses designed by Washington architect Hugh Jacobsen in Bolton Hill [138]. They have staggered facades and modern fenestration, but their ancestry is obvious.

Other outstanding groups of row houses are to be found on Stirling Street in Old Town, where a curving block of homes dating from the 1830s has been vigorously restored under the city's Urban Homesteading Program, which began there in 1974; the 1900 block of Mount Royal Terrace [145]; and the longest row of houses in the city, in the 2600 block of Wilkens Avenue, built around 1910.

Sometimes their form set them apart from their neighbors, as in the band-boxes, or half-houses at Montgomery and Leadenhall streets in South Baltimore. And there were attempts at decorating the facades, such as the homes nearby, with brick pilasters, at 631-633 South Paca Street.

Row houses in most cases, however, were not meant to be beautiful. They were economical and eminently practical. They saved land for the builder and heating and upkeep costs for the buyer. In fact, while many modern groups being built today—even in the suburbs—are advertised as "town houses," they are still row houses and are still built with the same economies in mind.

The average two-story row house of the early part of this century was 12 feet wide and about 40 feet long. One entered the living room directly from the front door. In back were the dining room and kitchen. Upstairs were the bedrooms and, generally, one bath.

Row houses have many advantages aside from those already mentioned. Their exteriors can be altered variously (though it was rare for a great deal of imagination to be used in Baltimore), and interior arrangements of rooms can vary, too. They can house people densely, but without tenement overcrowding. Their height, usually four stories at most, is low enough so that from the street they are human in scale; in turn, people on the inside do not lose contact with the street. Indeed, row houses seem to be made for leaning out of.

"The houses were not works of art," writes art historian Phoebe Stanton, "but the rows were. They gave the city its own anonymous, slow visual rhythm."

Some row houses are, however, neighborhood works of art. On a summer evening in the Patterson Park vicinity, for instance, the marble steps shine with an iridescent glow. Window screens are painted with views of forests and waterfalls, and vases appear in the basement windows of house after house, block after block, row upon row. It is the essence of the city.

115 ST. LUKE'S CHURCH
200 block North Carey Street
1853—Niernsee and Neilson and others

Several architects, including John W. Priest of New York,
had a hand in this Gothic church. When it was built it was
the largest Episcopal church in Baltimore. Its stained-glass
windows are especially fine.

116 PRATT LIBRARY BRANCH
1401 Hollins Street
1886—Architect unknown

This was one of the original branches of the Enoch Pratt
Free Library. It was designed in the Richardsonian Romanesque style two years after the original central library
building, a Victorian pile by Charles L. Carson which has
since disappeared.

117 LUSBY HOUSE (MOUNT ST. JOSEPH HIGH SCHOOL ADMINISTRATION BUILDING)
4430 Frederick Avenue
1863-1866?—Architect unknown

No one seems to know much about this funny building in what might, if only it were a little more fancy than it is, be called a Riverboat Victorian style. As it stands, the pink-red color is not right (yellow and white have been found underneath); it serves to emphasize the quoins, which are too big anyway. Whoever thought the building up obviously hedged his bets with the Palladian doorway. But it's amusing partly because of its inconsistencies.

118 OELLA

Oella was the site of the Union Manufacturing Company, the second cotton mill to begin operations in the state, in

1810. The company owned 1,670 acres of land, extending for three miles on both sides of the Patapsco River. In 1825, the town, with a population of 700, had 70 brick and stone dwellings, a company store, a schoolhouse, and a church. In 1887, the property was bought by the Dickey interests; the W. J. Dickey & Sons, Inc., woolen mill operated in Oella until 1972, when it was closed. At its peak in the 1900s, 500 mill employees lived in 110 company-owned houses. Nothing remains of the original mills, but Oella is an almost perfectly preserved nineteenth-century mill town. The houses are now privately owned.

119   ELLICOTT CITY STATION
Old Frederick Road, Ellicott City
1831—Jacob Small, Jr.

This is the country's oldest railroad station. It was built as a freight depot at what was then Ellicott's Mills, founded in 1772, and the initial western terminus of the Baltimore and Ohio Railroad.

The railroad hired Colonel Jacob Small, Jr., son of the architect of the Otterbein Church, in January 1831 to "furnish plans for improvements at company depots." A few months later, the directors approved his plan for a depot at Ellicott's Mills; "a stone building for the reception of produce, and which also includes a car house and office" was completed that year, according to the architect's subsequent reports.

The depot was built of granite from nearby quarries; the interior is framed in heavy timber. Originally, freight was brought in by wagon, hoisted up one floor to track level, and loaded on freight cars that entered the building on a spur track. Smoke funnels in the roof indicate that engines also laid over here.

Passengers of the day got off the trains across the street, at the Patapsco Hotel, which was a stagecoach stop on the old National Road, now Route 144. In 1856, the railroad considered erecting a separate passenger station at Ellicott's Mills but decided instead on a "refitting of the warehouse for passenger accommodations." Other minor changes were made around the 1890s. The building is now being renovated again, this time to recapture its appearance at the turn of the century.

Remains of the Oliver Viaduct, built contemporaneously with the station to carry the railroad over the turnpike, and of the old flour- and cotton-milling industries, linger in this extremely picturesque area.

120   DOUGHOREGAN MANOR
Off Route 144 in Howard County
1699 and later—No known architect

The real interest of the manor, which is never open to the public and which outsiders are emphatically discouraged from visiting, is that it is what remains of a once enormous plantation complex—an eighteenth-century family community.

The estate is still in the hands of the Carroll family, who have owned it since 1699, when it was granted to Charles

Carroll, grandfather of the signer of the Declaration of Independence. It once consisted of between 13,000 and 15,000 acres, on which were situated several houses of other members of the family. The complex also included slave quarters and numerous farm buildings, among which were the first sheep barns in Maryland (about 1780). Gradually much of the estate has been sold, but it still comprises about 2,500 acres.

While the Carrolls have steadily modernized the farming operation, there were until a few years ago four brick and stone-base barns dating to the eighteenth century, one of which, built in 1710, was the oldest building on the property. In 1968 these burned in a fire that destroyed five barns.

The manor house, dating from about 1717, has been added to by successive generations of Carrolls until it is now 300 feet long, with a center hall and a T-shaped wing on each end. One of these contains a small Gothic chapel, originally separate from the house but later joined to it. Catholic services are still held there on Sunday mornings.

121 EL MONTE
Junction, Routes 29 and 99, outside Ellicott City
ca. 1856-1858—Nathan G. Starkweather

As late as the 1960s, El Monte was the seat of a large estate
and dairy farm. Then it was sold, not quite half of the 285
acres going to the State Highway Administration and most

of the remainder to a development called Patapsco Park Estates.

The house, a large Italianate mansion, remains surrounded by about three acres of land. It was built of local granite by members of the Dorsey family. El Monte has large center halls running the length of each floor, 20 rooms, and seven marble fireplaces. The owners have made some renovations.

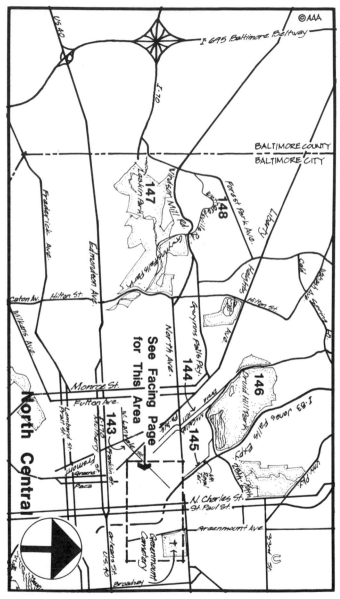

©AAA

I-695 Baltimore Beltway

US 40

I-70

BALTIMORE COUNTY
BALTIMORE CITY

147

148

Leakin Park

Winans Mill Rd.

Woodlawn

Forest Park Ave.

Liberty

Heights Ave.

Frederick Ave.

Edmondson Ave.

Caton Av.   Hilton St.

Wilkens Ave.

Hilton St.

Gwynns Falls Pkwy.

North Ave.

144

See Facing Page
for This Area

Druid Hill Park

146

I-83 Jones Falls Expy.

Monroe St.

Fulton Ave.

145

Mt. Royal

Reservoir Rd.

26th St.

Mt. Royal Ave.

Maryland Ave.

Falls Rd.

143

Lombard St.
Pratt St.

Lanvale St.

Mulberry St.

Franklin St.

Howard St.
Greene
Paca

N. Charles St.
St. Paul St.

Greenmount
Cemetery

Greenmount Ave.

33rd St.

Orleans St.
US 40

Broadway

North Central

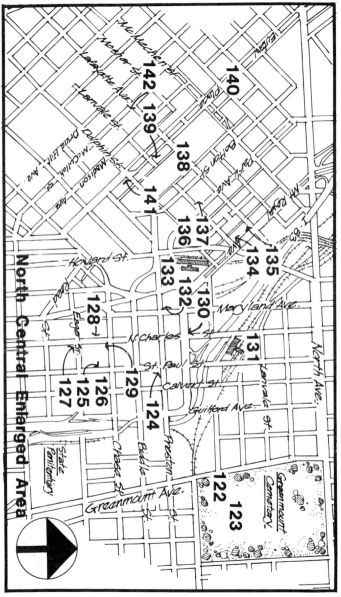

North Central Enlarged Area

State Penitentiary

Greenmount Cemetery

Greenmount Ave.

Howard St.

Maryland Ave.

N. Charles St.

St. Paul St.

Calvert St.

Guilford Ave.

North Ave.

Lanvale St.

McMechen St.

Mosher St.

Lafayette Ave.

Lanvale St.

Madison Ave.

McCulloh St.

Druid Hill Ave.

Dolphin St.

Temple St.

Druid Hill

Biddle St.

Preston St.

Eutaw St.

Chase St.

Etting St.

142 139 138 141 140 137 136 133 132 130 134 135 131 128 127 125 126 129 124 122 123

167

This tour illustrates several periods of Baltimore architecture. Curiously, some of the oldest buildings are the farthest from the center of town. The reason is simple: they were built as country houses and were later engulfed by the city. Upton is a late example of the Classical Revival style. The Family and Children's Society Building, erected only ten years after Upton, was Victorian in concept even before later additions made it more so. The Green Mount Cemetery gates and chapel are still more High Victorian.

But the most interesting buildings are those erected between 1887 and 1906, products of the examples set by Richardson, Sullivan, the young Frank Lloyd Wright, and others. American architects were creating a "free eclectic" style which, if it drew on European models, was at the same time reflective of a rapidly growing and confident America. The Winans House and the Maryland Club, particularly, show the new qualities of individuality that enjoyed popularity at the close of the old century and the beginning of the new.

Many of these buildings became impractical for their original purposes and have been turned to new uses. This is in part because the north central area of the city has changed greatly in the last three-quarters of a century. Thus the Winans House 'now houses doctors' offices, the Garage is part of a university, Mount Royal Station is part of an art college, the Thom House (though still in a residential neighborhood) is a charitable institution (the Family and Children's Society), and the Eutaw Place Synagogue is a Masonic Temple. That these buildings have survived at all is due to the fact that they have continuously been needed for and adaptable to new purposes.

Finally, the Chambers Building shows how a good architect can create a new building which fits in with its older neighbors without losing its own sense of identity.

122 GREEN MOUNT CEMETERY GATES
Greenmount Avenue and Oliver Street
ca. 1846—Robert Cary Long, Jr.

Long's Tudor Gothic gatehouse, with its 40-foot towers, guards the entrance to the burial grounds of some of the city's most illustrious citizens (and some of the most notorious as well—John Wilkes Booth is buried here). The land was formerly the country estate of merchant Robert Oliver; the first burial took place in 1839.

123 MORTUARY CHAPEL
Green Mount Cemetery
1856—Niernsee and Neilson

This building is an octagon, the second story of which culminates in a small dome under the tower. Flying buttresses extend out to meet the surrounding pinnacles. A lofty tower is strongly buttressed and, with its traceried arches, remarkably open. The material is brownstone.

124   WINANS HOUSE
St. Paul and Preston streets
1887—McKim, Mead, and White

Built for a member of a family prominent in the construction of railroads in Baltimore and elsewhere, the Winans House is distinguished outside by its rugged compactness and rich surface patterns. Inside, its grand entrance hall and splendid use of materials recommend it to the lover of architecture.

The first story of the house is brownstone; the other three are of narrow, light red brick, with brownstone trim and panels of carved relief. The solid, carefully balanced design of the building, with its tower, wall dormers, fancy chimneys, and deep-set windows, makes it a good example of the

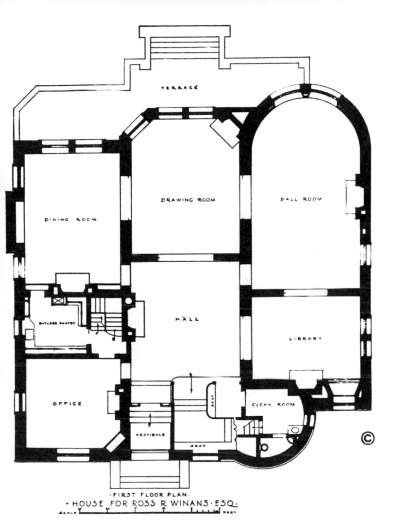

TERRACE

DINING ROOM

DRAWING ROOM

BALL ROOM

BUTLERS PANTRY

HALL

LIBRARY

OFFICE

VESTIBULE

CLOAK ROOM

SEAT

SEAT

©

·FIRST FLOOR PLAN·
· HOUSE FOR ROSS R WINANS · ESQ·
SCALE

Winans House Floor Plan

Chateau style, whose major practitioner was Richard Morris Hunt.

The entrance hall is paneled in oak with a shallow, open-beamed ceiling. A frieze of wood mosaic surrounds the hall, which runs the length of the first floor and terminates at the garden entrance in back. In front, a lavishly ornamented staircase with parquet walls is lighted by three large leaded windows and leads to the upstairs bedrooms. Throughout the house are ornate fireplaces, burnished metal decorations, and elegant oak, teak, and mahogany woodwork—all in the grand Stanford White manner. The building now houses doctors' offices.

125 1020 ST. PAUL STREET
1938—Charles Nes, Jr.

This appealing, simple building, with its clean lines and
Art Deco touches (especially notable in the entrance treatment), was inspired by the International style of Walter
Gropius and his followers. Young architect Charles Nes
created its simple lines and modern feeling for the architectural firm of Palmer and Lamdin, which first occupied the
building. (Nes is now a partner in a successor to that firm,
Nes, Campbell, and Partners.) The building originally had
an open driveway under the second floor south bay; it was
later filled in to give the present appearance.

126 BELVIDERE TERRACE
1000 block North Calvert Street
ca. 1882—Wyatt and Sperry; J. A. and W. T. Wilson

On the site of Belvidere, the John Eager Howard mansion, J. B. Noel Wyatt and others created, on both sides of Calvert Street, terraces of houses similar in aspect to Queen Anne-style houses of the period but different in treatment of windows and ornament. They avoid the monotony found in many blocks of row houses. The false gables on the east row actually mask a mansard roof. This side was designed by J. Appleton Wilson and William T. Wilson, the west side (shown in the photograph) by Wyatt and Sperry.

127 MARYLAND CLUB
Charles and Eager streets
1893—Baldwin and Pennington

With its large, low-arched entrance, its rough-cut Beaver Dam marble facade, and its asymmetrical but harmonious proportions, this is a good example of the Richardsonian Romanesque style. This style reflected a desire among American architects following H. H. Richardson to create something that was not simply a copy of European styles, yet used parts of them in freer ways to reflect what they regarded as the strength and spirit of America. The interiors are appointed with mahogany, Tennessee marble, and quartered oak.

128 CHAMBERS BUILDING
1010 North Charles Street
1964—Charles H. Richter; Fisher, Nes, Campbell, and Partners

Baltimore's architectural heritage was used imaginatively in the Chambers Building, which houses a local interior-design firm. The five strong, simply outlined arches are traditional in form (echoing the row-house doorways found across the street and throughout Baltimore), but the general design is contemporary.

Handmade brick was used to keep the building consonant with its surroundings. The construction is steel-frame with exterior load-bearing walls. The windows in the arches open the showrooms to public view; the slots between are carried up to the second floor, where the firm's offices and workshops are located, allowing light to enter and providing views of the street.

129 THE BELVEDERE
Charles and Chase streets
1903—Parker and Thomas

Beaux-Arts, a style of classicism which took its name from
the Ecole des Beaux-Arts in Paris, became popular in this
country at the end of the nineteenth century. Called "pictorial classicism," it is characterized by elaborately decorated, symmetrical facades, often with advancing and receding fronts, combinations of columns and arches, doubled
columns, and sculptured elements; it gives the viewer
"plenty to look at," as one observer noted.

Designed by the Boston and Baltimore firm of Parker and
Thomas, the Belvedere rises from a two-story rusticated
base with a cornice at the third-floor level through a main
body of brownish-pink brick with quoins and other embellishments to a massive cornice at the eleventh floor—all
this surmounted by a 35-foot-high mansard roof with broad
moldings at the hips and ornate dormers on the twelfth-
floor level. Much of the decoration is of terra-cotta and iron
simulating stone.

The interiors were done mostly in plasterwork described
in 1904 as "a free version of Louis XVI." An exception is the

lofty barroom, with its walls of patterned brickwork and its patterned ceiling.

After a period of decline and neglect, the Belvedere was thoroughly and for the most part successfully renovated in the late 1970s by the firm of Cochran, Stephenson, and Donkervoet for a new owner, Victor Frenkil, who has converted the building to apartments. Its grand public rooms, probably the finest in Baltimore, are again in use for many social and business functions.

130 THE GARAGE (UNIVERSITY OF BALTIMORE)
Charles Street and Mount Royal Avenue
1906—Beecher, Friz, and Gregg

In the early 1900s this neighborhood was a center of the new automobile culture. Several car showrooms, now largely converted to other uses, lined the streets. The model for most of them was the Garage, which was reflective of some of the early work of Frank Lloyd Wright.

The building is a three-story structure of reinforced concrete faced with brick. The original wide roof overhang and the row of small windows beneath it lent the building something of the Wright air of horizontality and strength. The comparison was more obvious before the second-floor balcony was removed in a recent remodeling, which dissipated some of the original strength of design. The changes, for which Allen Hopkins of Fisher, Nes, Campbell, and Partners was the architect, were completed in 1971. Baltimore Heritage, Inc., cited the building as the most important example of restoration-renovation in the city that year.

The Garage was built as a showroom and auto club. Originally it contained a bowling alley and roller-skating rink, gymnasium, and restaurant. It was later owned by an automobile dealer, then stood vacant until being turned into an academic center by the University of Baltimore.

131 PENNSYLVANIA STATION
1525 North Charles Street
1911—Kenneth W. Murchison

Murchison, a New York architect, chose Beaux-Arts classicism for the style of Baltimore's last major railroad station, the only one currently serving the passengers of Amtrak, which now owns it. The steel-frame structure is clad in granite and terra-cotta and has a cast-iron marquee running the length of the facade.

Inside is a two-story lobby, with railroad offices on the upper level, covered with three domical skylights of leaded glass, each 23 feet in diameter. There are also iron balconies, marble walls, mahogany benches, bronze candelabras and sconces, terrazzo floors with mosaic borders, and one of the few installations of Rookwood ceramic tiles remaining intact. The last was produced by the Rookwood Pottery Company, the country's foremost art-pottery manufacturer; it developed complete interior decorative schemes for churches, restaurants, hotels, and train stations. The tiles are visible around windows, wall-mounted lighting fixtures, and drinking fountains.

There have been some changes: the original marble ticket counter with iron grilles was replaced, and there were alterations during the war years. The station then entered a period of decline coinciding with the fortunes of the railroad that owned it.

In 1976, a $600,000 renovation program began, paid for by the federal government. The station was cleaned inside and out, the paint that darkened the skylights for blackout purposes during World War II was removed, and the exterior was landscaped. Major renovations are planned as part of the Northeast Rail Corridor improvement program passed by Congress in 1980.

132   GREEK ORTHODOX CHURCH
Preston Street and Maryland Avenue
1889—Charles E. Cassell

Although its Romanesque architecture seems admirably suited to its present occupants, this was built as a Congregationalist church and used as one until 1934. Constructed of Port Deposit granite at a cost of $137,000, it has been badly renovated inside. The interior consists of a single auditorium-style room with an ornate altar area, including a central icon screen in front and a curving balcony in back. The flat ceiling hides the trusses that support the roof.

133   MOUNT ROYAL STATION
Mount Royal Avenue and Cathedral Street
1896—Baldwin and Pennington

Built for the Baltimore and Ohio Railroad at the height of its power and as a symbol of that power, Mount Royal Station has always been striking. It is now additionally interesting as an example of how architecture no longer useful in its original role can be saved by imaginative redesign.

Baldwin and Pennington's Romanesque building owes much to Richardson's influence in its massive granite walls and high clock tower, but there is a signal of change here, too: the relative smoothness of the walls (compared to the rough-cut stone of the Maryland Club) and the Italian Renaissance Revival windows are harbingers of the Second Renaissance style taking hold in the second half of the 1890s.

The largest passenger station built to accommodate one line when it opened, Mount Royal combined a solidity of appearance with such lighter touches as its train shed girders. One of the few stations built at track level, its situation in a hollow—it is always seen from above—adds to its attractiveness.

The original interior was notable for the loftiness of its main waiting room. In 1964 the station was sold to the Maryland Institute, College of Art, which was seeking to expand from its building a block away [134]. The job of converting the building for maximum institute use while preserving the exterior was accomplished by Richard Donkervoet of Cochran, Stephenson, and Donkervoet.

The following is from an article by Alexander Cochran in *Historic Preservation* concerning the conversion: "The exterior was altered only by the enclosure of open roof areas. The interior was high enough to create two ample floors in much of the waiting room with the addition of a grand staircase on axis with a newly opened central space at the porte-cochere. Considerable interior architectural decoration was preserved *in toto*, such as the central columns, all the waiting room ceiling, much of the decorative floor and most of the exposed iron structure."

The building now houses studios, offices, a library, a gallery, and a lecture hall.

134 MARYLAND INSTITUTE BUILDING
Mount Royal Avenue and Lanvale Street
1908—Pell and Corbett

At the end of the nineteenth century there was a spate of architectural revivals in reaction to the half-generation of medieval throwbacks, Gothic and Romanesque. Almost at once appeared Beaux Arts classicism, a purer Neoclassical Revival, a Georgian Revival, and a second Renaissance Revival. To the last of these categories belongs the Maryland Institute Building, with its gleaming white marble facade, Florentine-palace second-floor windows, barrel-vaulted entry, imposing great hall, and grand but too steep stairway.

135   CORPUS CHRISTI CHURCH
Lafayette and Mount Royal avenues
1891—Patrick Charles Keely

Called "a landmark . . . a monument . . . a beautiful work of art," by Cardinal Gibbons when he consecrated it in 1891, Corpus Christi remains one of the handsomest of the city's Gothic Revival churches. It was built at a cost of $200,000 in memory of Thomas C. Jenkins, by his family and was formerly known as Jenkins Memorial Church.

The building was designed by a Brooklyn architect with several hundred churches to his credit. The proportions were vastly improved in 1912 when the original stumpy, square spire was replaced by a much taller, octagonal one, also paid for by the Jenkins family.

A baptistry, two side chapels, and two sacristies project from the church. Its walls are of Woodstock granite, two and a half feet thick, lined with brick inside. The windows are framed in Kentucky sandstone. In the interior can be seen rare stained-glass windows and mosaics, decorative marble from Tennessee and Siena, bronze doors, oak pews, and carved marble altars. The church fell into a state of neglect over the years, but a renovation program has recently been undertaken.

136   BOLTON HILL

The Bolton Hill neighborhood is now an historical and architectural preservation district. It is almost exclusively nineteenth-century in character, from the 1850s houses in the 1300 block of John Street to the 1890s town houses in the 1600 and 1700 blocks of Park Avenue. A walk around offers an idea of the variety of row-house styles popular during the century. This was a middle- and upper-middle-class area; it does not boast the rich people's houses of Mount Vernon and Eutaw places. After deteriorating for a number of years, Bolton Hill is a fashionable residential neighborhood again, but only a minority of the houses are now one-family owned and occupied.

137   FAMILY AND CHILDREN'S SOCIETY
Park Avenue and Lanvale Street
1840s—Enlarged and altered by Edmund Lind, 1866

A "Gothick Cottage" of the second quarter of the nineteenth
century, this was typical of the type that dotted the area in
the 1840s and 1850s. It is two and a half stories, of brick
which has always been painted. The doorway, window, and
roof trim are original.

   In 1866 the bay window in the west side of the house and
the "enclosed verandas" on each side of the entrance porch
were added. Since 1937 the house has been the headquarters of the Family and Children's Society.

138   BOLTON COMMON
200 block West Lafayette Avenue, 1400 blocks of Jordan and Mason streets
1968—Hugh Newell Jacobsen

This complex of 35 town houses arranged roughly in an omega shape with a private oval park in the center has won awards for town-house design and land use, including a national American Institute of Architects award in 1969.

The architect created modern houses which are nevertheless in harmony with the nineteenth-century row houses of the neighboring Bolton Hill area. This involved the use of North Carolina brick and other materials more expensive than but aesthetically preferable to local materials.

The houses look similar in size from the front, but there is actually a wide variance from 18- by 30-foot, two-bedroom houses to 20- by 40-foot, four-bedroom houses with two-story living rooms. Each house has a private walled garden in the rear.

The architect and the builder, Stanley I. Panitz, were responsible for touches that usually go unnoticed, such as completely concealed rain gutters and underground telephone and electric wires. They help make this a remarkably attractive grouping.

139   EUTAW PLACE TEMPLE
Eutaw Place and Lanvale Street
1893—Joseph E. Sperry

With the sun behind them in the evening, the tiled domes of
the old Eutaw Place temple (or Oheb Shalom Synagogue)
form one of the outstanding features of the Baltimore skyline. The style of the building is clearly Byzantine, with
three domes and a mosquelike interior. The latter consists
of a large room, roughly 82 feet square, under a series of
half-domes, arches, and vaults. With galleries on three
sides, the room can seat 2,200 people.

The exterior walls are of Beaver Dam marble; the inside
woodwork is quartered oak. The light, spacious wood and
plaster interior is in marked contrast to the heavy, almost
fortresslike exterior.

In 1892 the temple cost about $225,000 to build. In 1961 it
was purchased by the Prince Hall Masons and is now used
for meetings and concerts.

140 EUTAW PLACE

The purpose behind creating boulevards, or broad, land-scaped thoroughfares as was done here and on North Broadway and Park Avenue, was to encourage residential development and enhance prospective values. It worked on Eutaw Place as well as anywhere, for in the last part of the nineteenth century this became one of the most fashionable sections of Baltimore in which to live. Some of the grandest town houses of the era were built here.

Unfortunately, after World War II, urban renewal all but destroyed the effect by tearing down parts of many of the rows and putting up public housing, a school, and other such standard buildings. But in recent years, preservation has reared its welcome head, and it appears that what is left will be preserved.

141 EUTAW PLACE BAPTIST CHURCH
Eutaw Place and Dolphin Street
1871—Thomas U. Walter

A Gothic Revival church in white marble, this is the only building in Baltimore by the architect responsible for the dome and extensions of the wings of the United States Capitol. The church is dominated by a 190-foot tower and is asymmetrical to the point of appearing foreshortened.

142 OLD WESTERN HIGH SCHOOL
Lafayette Avenue and McCulloh Street
1895—Alfred Mason

The school is one of the finest remaining local examples of the Romanesque Revival style. Built of red brick and embellished with carved Seneca stone, it housed, besides classrooms, a gymnasium, assembly rooms, and laboratories. The tower is functional as well as decorative, its windows providing extra light for the corner rooms. Later additions date from 1911 and 1951. The building was threatened with destruction but is now to be retained as a school.

143   UPTON
811 West Lanvale Street
1838—Architect unknown

Upton is one of the few surviving examples in Baltimore of the Greek Revival country house. Built for David Stewart, who served for a time in the United States Senate, the house was admirably suited for entertaining. To the left of the main entrance hall that divides it in two are two rooms, originally connected, that served as the main banquet hall.

Greek Revival details are seen in the cornice and in the entrance porch, framed by large Doric columns. The original portico on the opposite side, facing the harbor, has been replaced by a brick stair tower.

By and large the changes to the building were minimal as it became, successively after the death of Stewart in 1858, a private home, a hospital, a radio station, an interracial music conservatory, and a special school.

144 DRUID HILL CABLE RAILWAY POWER HOUSE
Druid Hill Avenue and Retreat Street
1891—Architect unknown

Built in the Romanesque Revival style, this ornate fortress of brick and stone has a large, arched entrance and an odd roofline made up of turrets and dormers. As the northern terminus of the Baltimore Traction Company's cable-car route, between Druid Hill and Patterson parks, the building once housed cars, cable machinery driven by two 500-horsepower Corliss engines, and other equipment. It currently serves as a warehouse.

145 MOUNT ROYAL TERRACE HOUSES
1900 block Mount Royal Terrace
ca. 1885—Architects unknown

The variety of color and texture in surface materials characteristic of the Queen Anne style and the furniture-like columns and porch spindles of the Eastlake style can be seen in repeated patterns in the 19 houses that make up Mount Royal Terrace. Usually these styles occur in suburban homes [181], but here they were adapted to the Baltimore row house, making this block unique in the city.

146   DRUID HILL PARK
1860 and after—Howard Daniels; George A. Frederick; others

One of Baltimore's great amentities is its collection of public parks, 30 in all, covering (according to a 1980 figure given by the Department of Parks and Recreation) 6,134.157 acres. Many of these parks, of course, are small areas under the parks department's jurisdiction, such as the four squares in Mount Vernon and Washington places. But the ten large parks are something else again, and the principal reason Baltimore has them is that a remarkably consistent and forward-looking parks board acquired by gift or purchase seven major estates between 1827 and 1942, as the city moved outward. The first of these was a portion of what is now Patterson Park, given in 1827 by the father of Betsy Patterson Bonaparte (famous for having married Napoleon's brother Jerome). The last was Cylburn, bought in 1942 for $42,000—it is staggering to imagine what a 180-acre tract of prime northwest Baltimore land would bring today on the open market.

Another factor to be credited to the parks board is that it retained a number of the imposing estate mansions built in the eighteenth and nineteenth centuries and converted them to park use, thus preserving several architecturally

important buildings. These include the mansion house in Druid Hill Park, Clifton in Clifton Park, Cylburn in Cylburn Park, Crimea in Leakin Park, and Mount Clare in Carroll Park (all included in this book). Mount Clare is an exception to the parks-use category; it has become a house museum.

Druid Hill, at something over 600 acres, is not the largest of the city parks; that honor goes to Gwynns Falls park (about 700 acres). But Druid Hill is rightly the most celebrated of all. Thanks to its creative natural landscaping and the wealth of interesting buildings that have been created and preserved there, it is both the most beautiful and the most interesting. It is also a good example of how the parks were developed from estates.

In 1860 Lloyd Nicholas Rogers sold his estate, Druid Hill, and the charming Federal mansion built on it by his father in the late 1790s, to the city for $475,000 ($1,000 an acre—the park has since been expanded).

Under the supervision of Augustus Faul, the estate was landscaped for a park along its natural lines by Howard Daniels, who took advantage of the hills and valleys to create lakes, scenic views, picnic groves, pathways, and promenades (see Introduction). George A. Frederick de-

signed a number of fanciful pavilions, most of which still remain and are believed to be the oldest park buildings in the country; these originally served as stops along a small railway that wound through the park and that has long since been discontinued. Either Frederick or John H. B. Latrobe (both claimed it) designed the imposing gateway to the park at the end of Madison Avenue.

The Rogers house (usually called the mansion house) has been through a number of renovations. In the early 1860s, the city tore out its middle section, replaced it with a Victorian section, and created a wide, open pavilion all around the building. This would be thought architectural desecration today, but the building has worked well for the purposes to which it has been put. The surrounding pavilions were enclosed in the 1930s. Recently, the house vastly benefited from an $850,000 restoration under the direction of Michael F. Trostel of the firm of Edmunds and Hyde. It houses the headquarters of the Baltimore Zoo, which is located in the park.

In the early 1890s the conservatory, a large greenhouse of metal construction, was added. A building which had been the Maryland pavilion at the Philadelphia Exposition of 1876 was at some point transplanted to a knoll near the mansion, where it now serves as headquarters of the Baltimore Zoological Society. One other building should be mentioned: the large pool house of 1924, by Josias and Hall P. Pennington.

During the Depression and World War II and for some years thereafter, the park declined somewhat, but the decline seems to have been reversed. The zoological society has undertaken an ambitious 20-year plan to improve the zoo, and many of the park pavilions have recently been restored.

147   CRIMEA
Windsor Mill Road
ca. 1860—Architect unknown

In a spectacular setting on the west side of the city, Thomas De Kay Winans built one of his Baltimore mansions (the other was Alexandroffsky on West Baltimore Street, designed by Niernsee and Neilson and razed in 1926).

Mr. Winans was the son of Ross Winans, builder of railroad locomotives. About 1850, the elder Winans, in partnership with a Philadelphian, signed a contract with the Russian imperial government to equip a new rail line from St. Petersburg to Moscow. The Winans sons, including Thomas, carried out the project for a reported $10,000,000.

The house Thomas Winans built sits on the high point of an estate that once encompassed nearly 1,000 acres. The building is of ashlar stone construction with a basement which, due to the slope of the land, makes a fourth story on the south side. The most outstanding exterior features aside from the stone itself are the large verandas that extend around three sides of the building.

In 1940 the city bought 200 acres of the Crimea property, including the house, for roughly $108,000. The park is now called Leakin Park; the first floor of the mansion is used for park offices. Also on the grounds and built in the same style as the house are a stable and servants' quarters (now occupied by the park superintendent). Near the entrance to the Crimea is a small wooden chapel with round-arched windows and a steeply sloping roof with bargeboards.

148 DICKEYVILLE
Wetheredsville Road near Forest Park Avenue

Dickeyville is less important for architecture than for atmosphere. It grew up around several mills that once occupied the banks of the stream (Gwynns Falls) that flows through town. In 1762, Wimbert Tschudi, a Swiss, built a stone house and a grist mill on its banks. Around 1812 the Franklin Company erected a factory and paper mill; some of the village's stone houses date from this period.

The Wethered family bought the factory in 1829 and changed it to a woolen mill. The town, (taking the name of Wetheredsville), prospered, and its wool cloth won prizes. Later, a cotton mill was added; at one time it employed 210 hands.

In 1854, the mills burned to the ground and were rebuilt. Three years later a dam was washed away upstream; the resulting flood caused $100,000 worth of damage to the mills. In 1868 there was another "great freshet," which demolished a covered bridge at Wetheredsville and carried away part of the schoolhouse. Later there were fires in the mills again.

In 1871 the Wethereds sold three mills, several stone houses, and 300 acres to William J. Dickey for $82,000. The new owner added several frame mill houses, a warehouse of dark gray rubble stone with red brick trim on Pickwick Road, and, in 1885, the white clapboard Dickey Memorial Presbyterian Church on Wetheredsville Road. (The former Ashland Chapel at Pickwick and Wetheredsville roads, built in 1849, is now a private home, as is the old mill office and jail at 2435 Pickwick Road.) In the 1880s, 400 hands worked in the mills, and the town entered a period of prosperity that lasted until 1909, when the Dickeys sold out. The village subsequently went into an economic decline that was aggravated by the Depression.

In 1934, the town was sold at auction to the Maryland Title Guarantee Company; the company paid $42,000 for 65 acres of land, 81 stone, frame, and brick buildings, a mansion house, and three factories. The mills continued to produce everything from kitchen cabinets to gun covers until the 1950s (the Dickeys reacquired them in 1954). By that time, a new industry had sprung up—providing housing for people attracted by Dickeyville's bucolic charm.

The Dickeyville Improvement Association was formed in 1937; as one walks along the falls today, the feeling of the town is different. The mills are gone and the houses, with their black shutters and white picket fences, have been altered to a condition they probably never enjoyed in mill days. The only mill left standing is the old Ballymena Woolen Mill, named for the town in Ireland from which the Dickey family emigrated. The mill is a two-story structure with double windows overlooking Wetheredsville Road. Milling operations were ended in 1967, when production was shifted to South Carolina; the building, which dates from 1873, is now occupied by artists and craftspeople.

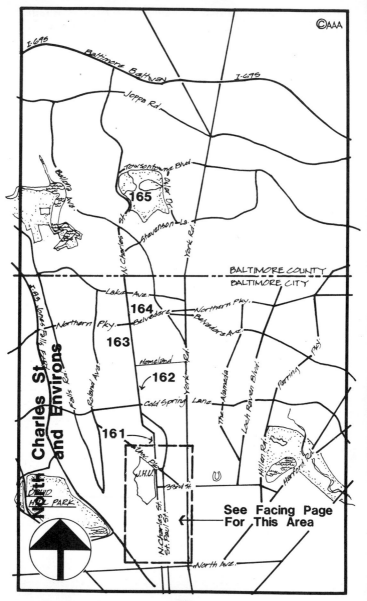

©AAA

I-695

Baltimore Beltway

I-695

Joppa Rd.

Towsontowne Blvd

Dular Dr.

Bellona Ave.

165

N. Charles St.

Stevenson La.

York Rd.

BALTIMORE COUNTY
BALTIMORE CITY

Lake Ave.

164

Northern Pky.

Belvedere

Northern Pky.

Belvedere Ave.

163

Northern Pky.

Roland Ave.

Falls Rd.

York Rd.

Homeland

162

The Alameda

Loch Raven Blvd.

Perring Pky.

Cold Spring Lane

Hillen Rd.

Harford Rd.

161

Univ. Pky.

J.H.U.

33rd St.

© North Charles St. and Environs

DRUID HILL PARK

N. Charles St.

St. Paul St.

See Facing Page For This Area

North Ave.

IVYMAN PARK

39th St.

158   160

San Martin Dr.

N. Charles St.

St. Paul St.

University

JOHNS HOPKINS
UNIVERSITY

159

Greenway

Blvd.

155

156

157

33rd St.

←154

32nd St.

31st. St.

30th St.

152 →   153

29th St.

28th St.

Howard St.

Maryland Ave.

N. Charles St.

St. Paul St.

N. Calvert St.

Guilford Ave.

Barclay St.

Greenmount Ave.

27th

26th

25th St.

24th.

150

149

151 23rd St.

22nd St.

North Charles St.
and Environs Enlarged Area

Tour K   North Charles Street and Environs (Driving)

Baltimore's north-south axis is Charles Street. Not only has the city grown up fairly equally on both sides of this thoroughfare, but some of its finest buildings lie along or near the street. The city grew toward some of the examples on this tour, such as Homewood; more were built where they were because Charles Street has always been the most important street in town.

Almost a century after Homewood Stanford White's Lovely Lane Methodist Church, although Romanesque in flavor, was a reflection of the attempt to find an American style through "free eclecticism." Forty years after that, John Russell Pope's Baltimore Museum, University Baptist Church, and Scottish Rite Temple used classical models when the Bauhaus style was flowering. When the products of the Bauhaus finally arrived in Baltimore in the 1960s, as at Highfield House, the style was so familiar that it had attained a kind of classicism of its own. Other buildings are notable for their attempt to be modern without outraging their surroundings: the Church of the Redeemer by Pietro Belluschi and RTKL Associates, Inc., is a good example.

Baltimore has often been called an ugly city, and some of it certainly is. Much of the best it has to offer in terms of neighborhood—Homeland, Guilford, Roland Park—lies along Charles Street from University Parkway north to the city line. Charles Street itself has been thought of as something of a showplace, from the downtown shopping center to the northern suburbs; a ride along it will show that with some exceptions those who have built along Charles Street have at least made some attempt to live up to its rich if somewhat conservative character.

149   LOVELY LANE METHODIST CHURCH
St. Paul and Twenty-second streets
1887—Stanford White

For his only church building in Baltimore, White borrowed from several churches in Ravenna, Italy, and fused the elements into a composition of stark simplicity and boldness. The nine-story bell tower, with its conical tiled roof (186 feet high, it contains 6,000 tons of rough-hewn Port Deposit granite), was modeled after the campanile of Santa Maria, a twelfth-century brick church near Ravenna.

The nave of the church is an oval-shaped auditorium with a curving balcony that extends around three sides. The space was designed to be used both for religious services and special programs such as pageants and concerts.

The first-floor windows contain the names of the pastors of the church beginning with Francis Asbury. The clerestory windows above reproduce the patterns of mosaics from Ravenna's mausoleum of Galla Placidia. Over the whole is a ceiling on which has been painted a star chart, prepared by the noted American astronomer Simon Newcomb, which represents the heavens as they appeared on

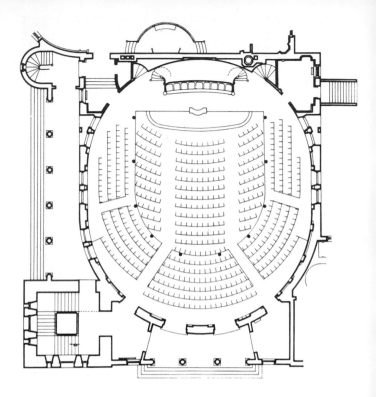

the night the church was dedicated. The interior was originally lit with 340 gas jets; White's lighting arrangement, which cast no shadows, was copied from still another church in Ravenna, San Vitale.

The building of Lovely Lane, which is now considered the mother church of American Methodism, was contemporaneous with the beginning of Goucher College. Several of the buildings in the area were once part of the college.

150 GOUCHER HALL
St. Paul Street between Twenty-second and Twenty-third streets
1888—Charles L. Carson

The building for the Woman's College of Baltimore (later named Goucher College after its first president, John F. Goucher) was built of granite, roofed with red tiles, and designed by Carson in the Romanesque style to blend with White's church.

Across the street to the north is Bennett Hall, which once housed the college's gymnasium and swimming pool. Also of granite, with a hipped roof and polygonal tower, it is by the firm of McKim, Mead, and White.

151 GOUCHER HOUSE
2313 St. Paul Street
1892—McKim, Mead, and White

The house built for Dr. Goucher (who was pastor of Lovely Lane as well as president of the college) is of Pompeian brick and has an Italian Renaissance facade. The interior is laid out around a central hall with an oak staircase. Elsewhere in the house, now used for offices, are some of the opulent materials that were characteristic of the firm's work: Mexican onyx, Siena marble, exotic woods.

152 OAKLAND SPRING HOUSE
Museum Drive, Wyman Park
1827—Benjamin H. Latrobe

Except for the Basilica of the Assumption [22], this little building is the only known example of Latrobe's work left in Baltimore. It is the simplest of structures—an Ionic porch with pediment leads to an unadorned rectangular room.

The classical design is of course typical of Latrobe.

Originally located at Oakland, the estate of Senator Robert Goodloe Harper (now part of Roland Park), the spring house was moved to its present location some years ago. Harper, a major patron of Latrobe, was the son-in-law of Charles Carroll of Carrollton, who paid for Oakland.

153   BALTIMORE MUSEUM OF ART
Museum Drive, Wyman Park
1929—John Russell Pope

Pope, the chief museum architect of his day, and best known now for his later National Gallery in Washington, was principally famous for his classical buildings. He created a flexible design here; when first built, it consisted of only the front galleries flanking the main hall. But there were plans for building additional wings around a central court, some of which have been built.

The pleasantest feature of the building is the Antioch court, a square courtyard surrounded by an enclosed, cloisterlike walkway whose walls contain fragments excavated at Antioch. From this court are entrances to the main building and the major wings.

In 1979, a major renovation and expansion began at the museum; it is scheduled for completion in 1982. Included in the plan are major alterations to the original building, plus addition of a sculpture garden and a new wing, by the architectural firm of Bower, Fradley, Lewis, Thrower of Philadelphia.

154   WOLMAN HOUSE
3213 North Charles Street
1939—Laurence Hall Fowler

Set modestly back from the street between two larger buildings, this house still stands out because of its superior design. The size of the lot (40 feet wide by 156 feet deep) dictated the shape of the house. It is a narrow rectangular box with an interesting arrangement of windows—especially the oriel set in the middle of the front of the house.

Built on the English basement plan, the second floor contains the main living spaces, a living room, and master bedroom. On the first floor are the dining room and kitchen, and on the third are a guest bedroom and study. There is a fourth level in back—a basement room that opens onto a small enclosed garden.

155 HOMEWOOD
Charles and Thirty-fourth streets
ca. 1803—Charles Carroll, Jr.,? Robert and William Edwards, builders

The latest and most refined of the surviving Federal period country houses built near Baltimore is Homewood. Its owner, Charles Carroll, Jr. (son of Charles Carroll of Carrollton), was probably responsible for its Regency flavor and Adamesque touches.

It is a five-part structure, the dependencies joined to the main body of the house by sections deep enough to contain bedrooms. Made of brick with marble trim, the house is basically a one-story design with a high cellar and a small attic story over the central section, the latter indicated by the unusual, unpedimented dormers.

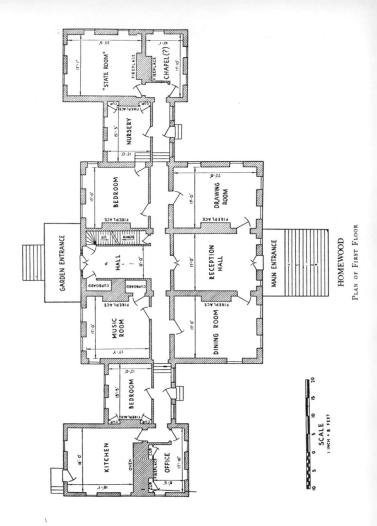

HOMEWOOD

PLAN OF FIRST FLOOR

SCALE
1 INCH = 8 FEET

Approaching the building from the Charles Street side, one sees much of the thought that went into the beautiful facade. The windows are carefully proportioned to the sizes of the various sections. The height of the walls above the windows in the central section, necessitated by the attic story, is minimized by the deep cornices and by the marble panels above each window. The pedimented portico contains a delicate frieze with a shield-shaped window in the center. The doorway, with its attached columns, coffered arch, fanlight, and carved cornice, is rich without being gaudy. The northwest front of the house is also handsome, less formal, and appropriate to a garden facade.

The interior is notable for its detailed woodwork, in which Gothic and classical touches blend. But no less impressive than its looks is the eminently practical plan of the house. A cross-hall runs the length of the house with all rooms opening from it, so that it is never necessary to go through one room to get to another. The large number of closets attest as well to the fact that the requirements of comfort were not sacrificed to the desire for elegance.

Though not a large house, Homewood cost a small fortune for its time: originally budgeted for $10,000, it finally cost $40,000. For 60 years it has been the property of the Johns Hopkins University. In 1980 a major restoration began.

156   GILMAN HALL
Hopkins Campus
1904—Parker and Thomas

The Hopkins Homewood campus was executed in the neo-Colonial or Georgian Revival style popular at the turn of the century. Gilman Hall, which shows touches of Homewood in its rounded dormers, was the most important building in the plan. The Colonial look was more or less adhered to in later buildings until the 1960s.

157   UNIVERSITY BAPTIST CHURCH
Charles and Thirty-fourth streets
1926—John Russell Pope

Another example of Pope's neoclassicism, the University Baptist Church fits its site well. But here there is something of a Renaissance feeling too, especially in the octagonal dome and the arcade on the Charles Street side.

158   CARNEGIE INSTITUTE EMBRYOLOGY BUILDING
University Parkway and San Martin Drive
1962—William E. Haible of Anderson, Beckwith, and Haible

This brick and concrete building blends well with its wooded surroundings and has features that have been copied in more recent bio-science buildings. Another welcome departure from the prevailing Georgian Revival style is Donald L. Sickler's 1974 glass pavilion, an addition to Levering Hall.

159   CATHEDRAL OF THE INCARNATION (Episcopal)
University Parkway and St. Paul Street
1909-1947—Various architects

This English Gothic church atop a Norman crypt was the
subject of much controversy and is actually only a fragment
of the building originally planned.

In 1909 Henry Vaughn submitted the first plan. Ten
years later Bertram G. Goodhue submitted a design for a
huge church similar to the Episcopal cathedrals in New
York and Washington. But the Maryland diocese never had
the money to carry out such an elaborate project, and finally the present building, representing no more than one
transept of the grand design, was built to a design by Frohman, Robb, and Little. Philip Frohman was the main architect of the Washington Cathedral.

160   SCOTTISH RITE TEMPLE OF FREEMASONRY
Charles and Thirty-ninth streets
1932—Clyde N. Friz, with John Russell Pope, consultant

Pope's neoclassicism is here Corinthian. The columns and barrel vault of the portico are particularly imposing.

161   HIGHFIELD HOUSE
4000 North Charles Street
1964—Mies van der Rohe

The second Mies building in Baltimore, like his first [37], is a free-standing tower set on a platform. The glass-enclosed lobby, containing elevators, lounges, and reception desk, occupies less than a third of the ground level; the rest, with the exception of stair enclosures, is open space defined by the columns that raise the building 20 feet above the platform. Down below are underground parking facilities and a glass-walled recreation room, the floor of which extends out in back of the building to become a large plaza with a swimming pool-fountain.

The building is of reinforced concrete, which the architect arranged in a wide-bayed grid of finely proportioned members. Although the tower has the refined precision and meticulous planning that characterizes Mies van der Rohe's work, two concessions were made to the character of the neighborhood. The column-to-column windows give the building a horizontal feeling, making its height (13 apartment floors plus a two-story lobby) less noticeable in an area of moderate-sized apartment houses and individual homes. In addition, the panels above the spandrels are of buff face brick, also in keeping with the more traditional surroundings.

162 EVERGREEN
4545 North Charles Street
ca. 1855, with later additions—Original architect unknown

A free classical design with an asymmetrical floor plan and moody interiors, this house was originally built for a family named Broadbent and was supposedly modeled after Melville Park, a former country estate east of Old York Road. The finest single feature of the house is the magnificent Corinthian portico.

The house was bought by T. Harrison Garrett in 1878, and the Garrett family added to it considerably. John W. Garrett added the north archway and wing, designed by Charles L. Carson, in the 1880s. The wing contains the recently restored theater decorated by Bakst, the famous stage designer for the Russian ballet.

The library, with its slightly domed ceiling, hand-carved walnut paneling, and floor-to-ceiling bookcases, was designed by Laurence Hall Fowler and added in 1928.

Now owned by the Johns Hopkins University and administered as a research facility for the university and the city of Baltimore, Evergreen contains the collections of generations of Garretts, from Victorian pieces through Louis Comfort Tiffany to Picasso. There is also a rare book collection. The Garrett coin collection, one of the finest in the world, was housed at Evergreen until it was sold by the university.

163 CATHEDRAL OF MARY OUR QUEEN
5200 North Charles Street
1959—Maginnis and Walsh

An earlier Romanesque plan of the thirties was never built; the architects termed the present edifice "an adaptation of Gothic principles to modern expression." It is 373 feet long and 239 feet wide at its fullest extension and has two stone towers 128 feet high on the eastern facade. The cathedral is built of brick faced with limestone and granite. There is Art Deco-like decoration on both the cathedral building and the rectory to the north. An interesting feature of the cathedral design is that it has two independent chapels to the north and south of the nave but no real transepts.

The cost of the cathedral was about $8,500,000.

164   CHURCH OF THE REDEEMER
Charles Street and Melrose Avenue
1958—Pietro Belluschi, RTKL Associates, Inc.

Belluschi, the noted contemporary architect, here tackled a difficult commission and created a masterpiece. The problem, as the church committee presented it, was to build a church several times as large as the original century-old church, which was to remain as a chapel, without dwarfing it, and to build a thoroughly contemporary structure in harmony with its Gothic-style neighbor (which was designed by R. Snowden Andrews).

Belluschi created a church that embraces the ground. The low walls, built of the same local stone used in the old church, are separated by a row of windows from a steeply pitched roof. The whole church, though massive, is lower than the top of the old church's spire, and the eye travels easily from the one to the other.

The interior satisfies the congregation's desire that the church "give expression to the building's function as the link between heaven and earth." The Gothic contours of the huge wooden arches echo those of the old church but are structural here. Though they support the roof, they do not rise to the top of it—"it being felt that separation between arches and rooftop would symbolize the spiritual."

The great wooden arches themselves connote both the power and the aspirations of man, and the effect is enhanced by the band of stained-glass windows separating walls and roof.

The large stained-glass window behind the altar was made at Chartres to a design by Gyorgy Kepes, professor of visual design at MIT. It appears at first to be totally abstract, but there is the outline of a cross in the glass.

165   SHEPPARD AND ENOCH PRATT HOSPITAL
6501 North Charles Street
1858-1888—Dixon and Dixon with D. Tilden Brown, Calvert Vaux

When Quaker philanthropist Moses Sheppard died, he left a bequest of $571,000 for the building and operation of a hospital for the insane. His principal stipulations were two: having witnessed the inhumane conditions to which the mentally ill were subjected in his time, he directed the trustees to "put first the comfort of the patient," and specifically stated that there should be plenty of light and fresh air everywhere; and he required that only the income from his bequest ever be used to support the hospital.

It is probable that both these conditions were responsible for the remarkable Victorian buildings which grew over a period of 30 years on the Baltimore County site chosen for the hospital. The two identical original buildings, each 360 feet long, are noted for the spacious, airy, light-filled quality of their interiors, and the fact that the buildings only proceeded as income from the bequest became available surely meant that every care could be taken in their construction.

The extended gabled and dormered brick buildings, which were constructed with iron girders and stairways, slate roofs, and stone foundations—chosen to make the buildings as fireproof as possible—are visually enhanced by the two unequal towers of each, the taller ones six stories high with steep, wedge-shaped roofs. Altogether, in an era when large buildings were often forbidding in appearance, these managed a charming complexity of facade which positively invites one to enter and explore. No doubt this quality was one reason the Dixons' design was chosen from those submitted in the architectural competition held by the trustees. The amusing gatehouse on Charles Street is also by Dixon and Dixon. Calvert Vaux, a well-known landscape architect who collaborated with Frederick Law Olmsted on the design of Central Park in New York, was named associate architect of Sheppard Pratt.

It is interesting to note that the two principal materials used in the buildings, brick and stone, came from the property, which had been an estate called Mount Airy. The stone was quarried from one portion of the land, and elsewhere was found excellent brick clay from which 11 million bricks were fired in kilns constructed at the site.

In the late 1960s and early 1970s a complete renovation of the two main buildings was undertaken by the engineering firm of Fred vonBehren, Inc., during which much long-unused space in the original buildings was reclaimed. At the same time the space between them was filled with a new central building designed by Anthony J. Ianniello.

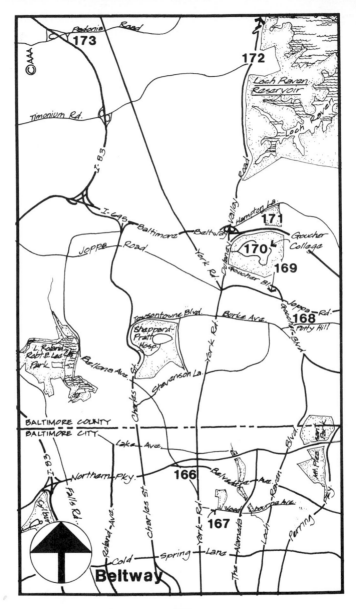

Padonia Road

173

172

Loch Raven Reservoir

Timonium Rd.

I-83

Loch Raven Road

I-695

Baltimore Beltway

Dulaney Valley Road

Hampton La.

171

Goucher College

170

169

Joppa Road

York Rd.

Goucher Bl.

Joppa Rd.

Towsontowne Blvd.

Burke Ave.

168

Goucher Blvd.

Putty Hill

Sheppard Pratt Hosp.

L. Roland Robt. E. Lee Park

Bellona Ave.

Charles St.

Stevenson La.

York Rd.

BALTIMORE COUNTY

BALTIMORE CITY

Lake Ave.

I-83

Northern Pky.

Falls Rd.

166

Belvedere Ave.

Ft. Pleas

Loch Raven Blvd.

Pky.

Roland Ave.

Charles St.

York Rd.

Woodbourne Ave.

167

Falls Rd.

Cold Spring Lane

The Alameda

Perring

Beltway

Some of the Baltimore area's oldest, most eccentric buildings, sufficiently far from the city in the 1800s to qualify as genuine country manors, as well as a few new and wild examples of postmodern architecture, lie conveniently within reach of the Beltway, the new main street of the metropolitan area.

166   SENATOR THEATER
5904 York Road
1939—John J. Zink

Art Deco, a modernistic style of decoration that flourished in the 1920s and 1930s, reached its apogee with the Chrysler Building and Radio City Music Hall in New York. Ornamental rather than architectural, the characteristics of Art Deco included stylized sunbursts, ziggurats, waves, waterfalls, fountains, and thunderbolts. In the twenties these were generally depicted rectilinearly; in the thirties more rounded, streamlined shapes took over. Art Deco was to be seen not only on buildings but in the design of everything from light fixtures and furniture to dresses and cigarette lighters. Finally it died of twin causes: the boredom

and eventual revulsion produced by its ubiquity and the enormous amount of kitsch turned out in its name; and opposition to Germany's Nazi party, which appropriated many of its design elements.

Just as Art Deco was dying, what should appear in typically backward Baltimore but the Senator Theater, which has remained (along with the Maryland National Bank Building and Hutzler's) as one of the best surviving local examples of this style. With its exterior glass-brick upper walls, illuminated by colored lights at night, round lobby with sunburst panels beneath a lounge balcony and a mural depicting "the progress of visual entertainment" (the artist was Paul M. Roche), rounded columns and walnut-veneered walls, and the sunburst effect of the colored lighting display on the ceiling of the auditorium, echoed in the lighting fixtures of the upper-level lounge, the Senator Theater is, now that interest in Art Deco has revived, a treasure. Some elements, such as the gold leaf on the lobby and auditorium ceilings and the draped female statues on either side of the stage, have disappeared over the years. But enough remains.

John J. Zink was a theater architect of the twenties and thirties and a master of Art Deco embellishment. Among his commissions in Baltimore and Washington were several of the Durkee chain of movie theaters, including the Patterson, the Edgewood, and the Ambassador. This chain still owns and proudly maintains the Senator.

167   TIVOLI (WOODBOURNE CENTER, INC.)
1301 Woodbourne Avenue (between the Alameda and Loch Raven Boulevard)
ca. 1855?—Architect unknown

One of the summer houses built outside Baltimore in the second half of the nineteenth century, this was purchased by Enoch Pratt in 1870; he owned it until he died there in 1896. But the benefactor of the Enoch Pratt Free Library did not, apparently, build it. The present owners—it is now a home for emotionally disabled adolescents—claim that it was probably built about 1855 and shows "an Italian influence popular at the time." This stone structure, however, is rather severe to be called fully Italianate.

168   BEST PRODUCTS, INC.
1245 Eudowood Plaza, Joppa Road and Goucher Boulevard, Towson
1978—Site, Inc.

Most Best stores are normal suburban shopping center designs. The Towson "Tilt" project, however, has its 14-inch-thick, 450-ton masonry front wall lifted from ground level at one corner and angled smartly from the facade. The tilt is about 20 degrees in both planes. The bottom left corner of the wall rests on a caisson. The remainder of the weight is carried by cantilevered steel beams; the enclosure is visible from underneath about mid-point in the wall. The bottom edge, which looks as if it's hanging by itself, is actually a reinforced masonry beam, connected to the supporting structure with U-bolts. It was fabricated on the ground, then raised to the proper angle and tilted, and the rest of the blocks laid on top of it.

The store was designed by James Wines, a Towsonite and a sculptor, and Emilio Sousa; both are principals of Site, Inc., a New York firm. It is the fourth in a series of variations on a theme for the country's largest catalogue-showroom merchandiser. The other departures, also by Site, Inc., feature crumbling bricks, sliding entrances, and peeling facades, signifying . . . what? Commercial gimmickry, dearchitecture, apocalyptic visions—all have been suggested. At any rate, the Best Company, which finds the radical designs are good for business, is building more of them.

169   MARYLAND BLUE CROSS BUILDING
700 East Joppa Road, Towson
1972—Peterson and Brickbauer; Brown, Guenther, Battaglia, and Galvin

This striking building is the concept of the local architects responsible for the Sun Life and Mercantile buildings downtown. Inside, it is a typical office building, with a lobby on the lower level, ten office floors, and mechanical equipment on the roof, all supported by a structural steel frame. From the exterior, however, it looks like a giant cube of ice etched with black lines and reflecting the sky and the landscape around it. The surface is silver reflective glass in a black aluminum curtain wall, which emphasizes the cube and square motif of the building itself.

The reflecting glass serves two purposes, according to the architects—an esthetic one and a functional one. "The site is triangular and is the highest elevation in the area. The neighborhood is essentially residential and the mirrored cube was used to diminish the disparity in scale by becoming merely a reflection of the sky and the constantly changing cloud and light formations." Also, the reflecting glass considerably reduces air conditioning costs.

In order to preserve the integrity of the cube, a recessed circular entrance court allows for entrances from below ground level. The flame-red glazed-brick cube nearby houses mechanical apparatus and serves, in the architects' words, to create "in an abstract fashion a gigantic minimal sculpture."

170   GOUCHER COLLEGE CENTER
**Goucher College Campus off Dulaney Valley Road north of Towson
1960—Pietro Belluschi, RTKL Associates, Inc.**

Belluschi has combined fieldstone, wood, and concrete in an imaginative way in this grouping of buildings to create congenial spaces without sacrificing functionality. An auditorium, a lecture hall, administrative offices, and a student lounge are gathered around an open courtyard.

The complex itself presents no unified facade to the visitor. Wide stone stairs separating the auditorium and office buildings mount to the central court. The hexagonal auditorium, its bare concrete walls and floor softened by curved rows of seats sweeping unbroken from wall to wall, is an impressive interior.

171 HAMPTON
Hampton National Historic Site, off Dulaney Valley Road north of Towson
1783-1790—Architect unknown

This imposing mansion was the largest house in Maryland when it was completed for John Ridgely, ironmaster, after the Revolutionary War. The Ridgely family owned it until after World War II. The 175-by-55-foot house has a two-and-a-half story main section set off by one-story wings. The symmetrical design's stately appearance is mitigated somewhat by the decorative dormers and classical urns in the roof, which add lighter touches.

The front door, set off by tall pedimented windows, leads to a central hall. This hall runs the length of the house and was used as a picture gallery. There are two rooms of equal size on each side of the hall. The wings were used for the kitchen and other functional purposes. Throughout the house there is interesting architectural decoration.

The two significant elements of the house are the cupola, called "the first instance upon a colonial domestic building in which such a feature was treated with monumental importance", and the fact that the locally quarried field-stone walls were overlaid with stucco, one of the first instances of such use in the United States.

172   RAVENHURST
Ravenhurst Drive off Dulaney Valley Road
ca. 1850—Architect unknown

A curious 36-room Victorian mansion, this was the home of Major General Isaac Ridgeway Trimble, civil engineer, railroad executive, and Confederate officer. The house is distinguished by its vertical batten boards, the gable barge-boards with depending verticals at the ends, the Gothic windows in the dormers, and the cupola. All in all, a real Charles Addams creation.

173   JOHN DEERE COMPANY WAREHOUSE
York Expressway (I-83), near Padonia Road
1966—RTKL Associates, Inc.

A "big tent" is the way the architects refer to the structure of their warehouse, which turns its best face away from the road. The tent-ropes are one-and-a-half inch steel cables; they are tied to concrete anchors buried in the bank on the side facing the expressway. The cables run the length of the building and support, in three 131-foot spans, the precast concrete plank roof. They are anchored on the other side by concrete "buttresses." But unlike the buttresses of Gothic cathedrals, which push against the thrust, these pull to help support the roof; a similar roof system was used for Dulles Airport.

Most of the front of the building, thus freed of cables, is used for a loading platform. There are just two rows of interior columns, and large open spaces permit the free movement of the firm's products—large farm and industrial tractors and equipment. The front span houses the loading dock on a raised platform on one side and, on three successive levels, an auditorium-showroom space, a cafeteria, and classrooms and offices.

The warehouse sits on a 16-acre fan-shaped site and is itself shaped like a fan (the narrower portion faces the front), allowing for future expansion. The building, which encloses 197,000 square feet of space, clearly serves its purpose, yet it is also a dramatic departure from the conventional warehouse. The relationship between structure and form is particularly striking, the slender concrete "buttresses" on the front of the building giving the facade a Corbusian monumentality.

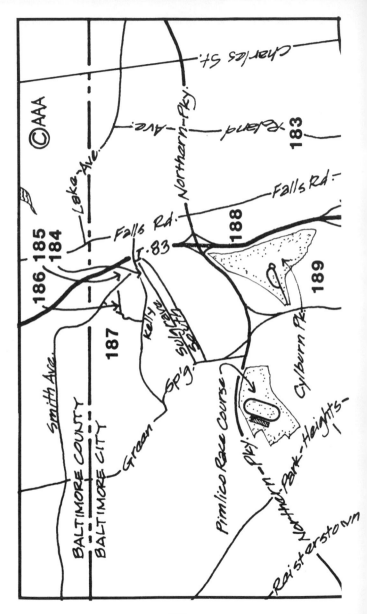

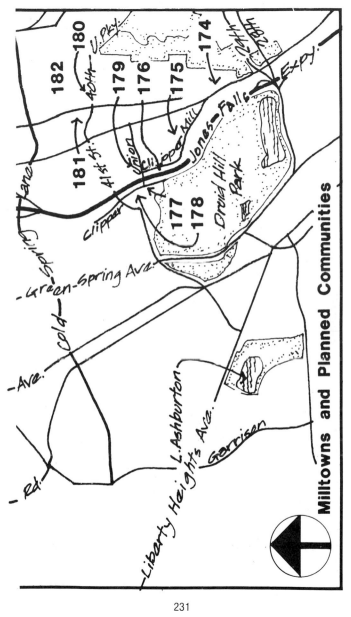

Milltowns and Planned Communities

182

180 — U. Pky.

40th —

179

176

175

174

174th

26th

L.

Expy.

181 —

41st St.

Union

Clipper-Mill

Jones-Falls

clipper

177

178

Druid Hill Park

Green-Spring Lane

Green-Spring Ave.

Cold-

-Ave.

-Rd.

L. Ashburton

Liberty Heights Ave.

Garrison

231

Tour M   Mill Towns and Planned Communities (Driving)

Engulfed and largely forgotten by the modern city, the lower Jones Falls valley is a treasure house of nineteenth-century industrial architecture. This is the result of the valley's traditional role as a transportation corridor and manufacturing center.

Falls Road was an early route through the valley between the city and the open country to the north. Railroads followed the same route; mills, attracted by the available transportation and water power, began appearing in the first half of the nineteenth century. By mid-century there were a number of milling firms in the valley.

The mill owners erected groups of houses for their workers; these grew into full-fledged communities and remain so today. Hampden and Mount Washington are examples. These communities in turn prompted the building of additional transportation facilities. In 1885, the Baltimore Union Passenger Railway Company operated the first commercial electric street railway in the country between Twenty-fifth Street and Hampden.

The cotton textile industry began in Maryland in 1810 when the Washington Cotton Manufacturing Company at Smith and Kelly avenues started operations. In 1839, Horatio Gambrill and David Carroll purchased an old flour mill and converted it into a cotton factory making yarn and cotton duck for sails. It was on the site of the present Clipper Mill. In 1842 Gambrill also purchased and converted the Woodberry Mill. The Clipper Mill, incidentally, took its name from the clipper ships, which were prime customers. Woodberry was the largest manufacturing town in the state during those years. Gambrill and William E. Hooper later erected other mills, including Mount Vernon in 1847, and Clipper and Druid in 1866. The history of these structures is complicated by the fact that they frequently burned and were rebuilt. Mill names and ownership also shifted frequently.

Iron was added to the valley's industries in 1853, when Poole and Hunt's Union Machine Shops were built on Union Avenue. The Poole and Hunt works employed about 400 men in the 1870s and manufactured steam boilers, mining and flour-milling machinery, and the iron columns supporting the dome of the United States Capitol. (More recently, the buildings were occupied by the Franklin-Balmar Tractor Company.)

The mills were then a long way from Baltimore and its labor pool; thus the company-owned communities of houses. The rents were cheap—$5 or $6 a month—but so was labor. In the early days, most of the work force at the cotton mills was made up of children aged 6 to 12; they put in 12 or more hours a day, six days a week for a little over half a cent an hour. "Strikes are unheard of," according to the contemporary Scharf's *Chronicles*, "and the only labor demonstration that has taken place in many years was a rejoicing, on February 19, 1874, over the passage by the Maryland Legislature of a law forbidding the employment of children under 16 years of age longer than 10 hours a day."

During their most prosperous and productive period from 1875 to 1890, the mills in the Jones Falls valley employed 3,000 people (adult wages ranged from $12 to $75 a month), consumed more than 25 million pounds of cotton a year, and produced more than half the world's cotton duck.

In this century the mills entered a decline. The owners moved their operations south to be nearer the source of cotton and to take advantage of cheaper labor. Mechanization took its toll of workers.

The last to succumb was the Mount Vernon Mills, which ceased the manufacture of synthetic yarns and fabrics in August 1972. Most of the mill houses have been sold. Today, the mill buildings are used to manufacture everything from brushes to raincoats.

To the north along Falls Road are Roland Park, one of the oldest planned communities in America, and Coldspring, one of the newest. Farther north and west is Mount Washington, another early planned suburb.

174 MOUNT VERNON MILL AND COMMUNITY
Falls Road
ca. 1843-1873

The main Mount Vernon mill building is a three-story brick structure with a tower at the south end (facing the bend in Falls Road), where a stone plaque identifies it as "Mt. Vernon Mills, No. 1." It was built in 1873 after its predecessor, dating from 1843, was destroyed by fire. Opposite the building that housed the main offices of the Mount Vernon Mills is a stone building that was the company store. There is another four-story brick mill building on Chestnut Avenue that dates from 1853.

In back of it, on East Darby Street and Elm Avenue, are houses built by the mill for its workers. The area is known as Brick Hill. Fronting on Pacific Avenue is another group of mill houses built about 1850. Known as Stone Hill, it is a cluster of 22 semidetached stone houses with yards, along five short streets with the only through traffic tangential to the cluster.

Another excellent feature of the plan is the height. The houses face southwest across the Jones Falls valley, far above the commotion of the mill and facing the prevailing summer breezes. It is a subdivision plan that would do credit to a modern builder.

175 EVERGREEN-ON-THE-FALLS
3300 Falls Road
ca. 1860—Architect unknown

Built by Henry Snyder, this Italianate mansion was occupied for most of the last half of the nineteenth century by members of the Hooper and Carroll families, who operated the nearby mills in Hampden and Woodberry. The Carrolls added landscaping and formal boxwood gardens that made the estate a showplace. In 1926, it was sold to the Maryland SPCA, which uses the house as its headquarters.

The house is white-painted brick, with bracketed canopies and other trim. The SPCA rebuilt the mansion after a serious fire in the early 1970s; a few original details, such as the main staircase (restored), marble mantels, and chandeliers, remain.

The stone valve house, built 1860-1861, once faced the Hampden Reservoir, since filled in; both were part of the city's early water supply system.

176 CLIPPER MILL
Clipper Mill Road, Woodberry
1866

Two earlier mills on the site burned. The third one is a handsome three-story brick building with a stelliform chimney and arched double windows. On either side of the road and on the ridge to the east are more stone mill houses, including two row-house groups of four houses each.

177 MEADOW MILL
Union Avenue and Seneca Street
1877

The Meadow Mill is a two- to four-story building with a distinctive brick and wooden bell tower identified by the letter *L* on the sides.

Across from the Meadow Mill, at Union Avenue and Clipper Road, is the old Union Machine Shops of the Poole and Hunt Foundry. The buildings, some dating from the 1850s, are now used for light industry.

The windows of both the Meadow and Mount Vernon mills were bricked up in modern times to help maintain interior temperature control.

178   PARK MILL
Clipper Road
1855

Farther north on Clipper Road are 37 two-and-a-half story mill houses. To their east is the Park Mill and the site of the old Woodberry Mill from which the community takes its name.

179   DRUID MILL
Union Avenue
1866; enlarged 1872

The Druid Mill, east of Clipper Mill Road, is the only one in the Italianate style. The building with the tower was built in 1866, the wing to the north in 1872.

180   GREENWAY COTTAGES
Fortieth Street between University Parkway and Roland Avenue

These are three handsome, solid, Victorian cottages, with particularly notable chimneys.

181 QUEEN ANNE STYLE HOUSES
4100 and 4200 blocks Roland Avenue
ca. 1875—Architect unknown

The picturesque Queen Anne style, inspired by Richard Norman Shaw, with its variegated gables, dormers, towers, and multicolored roofs, is shown to good advantage in four houses in the two blocks. They were all probably built about the same time, perhaps by the same hand.

182 POURED CONCRETE HOUSES
835-843 West University Parkway
1905—Architect unknown

These houses of exposed poured concrete were an innovation in their day. Indeed, Alexander Cochran, in his Introduction, asserts that the same use of material was not to occur again in Baltimore for 60 years. The houses are a great deal larger than they look from the street; the middle one, for example, contains eight bedrooms.

183   ROLAND PARK
1891 and later—Olmsted brothers and other planners and architects

The development of Roland Park, one of the earliest and still one of the finest planned suburban communities in the country, is discussed at some length in the Introduction. In brief, the famous landscape architectural firm who designed Roland Park for a syndicate of English speculators took advantage of the natural topography of the land, with its hills and ravines (especially to the west of Roland Avenue), and the houses were built largely out of plans provided by *The American Builder* and other magazines of the time. The three predominant styles to be seen here are the cottage in the Shingle style (shown in photograph 1), the Tudor half-timbered house (photograph 2), and a vaguely Queen Anne cottage. Of these, perhaps the most appropriate to the landscape is the Shingle, which seems to nestle into the trees and hillsides.

There is no great architectural distinction to most of the houses. As Howland and Spencer noted in *The Architecture of Baltimore*, "If they have any architectural features in common beyond a general studied picturesqueness, it would be in the sense of intimacy and comfort of family life expressed by the deep, capacious verandas, the wide bay windows, the substantial, decorative and functional chimneys, and a round tower on every other house."

Special mention should be given to the Roland Park Shopping Center (photograph 3), often called the first suburban shopping center in the United States. It was designed in the Tudor half-timbered style (also seen in several houses nearby) in 1896 by Wyatt and Nolting. The complex's gables and dormers, tall chimneys, and diamond-paned casement windows contribute to the overall interest and achieve a certain lightness which counteracts the mass. The shopping center was renovated in 1977 by James Colimore of Ekstrom, Colimore, and Doyle.

Roland Park is bounded roughly by University Parkway on the south, Northern Parkway on the north, Falls Road on the west and Charles Street on the east. It is divided by Roland Avenue.

184 MELE HOUSE
1709 Sulgrave Avenue
ca. 1855—Architect unknown

A brilliant-hued Victorian Gothic cottage that looks as if it came from a book of fairy tales, the Mele House, according to its present owner, was built as a summer home. It was one of the first houses in Mount Washington.

185 MOUNT WASHINGTON OCTAGON
Near Smith and Greeley avenues
1855—James and Thomas Dixon (?)

The design of the Mount Washington Octagon is straightforward to the point of plainness. The octagon was built under the direction of the Reverend Elias Heiner of the German Reformed Church and was used until 1861 as the Mount Washington Female College. The college failed after the Civil War, and in 1867 the Sisters of Mercy bought the building and opened a school called Mount St. Agnes. It later expanded to include 129 acres of land and several more buildings. In 1971, Mount St. Agnes merged with Loyola College and moved from the campus.

The octagon mode, which flourished in the United States during this period, was inspired by Orson Squire Fowler, a phrenologist who also wrote on health and marital happiness. The octagon's main advantage, according to Fowler, was that it enclosed more floor area. There are other examples of the style in the neighborhood.

186 MOUNT WASHINGTON PRESBYTERIAN CHURCH (School of the Chimes)
1801 Thornbury Road
1878—Thomas Dixon

This church, which cost $4,500 to build, according to Scharf's *History of Baltimore*, is an example of "Carpenter Gothic." The original church consists of the three-story shingled tower over the main entrance and a rather short nave. Attached to it at right angles is a newer, larger section housing a meeting room and kitchen in back.

The battens covering the wooden joints of the vertical siding and the wood buttresses, as well as the braces that suggest stone tracery, give the church a definite Gothic flavor. The triangular stained-glass clerestory windows are unusual.

The nave, with its dark wood trusses, is a small and intimate space. The altar and pews have been removed, as the building is no longer a church. It has been bought by the neighboring School of the Chimes for use in their training program for the retarded.

187   DIXON'S HILL
MOUNT WASHINGTON
1856-1878—Thomas Dixon and others

Mount Washington was one of the first of Baltimore's planned suburbs (see Introduction). It traces its origins to Washingtonville, the mill community that grew up around the Washington Cotton Manufacturing Company.

The Northern Central Railroad linked the mill town with Baltimore. This rail link was a main selling point of the Mount Washington developers, who offered rail commuting to the city.

These developers, George Gelbach, Jr., and Dr. Elias Heiner, also helped found the Mount Washington Female College. In 1854 they acquired a tract of about 190 acres west of the Northern Central rail line. Originally known as the Mount Washington Rural Retreat, it encompassed most of the present Mount Washington, including the old Mount St. Agnes Campus, The Terraces (another early development behind the campus), and part of Dixon's Hill.

According to an 1854 pamphlet, "The design of the enterprise is to furnish to those seeking it, a healthy, retired and respectable country residence, avoiding the monotony of a village, or the crowding and confinement of the city, yet retaining the advantages of a community; in short, having the conveniences of the city with the advantages of the country."

In succeeding years, as what began as a summer colony became a year-round place to live, various entrepreneurs purchased pieces of the original tract and built houses. Among them was Thomas Dixon, the architect of the Mount Washington Presbyterian Church, who in 1856 bought land near that building. Eventually, having acquired interest in a lumber company and seeing a ready market for his product, he built a number of houses in what is now known as Dixon's Hill (see Introduction).

Although an expressway now divides the original mill site from the original summer retreat, Mount Washington retains some of the character of an English village. Recently several small shops have opened in an area known as Mount Washington Village.

188 CROSS KEYS
Falls Road and Northern Parkway
1964—Various architects

Across the street from Roland Park—one of the oldest planned communities in the country—is one of the newest: the Village of Cross Keys, a carefully laid out "new town in town" planned for about 2,500 people.

Built by the Rouse Company (the developers of Columbia) on 72 acres of what was formerly the golf course of the Baltimore Country Club, the village took its name from an inn that once stood near the corner of Falls Road and Cold Spring Lane. The inn, whose signboard consisted of two large crossed keys, was a favorite stopping place for travelers from the outlying farms and villages.

The village square at the center of Cross Keys is now a favorite stopping place for the people who live there, as well as for neighboring suburbanites. Designed by Toronto architects Murray and Fleiss to resemble an old-fashioned village green, the landscaped square can accommodate concerts and art shows. Surrounding the square are 15 specialty shops with office space above them.

Richard C. Stauffer, an architect, and James W. Rouse, a mortgage banker, collaborated on the original site plan for Cross Keys. Stauffer and Collins-Kronstadt and Associates of Silver Spring designed the first town houses. Since then mid-rise apartment buildings and various amenities have been added, but due to the careful preservation of trees and natural landscape features, they still occupy an almost bucolic setting.

189　COLDSPRING
Cold Spring Lane and Springarden Drive
1977—Moshe Safdie

The major purpose of Coldspring, a new-town project designed by the architect of Montreal's Habitat, was to attract to the city middle-income residents who might otherwise live in the suburbs. So far, it has achieved its goal—the first 124 housing units have been sold, and 128 more are under construction.

When planning began for the project in the late 1960s, the Coldspring site was the largest vacant privately-owned area in the city. Bordered on the east by the Jones Falls Expressway and on the west by Greenspring Avenue, it stretches almost two miles between Cylburn and Woodberry and contains areas of dense hardwood forest, a city dump, and a stone quarry. The 375-acre site was undeveloped partly because of its difficult terrain.

In 1971, consultants, including Safdie and Lawrence Halprin, landscape architect, began work on a master plan for the area. Officially announced the following year, it called for 3,800 housing units to be built on 140 acres of land. A buffer zone was to be added between the new development and Cylburn, a nature preserve to the north; a town center was to be built in the middle of the site, at Cold Spring Lane; and the walls of the quarry near the southern end were to be lined with high-rise housing. Small lakes and parks and recreation areas were to be scattered throughout, including over the city dump.

Factory-produced housing units, like those that make up Habitat, were also part of the plan, and although the initial 124 "deckhouses" have been conventionally built, mass-produced housing has not been ruled out. F. D. Rich Corporation of Stamford, Connecticut, is the developer. Construction began in 1975, and the first families moved in in 1977.

The houses, stepped back in the rear and cantilevered in front, face each other over pedestrian decks, which in turn cover parking areas. The materials are mainly precast concrete and brick. The interiors are arranged in various configurations, but each unit has a private rear yard or terrace. The average purchase price was $45,000.

Coldspring currently represents about $40 million in private and public investment and is expected to cost about $200 million when it is completed in 10 or 15 years.

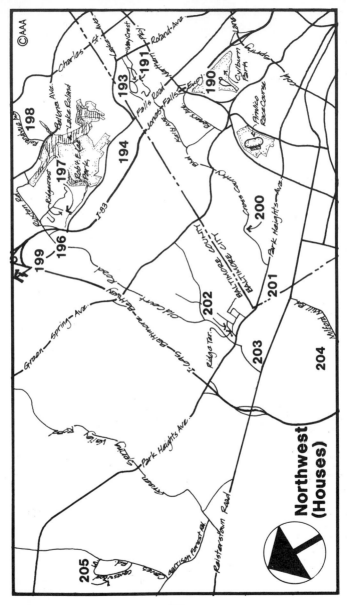

Northwest
(Houses)

Most of the buildings on this tour are houses. It is no accident that they occur in the north and northwest portions of Baltimore, for this is where wealthy persons emigrated when they left the center of the city. Several of the houses are located in Poplar Hill, north of Roland Park in the hills around Lake Roland, and in the Pikesville area.

Designed for purposes other than impressing passersby, these houses tend to turn away from the street and in on themselves. Some of the city's best modern architecture is to be found here.

190   CYLBURN
Cylburn Park, 4915 Greenspring Avenue
1889—George A. Frederick

Frederick's versatility as an architect is further illustrated by the Victorian mansion he did for Jesse Tyson, prominent member of a family involved in the mining and processing of chrome and copper. It was built of local stone as Tyson's country home.

"Cylburn was a showplace," noted a newspaper account. "The mansion, with its magnificent view of the city across Falls Road and its acres of formal gardens, was the scene of much formal entertaining."

The mansion and grounds were purchased by the city in 1942 for $42,300 for use as a park. The Cylburn area includes 176 acres, 70 of them now designated for a "wildflower preserve and garden center." The rooms of the house are presently used for offices, meeting rooms, and a nature museum.

191   EMORY NILES HOUSE
5600 Waycrest Lane
1938—John H. Scharf

Long and narrow with a flat roof and facing away from the street, the Niles House was considered modern for its time and surroundings.

192 DAVIS HOUSE
Address withheld at owner's request
1966—J. William Ilmanen

Combining the maximum exposure to wooded surroundings with the needs of a person who lives alone but often
entertains a large family, the architect has created a house
both comfortable and dramatic.

The open entrance deck separates two halves of the upper
level of the house; to one side, a door opens onto a balcony
with a circular staircase descending to a living room. Here a
24-foot slanting side wall is pierced by long strips of window
through which the room is lighted strikingly at night from
the outside. A sculptural fireplace separates the living
room from a long dining room, underneath the entrance
deck. The dining room windows make full use of the view.
Opposite the living room section of the house is the bedroom
section, with guest room on the ground level and master
bedroom-sitting room combination above.

The remarkable plan provides for a screened porch, an
open porch, and a sun deck. Owner and architect working
together have thought of every convenience, from a slide
projector concealed in a wall case and a screen that rises out
of the floor to a dumbwaiter to carry parcels from the garage
on the entrance level to the kitchen below.

Wooden frame construction was used, and the building was fitted out with a harmonious and utilitarian combination of woods, including Peruvian cypress, hackberry, oak, and Western red cedar.

The Davis House won a national award from *Architectural Record* in 1968.

193   COCHRAN HOUSE
901 West Lake Avenue
1975—Alexander S. Cochran

The architect's first house at 903 West Lake Avenue, built in 1951, was a "split-level" before the term became generic. It created a mild sensation in a neighborhood of more traditional homes. It also won a national American Institute of Architects design award. His family having become smaller since then, Cochran sold it and most of the five-acre lot to the Boys' Latin School and built a smaller house next door on the remaining acreage.

Brick has been substituted for stone, and the new house is on a single level, but some of the previous materials and features have been retained: living spaces with a southern exposure facing away from the street; a clerestory that allows natural light (augmented by fluorescent tubes) into the north side; and a cantilevered section that covers a sunken terrace. Bluestone, brick, and walnut paneling are some of the interior materials.

An atrium effect has been created in the rear, with a brick wall surrounding a large courtyard, sculpture garden, and a small pool, or "plunge." The wall has narrow vertical slots at 12-foot intervals, through which light plays in varying patterns.

William H. Potts, Jr., was the landscape architect.

194   BARE HILLS HOUSE
6222 Falls Road
ca. 1845—Architect unknown

With its pointed gables, porches, battens, and bargeboards, this picturesque house, set back from the road on 2.5 acres of land, is a prime example of the "rural Gothic" style popular in America in the mid-nineteenth century (see Introduction).

Set on a stone foundation, the house is built entirely of wood. Inside are four large rooms downstairs and two fireplaces; upstairs are five bedrooms and a central hall with odd planes and angles due to the steeply pitched gables.

The area is named Bare Hills because plants do not grow well in the rocky soil. In the mid- and late nineteenth century, several mines and quarries were active in the vicinity; commercial operations were begun in the 1800s by Isaac Tyson, Jr. Off Smith Avenue, toward Mount Washington, copper was mined; the area near Falls and Old Pimlico roads was a source of chromium and serpentine, the latter a dull green rock that was used in building the Mount Vernon Place Methodist Church [8].

195   HOOPER HOUSE
Address withheld at owner's request
1959—Marcel Breuer

Built to fit the area and not spoil its surroundings, the Hooper House, in a heavily wooded section overlooking Lake Roland, is by the renowned architect Marcel Breuer— contemporary of Gropius, member of the Bauhaus, designer of many architectural masterpieces.

The plan of the house is basically a rectangle, with a mid-court and entryway; the court is open to the sky between the sleeping and living areas. It is Breuer's bi-nuclear design, in which, according to the architect, "whole living areas are considered as unities. The result [is] . . . to separate and give privacy to distinct areas of a house."

The exterior is of rugged Maryland fieldstone taken from the site. The stone facade is broken only by the entry, two five-foot sliding glass doors permitting a view through the entry and court to Lake Roland beyond. The stone is an effective barrier to the western sun and helps orient the house to privacy and the eastern view.

The interior has stone floors and walls and acoustical tile ceilings. The furniture, much of it designed by Breuer, is spare so as not to compete with the beauty of the rooms themselves.

The house is spanned by steel beams resting on stone walls or on Lally columns and topped with 2-inch-by-10-inch wood joists. Floors are concrete slabs on grade or reinforced concrete where not supported by the ground.

196   ROCKLAND MILL, COMMUNITY AND HOUSE
Falls and Old Court roads
1810 and after

Between 1810 and 1813, the mill building at the corner of
Falls and Old Court roads was constructed to take advantage of the stream that passed by. An entire village sprang
up, of which the old stone houses across Old Court Road
remain; there were also a blacksmith shop, a wheelwright
shop, and other community amenities at one time. The
whole was owned by the Johnson family, who also owned
extensive property in the vicinity. In 1836 to 1837, they had
built for them a handsome early Greek Revival house; it
was subsequently enlarged with porches and an addition to
the back, both entirely in keeping with the original structure. The house still stands but is not visible from the road
and is not open to the public. It is still owned by the Johnson
family, who a few years ago sold the mill building and a
piece of property across Old Court Road (and a little way to
the west) to the firm of J. R. Azola and Son, builders. The
Azolas have handsomely renovated the mill building,
which now serves as their headquarters and other commercial offices. They have also constructed a housing community on the property across the road. The old stone houses still
belong to the Johnsons, who rent them out.

197   RICHTER HOUSE
2005 Ridgecrest Court
1963—Charles H. Richter, Jr.

This architect's house perches near the top of two acres of steeply sloping wooded land in Baltimore County. The interior spaces are simply and clearly defined, and all of them look out over the woods to the south through a wall of glass—creating the effect of a ski lodge in winter and a vacation cottage in summer. A wooden sun deck, with a grille allowing sunlight to penetrate to the lower level, extends out in back among the trees.

In fact, the whole house overhangs the trees; it is cantilevered on all four sides. Built into the hillside, railroad ties form the retaining walls for the two main levels and a series of intermediate terraces. The lower story is built of cinder block. The upper, supported by two transverse wooden beams, is faced on three sides with redwood siding. The house is set back from the road and approached by a winding path. A wooden footbridge crossing a shallow moat leads to the front door.

198 AZRAEL HOUSE
919 Rolandvue Road, Ruxton
1967—Walter D. Ramberg

This three-story house of wood and steel construction both complements its site and makes effective use of the land.

The owners wanted a summer house not far from the city but with the feel of the country: one that would enable them and their daughter to have separate living spaces and would provide a large central space for entertaining. Accordingly, the architect designed a house that descends a wooded ravine, its three stories looking into the woods from the side opposite the entrance.

The central story, on the entrance level, is almost exclusively a large living room, one end of which rises two stories to a skylight that runs the length of the room and provides light both for the living room and the upper-story balcony. The wall that rises to the skylight is a huge bookcase for the owners' large collection of books.

The upper story contains bedrooms for daughter and guests; the lower level is the owners' complex of bedroom, office, and sitting room, the latter with two glass walls. An enclosed porch on the lower level supports an open deck on the living room level.

199 BROOKLANDWOOD (ST. PAUL'S SCHOOL)
Falls Road north of the Beltway
ca. 1793—Architect unknown

Charles Carroll of Carrollton provided this Georgian house
on 1,400 acres of land for his daughter Polly and her hus-
band Richard Caton. The house was later owned by Alexander D. Brown, broker, and Captain Isaac E. Emerson, famous locally as the inventor of Bromo-Seltzer.

The various owners added sumptuously to the interior,
with an elaborate central staircase, carved mahogany
doors, and marble fireplaces—and they conducted lavish
pageants outside as well. The first Maryland Hunt Cup was
run here in 1894, and the estate is as notable for its re-
minders of a departed style of life as it is for its architecture.
It became the property of the school in 1952 and now houses
the headmaster's quarters and offices and reception rooms.

200 EUCHTMAN-MACHT HOUSE
6807 Cross Country Boulevard
ca. 1941—Frank Lloyd Wright

Built for Mr. and Mrs. Joseph Euchtman, this modest house
on a three-quarter-acre wooded lot is the only Wright building in Baltimore.

By the late 1930s Wright had become increasingly interested in middle-class housing. Hence the "Usonian"
house. (The name *Usonia*, which he preferred to *America*,
comes from Samuel Butler's term for "a nation of combined
states.")

Because Wright gave to his Usonian houses the same
measure of innovative design, careful planning and siting,
and attention to detail that he devoted to his larger projects,
the place has a special grandeur.

The first Usonian house was built for Herbert Jacobs
near Madison, Wisconsin, in 1937. Three years later the
Pope-Leighey House was built at Falls Church, Virginia.
(Under threat of an interstate highway, the latter house
has since been acquired by the National Trust for Historic

Preservation and moved.) The Euchtman-Macht House was built about the same time as the Pope-Leighey house; in fact, the same architect from Wright's Taliesin fellowship, Gordon Chadwick, supervised both projects.

All three Usonian houses were similar in plan. There is neither basement nor attic, the storage space and heating plant being incorporated on the ground floor. The houses are built on concrete slabs, with the radiant heating pipes embedded in the cement. The lighting is indirect. Interior spaces are defined not by doors and walls but by subtle changes in levels and ceiling heights.

Both the Virginia and Baltimore houses have two levels, reflecting their sloping sites. Flat roofs overhang the walls. The Baltimore building inspectors were skeptical of Wright's wall systems, which are sandwiches of cypress screwed to both sides of a plywood core. Accordingly, a sample four-foot wall panel was constructed and 23 hundred-pound bags of cement were loaded on it, about four times the required load. Unpersuaded by this practical demonstration of strength, the local inspectors were finally convinced by an engineering calculation.

Wright built not only fireplaces and bookshelves but also dining tables into his Usonian houses. He also designed the other furniture. A small storage room has been added to the back of the Euchtman-Macht house, and the interior was recently completely reconstructed, but it remains essentially as Wright planned it.

The long low line of the house, its incorporation into the landscape and its interior plan embody the essence of the Usonian idea. Wright believed that the horizontal line, being closer to the earth, was more natural than the vertical.

The interior plan defines yet brings together the various spaces. A bedroom (originally there were two) is in back. A narrow passage leads past the bathroom and down to the small kitchen, a model of compact, utilitarian design located in the center of the house—"an alcove of the living room," as Wright dictated. The passageway then opens out to the combined living and dining areas.

Natural brick, cypress, and floor-to-ceiling glass are the interior finishes. The house cost roughly $16,000 when it was built. It is now the home of an architect.

201 TEMPLE OHEB SHALOM
7013 Park Heights Avenue
1960—Sheldon I. Leavitt, architect, with Walter Gropius, consulting architect

Most distinctive among this building's features are the four great vaults designed by Gropius, which give both the facade and the interior of the sanctuary their character. Of

continuously poured concrete, a process new at the time, the arches taper from an eight-inch thickness at the bottom to a three-and-one-half-inch thickness at the top. The vaults carry through the sanctuary, creating a large open rectangle, 83 feet by 90 feet, seating 1,100 people.

The front part of the temple complex, of brick masonry construction, also includes a wide entrance hall and a rectangular auditorium on the same axis as the sanctuary. On major religious occasions the walls between the three areas slide back, creating a space capable of seating 2,400.

From this area the corridor or "spine" of the complex passes an enclosed garden and an office and board room area and continues in a covered walkway to the school beyond. The 23 classrooms of the school have a pan-type waffle-slab reinforced concrete roof and floor construction, with curtain walls of glass and concrete.

202   NEUMAN HOUSE
7800 Ridge Terrace, Baltimore County
1965—Charles H. Richter, Jr.

Built around a small atrium, the Neuman House is enclosed with its gardens within areas of brick walls that at once shut out the surrounding commotion and emphasize the continuum between interior spaces and garden areas.

The frame of the house is redwood, and redwood siding is used in sheltered locations (for example, around the atrium). The plan is zoned into separate but connected areas for the different activities of the resident family. The living and dining areas, the master bedroom, and the principal garden are to one side of the dividing kitchen, atrium, and entrance; the children's and maid's quarters complete the arrangement on the other side.

Brick walls surround both house and garden, and glass walls and continuous flagstone from interior to garden emphasize continuity between outside and inside.

203 PIKESVILLE STATE POLICE BARRACKS
Reisterstown and Old Court roads
1816—Architect unknown

This square complex of buildings is more notable for its history than its architecture. Even so, the older brick building on the left, facing Reisterstown Road, is a pleasant relief from the surrounding commercialism. The railings are cast iron. After serving as a military post and a home for Confederate veterans, the buildings are now used as headquarters of the Maryland State Police and other state offices.

204 SUDBROOK PARK
Sudbrook Lane

Sudbrook Park was laid out by Frederick Law Olmsted (see Introduction).

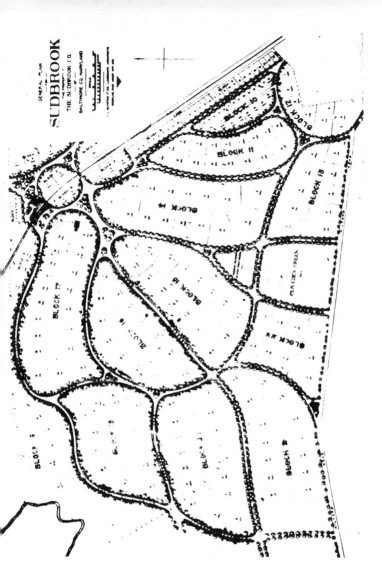

265

205   BLUM HOUSE
Caveswood Lane
ca. 1956—Marcel Breuer

Breuer oriented this house toward a view of the Caves valley to the northwest; for that reason the house is difficult to see from the street. (From the easternmost entrance to Caveswood Lane, the house is up the fourth driveway on the right.)

It was built on a 2.5-acre plot and is essentially a 40-by-80-foot one-story rectangle of glass, wood, and fieldstone. Portions of the rectangle have been scooped out to form courtyards and terraces.

The interior layout by which the architect separated the various living spaces is particularly ingenious, as is the design of the starkly functional but attractive kitchen and bathrooms. Breuer also designed built-in desks, bookcases, and cabinets throughout. The floors are Pennsylvania bluestone, under which radiant heating pipes have been installed. The living room features a clerestory window and a sculptural fireplace.

206   MILLER HOUSE
Address withheld at owner's request
1968—Charles H. Richter, Jr.

The house is composed of two linked pavilions and two floors, the lower one hidden by the slope of the land away from the house. The architect was thus able to minimize visually a very large house on a secluded woodland site. It is built of white brick with gray tinted glass and dark wood trim and was one of 20 houses in the United States by new architects selected for a 1969 award of excellence by *Architectural Record*.

Brief Biographies of Architects (Deceased)
Who Practiced in Baltimore

(Information on many of these architects is contained in
Biographical Dictionary of American Architects (Deceased)
by Henry F. Withey and Elsie Rathburn Withey, 1956, New
Age Publishing Company, Los Angeles, California.)

Andrews, R. Snowden (1830-1903). Andrews was born and
educated in Washington, D. C. After his family moved to
Baltimore, he began the study of architecture in the office of
Niernsee and Neilson. Later, with Eben Faxson, he formed
the firm of Andrews and Faxson. Andrews fought for the
Confederacy during the Civil War and shortly thereafter
gave up the practice of architecture. His extant works in
Baltimore include the Franklin Street Presbyterian
Church manse (1859) [21], the Eastern Female High School
[85], and the original Church of the Redeemer [164]. He also
designed the Governor's Mansion in Annapolis, later radi-
cally altered, and the south wing of the Treasury Department in Washington, D. C. Faxson is chiefly known for his
work on the portico of the Basilica of the Assumption [22].

Baldwin, E. Francis (1837-1916). The son of a Troy, New York,
civil engineer, Baldwin attended public schools in Baltimore after the family moved here and then studied architecture and engineering at Troy's Rensselaer Polytechnic Institute. Before the Civil War, he entered the Baltimore office of John R. Niernsee. After a brief association
with Bruce Price, he formed a partnership with Josias Pennington in 1883 that lasted until his death. (Pennington
died in 1929.) In addition to the Maryland Club [127], the
Fidelity Building [35], and the Mount Royal Station [133],
Baldwin and Pennington designed the 1895 City College
Building at Howard and Centre streets and the Maryland
Trust Building, now the Maryland National Bank, at Calvert and Redwood streets. Baldwin also designed the B&O

Railroad Central Building that stood on the northwest corner of Calvert and Baltimore streets and the Rennert Hotel at Cathedral and Saratoga streets. (Both have since disappeared.) For many years he was the house architect for the Baltimore and Ohio Railroad, designing numerous warehouses and other railroad structures in the city and stations along its main and branch lines. Several of the latter remain, the ones at Point of Rocks and Oakland, Maryland, being particularly well-known.

Bollman, Wendel (1814-1884). Bollman, the pioneer builder of iron truss bridges in America, had a strong influence on architects (see Frederick) and on the technology of construction. Born in Baltimore of German parentage, he began his career as a carpenter with the Baltimore and Ohio Railroad and participated in laying the first track. He subsequently was put in charge of bridges. Bollman, whose engineering training was largely self-acquired, patented his unique truss system [107] in 1852 while working for the B&O and in 1858 formed his own firm, W. Bollman and Company, and later the Patapsco Bridge and Iron Works, which built bridges throughout the east and in Mexico. Bollman also developed the precursor of the Phoenix column, a wrought-iron column fabricated in sections and bolted together. It was in standard use in construction until about 1900 when other, and larger, column shapes came into favor.

Burnham, Daniel H. (1846-1912). Architect and city planner, Burnham, in partnership with John Wellborn Root and others, had a major role in the development of the Commercial style in Chicago and in the construction of some of that city's most significant buildings: the Rookery, the Monadnock, and the Reliance among many others. Burnham "thoroughly mastered the technical, utilitarian, and financial aspects of building," according to Carl W. Condit in *The Chicago School of Architecture*, and left most of the designing to others. He was an architectural "impresario," as Frank Lloyd Wright described him, and a highly effective one. Burnham was largely responsible for the architecture of the Columbian Exposition in Chicago in 1893 which had a far-reaching effect on American civic design, and for the development scheme for Chicago's lakefront and circumferential system of forest preserves in 1909, the first comprehensive plan for an American city. "Make no little plans;" he said, "they have no magic to stir men's minds." Between 1896 and 1912, D. H. Burnham and Company, which was formed after Root's death, designed buildings for almost every major city in the country, including the Continental Trust Building in Baltimore (now the One South Calvert Building [54]) and Union Station in Washington, D. C.

Carson, Charles L. (1847-1891). Carson, the son of the developer of Waverly Terrace [114], was born in Baltimore and designed some of the city's impressive Richardsonian Romanesque structures, such as Goucher Hall [150], completed in 1888. In the same style, a few years earlier, he designed the first Enoch Pratt Free Library building on Mulberry Street, and most likely the original branches (see [116]). In addition, he was responsible for several churches, the Strawbridge Methodist Church on Bolton Hill among them. Others were done in partnership with Thomas Dixon. Later, with Joseph E. Sperry, he designed the Equitable Building [50]. Carson taught architecture for a time at the Maryland Institute.

Cassell, Charles E. (died ca. 1916). A charter member of the Baltimore Chapter of the American Institute of Architects, Cassell designed numerous houses and churches in the city. Besides the Graham-Hughes House [9] and the Greek Orthodox Church [132], he was the architect of the Stafford Hotel and Severn Apartments, both on Mount Vernon Place.

Davis, Francis (Frank) E. (1839-1921). Born in Ellicott City, Maryland, Davis began architectural practice in Baltimore with his brother, Henry R. Davis. He designed the Odd Fellows Hall, now Cathedral Place [31], an 1880s section of the Orchard Street Methodist Church as well as schools and other public buildings, including the Pine Street Police Station [111]. He later moved to Los Angeles where two of his sons became practicing architects.

Dixon, Thomas and James M. The Dixon brothers designed the Baltimore City Jail of which only the gatehouse remains [75]. Thomas Dixon subsequently, in partnership with Charles L. Carson, produced plans for several churches in Baltimore. He also designed the Mount Washington Presbyterian Church [186], and was largely responsible for Dixon's Hill in Mount Washington [187].

Faxson, Eben. See Andrews, Richard Snowden.

Fowler, Laurence Hall (1877-1971). Fowler executed a few large commissions such as the addition to the Safe Deposit and Trust Company Building [51] and the War Memorial Building and Plaza (see City Hall [61]), but the private home was his true metier. He designed some 80 houses up and down the East Coast, most of them in his native Maryland.

Fowler was born in Catonsville, the son of a judge. He graduated from Johns Hopkins University in 1898, did graduate work at Columbia University, and although admitted to the Ecole des Beaux Arts in Paris, returned to Baltimore where he worked briefly with Wyatt and Nolting before starting his own practice in 1906. The Wolman House [154], his own home north of Johns Hopkins University, and a 1941 house for Owen Lattimore in Ruxton are some of his designs which are characterized by subtle refinement, elegant proportions, and careful attention to landscaping.

Fowler advised the Roland Park Company on its development of Guilford and Homeland and was one of the organizers of the Baltimore Museum of Art. He amassed a large collection of drawings and rare books on architecture which he left to Johns Hopkins University (the collection is now housed at Evergreen). Fowler also published several articles and made extensive notes for a history of local architecture.

Frederick, George A. (1842-1924). A prolific architect who was comfortable in a variety of styles, Frederick produced some of Baltimore's finest municipal buildings and warehouses. He also designed churches, park buildings (see [146]), and was responsible in the 1870s for extensive renovations to the State Capitol in Annapolis. Born in Baltimore, Frederick began his architectural career at the age of 16 in the office of Edmund G. Lind and William T. Murdoch. He established his own practice in 1862 and soon thereafter began work on the City Hall [61], a commission he won through a competition. Frederick credited Wendel Bollman, the engineer who designed the City Hall dome, as the source of much of his knowledge concerning structure and the strength of materials.

Friz, Clyde N. (1867-1942). The Enoch Pratt Free Library [23], the Garage [130], and the Scottish Rite Temple of Freemasonry [160] are the major buildings in Baltimore by this Michigan-born architect. Friz studied architecture at the Massachusetts Institute of Technology and worked for various architectural firms in St. Louis before moving to Baltimore in 1900, where he joined the firm of Wyatt and Nolting before opening his own office in 1925.

Glidden, Edward H. (1873-1924). Glidden, son of the founder of the Glidden Varnish Works, was born in Cleveland, Ohio, studied architecture in Paris for four years, and came to Baltimore in 1912. Shortly thereafter he set up his own firm and designed several apartment houses including the Washington Apartments on Mount Vernon Place. He is chiefly known as the architect of the Furness House [58].

Godefroy, Maximilian (1765-ca. 1838). After Latrobe, Godefroy was the most important architect to practice in Baltimore in the nineteenth century. Widely read and classically educated, he worked for a time as a civil engineer in his native France until he was arrested and imprisoned for his opposition to the Napoleonic regime. He was then exiled, arriving in America in 1805.

At the end of that year, Godefroy came to Baltimore to teach drawing, architecture, and fortification at St. Mary's College. He also began a friendship with Latrobe and in 1808 married the socially prominent Eliza Crawford Anderson through whom he became acquainted with many of Baltimore's leading families, some of them later becoming his clients.

By this time (1808) he had completed the Gothic Revival St. Mary's Seminary Chapel [109]. A fews year later he contributed designs for the Washington Monument. His Commercial and Farmers Bank at Howard and German (now Redwood) streets was built about 1810. In his design for a Masonic Hall, ca. 1812 (later completed by the Smalls), he began to develop the sense of three-dimensional geometric form he was to perfect in his masterpiece of Romantic Classicism, the First Unitarian Church [20]. Previous to that, Godefroy designed the sally port at Fort McHenry (1814) and the cemetery gates with an Egyptian motif at the First Presbyterian (now Westminster) churchyard (1815), one of which remains, facing Greene Street. Several vaults in the churchyard as well, one of them a pyramid, are by Godefroy. Also in 1815, he completed the Battle Monument [49], the first great civic monument built in the United States. And, that same year, he began work on the Merchants' Exchange with Latrobe.

However, they quarrelled irreconcilably over the design, Latrobe's being adopted, and the brief collaboration ended in great bitterness on Godefroy's part. A proud, impulsive, and vindictive man, he sailed with his family for Europe about 1819, blaming Latrobe for his inability to find more work in America. His daughter died of yellow fever while leaving the Chesapeake Bay, and customs officials seized his books and drawings on his arrival in England.

Godefroy lived for a time in London but later returned to France, his architectural career continuing to decline. In 1838 at age 73 he was working in the mud and cold laying out new streets in Laval, France, where he was the municipal architect. The time, place, and circumstances of his death are unknown.

Godefroy designed structures in Richmond and other American cities, but his major architectural legacy is in Baltimore. Robert L. Alexander's *The Architecture of Maximilian Godefroy* is a thorough account of his life and work.

Hornblower, Joseph C. (1848-1908). Hornblower was born in Paterson, New Jersey, attended Yale University, and studied architecture at the Ecole des Beaux Arts in France, finishing in 1871. In 1883 he formed a partnership with John R. Marshall who had studied architecture at Rutgers University, also completing his studies in 1871. The firm of Hornblower and Marshall designed several buildings in Washington, D. C., including the Natural History Museum of the Smithsonian Institution. Their only work in Baltimore is the United States Custom House [60].

Keely, Patrick C. (1816-1896). Born in Kilkenny, Ireland, the son of a builder, Keely came to the United States in 1842 and began work as a carpenter in Brooklyn, New York. He designed his first church on Long Island and then began to get commissions from several states in the East. Keely is credited with over 600 churches from Montreal to New Orleans. He designed most of the churches and institutions for the Dominicans and many for the Jesuits. The cathedrals of Boston, Massachusetts, Hartford, Connecticut, and Charleston, South Carolina, are some of his major works. The Corpus Christi Church in Baltimore [135] was done toward the end of his career. Keely was active until his death.

Latrobe, Benjamin H. (1764-1820). America's Leonardo, Benjamin Henry Latrobe was described by his son John H. B. Latrobe as "an artist as well as an architect, botanist, geologist, entomologist, mathematician, poet, musician, and composer . . . ." To this list could be added surveyor, town planner, engineer, and linguist; Latrobe was fluent in four modern languages and could read and write Greek and Latin. He was also a superb observer whose letters, journals, and watercolors comprise a unique landscape of the United States during the Federal period.

Latrobe, whose ancestors were French, was born in Yorkshire, England. He was educated at the University of Leipzig, Germany, served a term in the Prussian army, was wounded in battle, and returned to England. There he studied architecture under S. P. Cockerell and engineering with

John Smeaton, the first modern civil engineer. In 1789, he became surveyor of public office and engineer of London.

Following the death of his wife, Latrobe came to the United States in 1796 and embarked on an American career that is unrivalled for its technical virtuosity. He was this country's first trained architect and engineer. In 1800 after work in Norfolk and Richmond, he designed Philadelphia's Bank of Pennsylvania, the first Greek Revival structure in America and the first to use masonry vaults for architectural effect. In partnership with Nicholas Roosevelt, he built that city's first waterworks powered by steam engines. Later he surveyed canals, wrote the first report on railroads received by the Congress in 1808, and built steamboats in Pittsburgh with Robert Fulton.

A few years later, Latrobe produced Baltimore's Catholic Cathedral [22], his finest remaining building with the possible exception of the Capitol in Washington, D. C. Having been appointed Surveyor of Public Buildings by Jefferson in 1803, Latrobe designed the Capitol's most distinctive spaces, including the original domed and vaulted Supreme Court and House and Senate chambers, with their famous tobacco leaf and cornstalk capitals. He rebuilt the building after the British set fire to it in 1814, but his work has been somewhat overwhelmed by that of his successors. (Latrobe also designed the porticoes of the White House.)

Some of the young nation's most prominent architects, for example Robert Mills and William Strickland, received their initial training in Latrobe's office. In 1815 in partnership with his colleague, Maximilian Godefroy, he began work on the Merchants' Exchange in Baltimore. It was designed in the shape of the letter H, and the wing facing Gay Street, built by Col. Jacob Small, was completed in 1820. The main feature of the Exchange was its coffered dome, 115 feet high and 53 feet in diameter. The building was razed in 1904 to make way for the United States Custom House [60]. Latrobe's only other building in Baltimore is the Oakland Spring House [152].

The partnership between Latrobe and Godefroy ended badly. Godefroy was to have made the working drawings and supervised the construction of the Exchange, but instead attempted to substitute his own designs and to undercut Latrobe's relationship with the trustees, according to

Talbot Hamlin, whose *Benjamin Henry Latrobe* is the standard biography. Godefroy withdrew from the work and later blamed Latrobe for the subsequent failure of his career in America. For his part, Latrobe gave his old friend credit for the main front of the Exchange and refused to compete against him for the design of the Unitarian Church [20], Godefroy's major structure in Baltimore.

Latrobe, whose own career suffered from the intrigues of political enemies, poor pay, and lack of recognition, vented his spleen in his letters and journals: "I nauseate beef and society at the same time." Yet he never lost his intellectual enthusiasm. In New Orleans where a new waterworks was being built under his supervision, he made scientific sketches of mosquitoes, including the variety discovered near the end of the century to be the one that carried yellow fever which killed him in 1820.

Latrobe has only recently been recognized for his genius. Scholars at the Maryland Historical Society are now editing and publishing his papers and sketches, many of which are housed there.

Latrobe, Benjamin H., the younger (1806-1878). One of the architect's sons, Benjamin H. Latrobe, began his career as a lawyer, but later became one of the country's foremost civil engineers and bridge designers. He spent most of his professional life with the Baltimore and Ohio Railroad, becoming its chief engineer, and laying out the line from Harpers Ferry to Wheeling, West Virginia. He also surveyed the Baltimore and Ohio line from Baltimore to Washington, and designed the masterful Thomas Viaduct at Relay [106]. Latrobe was later a consultant on the Hoosac Tunnel in Massachusetts and to the Roeblings on the Brooklyn Bridge.

Born in Philadelphia, he attended St. Mary's College in Baltimore and Georgetown University in Washington, D. C., before beginning his study of the law. However, he soon found he was more interested in engineering and got a job on the railroad with the help of his brother, John H. B. Latrobe, the Baltimore and Ohio's lawyer. He was shortly at work on the viaduct. Latrobe had had no formal engineering courses, but his journals show that he read Perronet's books on bridges in French and other borrowed works. Meanwhile, he was supervising workmen on the bridge. Nothing inspires the acquisition of knowledge like the need to impart it to others, he told a friend. His son, Charles H. Latrobe, also a civil engineer, designed several of the early iron bridges over the Jones Falls and the Patterson Park Observatory [90].

Latrobe, John H. B. (1803-1891). A sometime architect, John H. B. Latrobe worked on his father's drawings for St. John's Church and the Capitol in Washington, D. C., and had a hand in the design of the portico of Baltimore's Basilica of the Assumption [22] and the entrance to Druid Hill Park [146]. He was also an artist, an inventor (of the Latrobe stove), an organizer (of the Maryland Institute and the Maryland Historical Society), and an advocate of the African colonization of American Negroes. (The movement resulted in the founding of Liberia, for which John H. B. Latrobe supplied many of the place names.)

Born in Philadelphia, he attended the same schools as his brother Benjamin and was about to graduate at the head of his class from West Point, where he was studying engineering, when his father died. Latrobe left college to begin the study of law and served as general counsel for the Baltimore and Ohio Railroad from its beginnings in 1828 until near his death.

In the late 1850s, Latrobe spent several months in Russia as the emissary of the Winans railroad interests to the imperial court. A poet and writer of fiction, he was one of the first to recognize the literary talents of Edgar Allan Poe. He was intimately acquainted with many of the fascinating figures of the nineteenth century, from Daniel Webster to Samuel F. B. Morse. His son, Ferdinand C. Latrobe, served several terms as mayor of Baltimore between 1875 and 1893.

Lind, Edmund G. (1829-1909). Lind was born and educated in London and worked as a draftsman there before coming to Baltimore in 1859 to join the office of Nathan G. Starkweather. There he helped prepare the plans for the First

Presbyterian Church [12] and supervised its erection. Lind had a short partnership with William T. Murdoch and about the time of the Civil War, formed his own office. Best known as the architect of the Peabody Institute [2], he also designed the Brown Memorial Church and parsonage on Bolton Hill and a handsome iron front for a dry goods firm on Baltimore Street. An early organizer of the American Institute of Architects, Lind served for a time as the president of the Baltimore Chapter.

Long, Robert Cary, Sr. (1772-1835). A Marylander, Long was apprenticed to a carpenter in Baltimore before graduating into architecture. His extant buildings are Davidge Hall [74] and the Peale Museum [63]. Long is thought to have designed the Hamilton Street Rowhouses [19] as well. He also designed the Classical Revival Old St. Paul's Church with a tower, the Holliday Street Theater which stood across from City Hall, the Greek Revival Union Bank at Charles and Fayette streets, and a house for merchant Robert Oliver on Gay Street. He was one of the founders in 1816 of the Gas Light Company of Baltimore, the first in the country to manufacture gas for street lighting.

Long, Robert Cary, Jr. (1810-1849). Long's son Robert Cary, Jr., was born in Baltimore, attended St. Mary's College, and worked in a New York architectural office before returning to the city where he designed several churches and other structures. They were all done in the mid-1840s in a variety of styles. They are: the Green Mount Cemetery Gate [122], St. Alphonsus' Church [32], the Franklin Street Presbyterian Church [21], the Lloyd Street Synagogue [82], and St. Peter the Apostle Church [112]. Long, Jr., was a student of architectural history, had literary aspirations, and lectured on art. After he had gone back to New York to continue his career, his life was cut short by cholera at age 39.

Marshall, John R. (1851-1927). See Hornblower, Joseph C.

Mies van der Rohe, Ludwig (1886-1969). Mies van der Rohe was one of the founders of modern architecture and a principal of the International style. Born in Aachen, Germany, Ludwig Mies, who added his mother's surname, van der Rohe, when he became an architect, said that he never had any formal architectural training. He worked for his father, a stonemason and bricklayer, and for a furniture designer, before 1910, when he became an apprentice, with Walter Gropius and Le Corbusier, in the Berlin office of architect Peter Behrens. Inspired by Schinkel's logic and clarity and the new building materials, he designed revolutionary steel and glass skyscrapers in 1920, versions of which were later built in Chicago, and in 1929 the German Pavilion for the Barcelona Exhibition, for which he also produced the Barcelona chair. From 1930 to 1933, he was director of the Bauhaus until it closed under pressure from the Nazis. Mies van der Rohe left Germany in 1937 and the following year was named Professor of Architecture at the Armour Institute (now the Illinois Institute) of Technology in Chicago. There he designed a new campus for the Institute and several of its buildings. Other structures which illustrate his principles of skin-and-bones high-rise construction, precise details, and unobstructed interior space are the 860-880 Lake Shore Drive Apartments and the Federal Center in Chicago and the Seagram Building in New York. Baltimore's One Charles Center [37] is in this tradition. Mies van der Rohe's other local building is Highfield House [161].

Mills, Robert (1781-1855). Mills was America's first native-born trained architect, a Classical Revivalist who is perhaps best known for his monumental architecture: the Washington Monument in Baltimore, the Washington Monument in Washington, and the Bunker Hill Monument in Boston. However, he designed numerous other buildings including churches, courthouses, and private homes in several seaboard states. Mills was also an engineer who built bridges, surveyed canals, and was an early advocate of railroads.

He was born in Charleston, South Carolina; his father was Scotch, his mother American. Mills attended the College of Charleston and at age 19 began the study of architecture in Washington, D. C., with James Hoban, designer of the White House. He was later associated as an architectural apprentice with Thomas Jefferson and Benjamin H. Latrobe. From the latter he gained his knowledge of Greek forms, principles of professional practice, and engineering skill.

Mills began to design buildings in Charleston and Richmond and in 1808 established his own office in Philadelphia. There he added two wings to Independence Hall and in 1812 collaborated with Lewis Wernwag, early builder of wooden bridges, on the design of the Colossus, a 340-foot, single-span, arched truss over the Schuylkill River that was longer than any bridge then known.

By 1814 Mills had moved to Baltimore and was shortly at work on the Washington Monument [1]. To hoist Causici's 30-ton statue of Washington to the top, he devised his own pair of timber shears and accomplished the job before the eyes of several thousand people gathered in the square below. He was appointed the city's engineer of waterworks, and worked on street surveys as well. Also in Baltimore, Mills designed in 1815 the houses on Calvert Street east of the Monument, known as Waterloo Row (demolished 1960s), and in 1817 the Pantheonesque First Baptist Church at Sharp and Lombard streets (demolished 1877).

Mills moved back to Charleston in 1820 and primarily produced churches and public buildings there. In 1830 he moved to Washington where Andrew Jackson appointed him Architect of Public Buildings. In this capacity Mills designed and supervised the construction of the Treasury Building in 1836 and the Patent Office and the old Post Office, both begun 1839. His Washington Monument for that city was started in 1848 and finally completed in 1884. Mills's career is described in *Robert Mills, Architect of the Washington Monument, 1781-1855*, by H. M. Pierce Gallagher.

Mottu, Howard M. See White, Henry S. Taylor.

Murchison, Kenneth W. (1872-1938). A New Yorker, Murchison graduated from Columbia University in 1894 and from the Ecole des Beaux Arts in Paris in 1900. He opened an office in New York in 1902, and his first major commission was for railroad terminal buildings in Hoboken and Buffalo. Pennsylvania Station [131], his only building in Baltimore, was completed in 1911. Murchison later designed hotels, country clubs, and commercial buildings along the East Coast from Rhode Island to Florida.

Neilson, J. Crawford (1816-1900). See Niernsee, John R.

Niernsee, John R. (1814-1883). An Austrian, Niernsee was trained as an engineer at the Polytechnic Institute of Vienna and continued his studies in Prague from which city he emigrated to the United States in 1838. One of his first jobs here was helping to survey a projected railroad from Pensacola, Florida, to Montgomery, Alabama. The scheme went no further, and Niernsee ended up in New York. In 1839, Benjamin H. Latrobe, the younger, hired him to draw plans and maps of the new routes of the Baltimore and Ohio Railroad. In 1842, Niernsee and J. Crawford Neilson were both listed as $3 per day Baltimore and Ohio employees, Niernsee as office draftsman and Neilson as resident engineer.

Neilson had been trained in Belgium and had worked for other railroads before joining the Baltimore and Ohio Railroad, where he also drew maps and profiles for the new lines. Niernsee, while with the railroad, designed a series of prefabricated iron roofs for freight houses, locomotive sheds, and stations which are the earliest known instances of composite iron roofs in this country. He described their construction in a series of articles for an Austrian engineering publication.

When Niernsee and Neilson formed their architectural partnership in 1848, it was perhaps natural that some of their most significant work would be for railroad interests: the Italianate style Calvert Station which stood on the site of the Sunpapers; Alexandroffsky, Thomas Winans's mansion formerly located in West Baltimore, and Camden Station [99]. During the 1840s and 1850s, theirs was the largest and most successful architectural firm in Baltimore.

Although much of their work has subsequently disappeared, the list of what remains is impressive both in extent and quality: the Thomas-Jencks-Gladding House [17], Asbury House [7], St. John the Evangelist Church [87], Emmanuel Episcopal Church [10], Grace and St. Peter's Church [13], 700 Cathedral Street [14], the old YMCA Building [29], St. Luke's Church [115], and the Green Mount Cemetery Chapel [123].

In 1855, Niernsee was named architect of the Capitol of South Carolina. While he was serving in the Confederate Army during the Civil War, Sherman's troops burned the partially completed building, along with the architect's drawings. After the war, Niernsee returned to Baltimore and continued his architectural work with Neilson. In 1885 he went back to Columbia, South Carolina, but died before the work on the Capitol was completed.

Nolting, William G. (1866-1940). Nolting was born in Baltimore and educated in Richmond, Virginia. His early ambition was to be a chemist, and he spent his time as a young man planning imaginary buildings to house his future companies. Nolting began his architectural career in Richmond, continued it in Washington, D. C., and finally returned to Baltimore where in 1887 he formed a partnership with J. B. Noel Wyatt. Their firm designed numerous buildings in Baltimore and in Washington, D. C., and Virginia. (See Wyatt, J. B. Noel). After Wyatt's death, Nolting was associated in the 1930s with John H. Scarf.

Olmsted, Frederick Law (1822-1903). Olmsted was America's foremost landscape architect. Born in Hartford, Connecticut, he dropped out of Yale University, caught a ship to China, and on his return became a gentleman farmer and a reporter for the *New York Times*. He was first well-known as a writer; his *Journey Through The Seaboard Slave States* of 1856 was a vivid depiction of pre-Civil War society, and he wrote several other books based on his travels and experiences. Olmsted and Calvert Vaux prepared the plan for New York's Central Park, and in 1857 Olmsted was made superintendent. The plan set the pattern for several other parks in North America; by 1890, Olmsted and his associates had completed 17 of them, from Montreal to San Francisco. In 1893 Olmsted laid out the grounds for the World's Columbian Exposition in Chicago.

His son, Frederick Law Olmsted, Jr. (1870-1957), was also a landscape architect. Born in Staten Island, New York, he graduated from Harvard University, studied with his father, and began practice with him in 1895.

In Baltimore, Sudbrook [204] was the work of Olmsted, Sr., and Frederick Law Olmsted, Jr., was involved in the planning for Roland Park [183]. Olmsted Brothers, as the firm later became known, in 1904 published their report on the development of parks in Baltimore. Updated in 1926, it formed the basis for the city's system of stream-valley parks and continues as the framework for open space and park development in the city and surrounding area.

Parker, J. Harleston (1873-1930). Parker was the senior member of Parker, Thomas, and Rice, a leading architectural firm of the early 1900s. He was born in Boston, graduated from Harvard University in 1893, and completed four years at the Ecole des Beaux Arts in 1900. The following year, with Douglas H. Thomas (1872-1915) from Baltimore, he formed Parker and Thomas, and they opened offices in both cities. (Thomas had attended the Johns Hopkins University, the Massachusetts Institute of Technology, and the Ecole des Beaux Arts.) The new office soon had a large number of commissions.

In Baltimore the firm designed the Baltimore Gas and Electric Company Building [38], the Alex. Brown and Sons Building [53], the Belvedere [129], Gilman Hall [156], and the Baltimore and Ohio Railroad Central Office Building at Charles and Baltimore streets (1906).

Arthur W. Rice (1869-1938), a Bostonian, joined the firm in 1907. Parker, Thomas, and Rice designed the Hansa Haus [42] and the Savings Bank of Baltimore [43], as well as several major buildings in Boston and other cities.

Pennington, Josias (d. 1929). See Baldwin, E. Francis.

Pietsch, Theodore W. (1868-1930). Born in Chicago, Pietsch studied architecture at the Massachusetts Institute of Technology and the Ecole des Beaux Arts. In 1904 he opened an architectural office in Baltimore. He was associated with Otto Simonson (1862-1922) in the design of several local buildings, including the Paca-Pratt Building [73]; the Maryland Casualty Company, 711 West 40th Street (now the Rotunda); and the Southern Hotel, Light and Redwood streets, now the Calhoon MEBA Engineering School. In addition Pietsch designed the Broadway Recreation Pier in 1914.

Pope, John Russell (1874-1937). Pope, a New Yorker, attended the College of the City of New York and Columbia University's School of Mines before winning a fellowship to the American Academy in Rome where he spent two years. From there he went to Paris to the Ecole des Beaux Arts, completing his studies in 1900. After returning to New York, Pope worked for Charles F. McKim of McKim, Mead, and White and later opened his own office. His classical training is reflected in a number of buildings he designed. Among them are the Scottish Rite Temple, the National Archives Building, DAR Constitution Hall and the National Gallery of Art, in Washington, D. C. His buildings in Baltimore are: the Engineering Center (with Stanford White) [16], the Baltimore Museum of Art [153], the University Baptist Church [157], the Scottish Rite Temple of Freemasonry, with Clyde N. Friz [160], and Charlcote House in Guilford.

Rice, Arthur W. (1869-1938). See Parker, J. Harleston.

Simonson, Otto (1862-1922). See Pietsch, Theodore W.

Small, Jacob. A self-taught designer and builder, Small completed the Otterbein Church [101] in 1785 and the following year built a wooden bridge that spanned the Jones Falls at

Baltimore Street with a single, 90-foot segmental arch. He is also credited with finishing, from a design by Maximilian Godefroy, the old Masonic Hall that stood until 1895 on the site of the present Baltimore Courthouse.

Small, Jacob., Jr. (1772-1851). An 1833 guide to Baltimore lists Jacob Small, Jr., as an "architect and practical builder" who had an office on Conway Street between Hanover and Sharp Streets. Also known as Colonel Small, having served in the War of 1812, he later became a successful lumber merchant and politician. Colonel Small was Mayor of Baltimore from 1826 to 1831. He was the builder of the Merchants' Exchange and was consulted by Benjamin H. Latrobe on problems at the Capitol in Washington, D. C. The Baltimore and Ohio Railroad hired him in 1831 as their architect and superintendent of depots. Small left shortly to run again for Mayor. However, during the year he was with the railroad, Small designed the Ellicott City Railroad Station [119], his only remaining building.

Small, William F. (1798-1832). The son of Jacob Small, Jr., William F. Small was the first Baltimorean to be professionally trained as an architect. He designed several structures in the city, only two of which remain: the Archbishop's Residence [25], and (with William Howard), the McKim Free School [83].

Sperry, Joseph E. (1854-1930). From South Carolina originally, Sperry moved to Baltimore at an early age and went to work for Charles L. Carson with whom he later designed the 1893 Masonic Temple [34] and the Equitable Building [50]. In the 1880s he was associated with J. B. Noel Wyatt (see Wyatt). After 1886-87, when his partnership with Wyatt ended, Sperry worked on several buildings including the renovations to the First Unitarian Church [20], the renovations to the old YMCA Building [29], the Masonic Temple [34], the Provident Savings Bank [67], the Emerson Tower [71], and the Eutaw Place Temple [139].

Stone, Edward Durrell (1902-1978). Once considered the American heir to Frank Lloyd Wright, who praised his buildings, Stone at the height of his career had an office with 200 people and an international practice. He was born in Fayetteville, Arkansas, and later moved to Boston where his brother was a practicing architect. He won scholarships to Harvard University and the Massachusetts Institute of Technology, then studied architecture in Europe for two years. Returning to New York he worked on Rockefeller Center and Radio City Music Hall before designing, with Philip L. Goodwin, the Museum of Modern Art, one of the country's first International style buildings. Stone won renown for his 1959 design of the United States Embassy in New Delhi, India, in which he used grilles and the romanticized classical forms that were to become his trademarks. He designed the United States Pavilion at the Brussels World's Fair and the John F. Kennedy Center for the Performing Arts in Washington, D. C., among many other projects. In Baltimore, Stone was the architect for the Peabody Dormitory [4] and was involved in the early plans for the Maryland Academy of Sciences.

Thomas, Douglas H. (1872-1915). See Parker, J. Harleston.

Upjohn, Richard (1802-1878). Born in England, Upjohn came to the United States in 1829 and established himself in New York State as a skilled cabinetmaker and draftsman. He moved to Massachusetts and became an architect, designing several churches. In 1839 he was hired to rebuild Trinity Church in New York City, where he set up an office. When completed in 1846, the church inaugurated a new phase in the Gothic Revival. Upjohn designed other churches in the New York area and in the mid-1850s, St. Paul's Church in Baltimore [27]. While in Baltimore, Upjohn proselytized for the American Institute of Architects, of which he was a founder and the first president.

Walter, Thomas U. (1804-1887). Walter was the leading American architect of his time. Succeeding Robert Mills as government architect in 1851, he added the House and Senate wings, the cast-iron central dome, and rebuilt the west front of the United States Capitol. One of the original organizers of the American Institute of Architects in 1857, he served also as its president from 1867 until he died.

Walter was born in Philadelphia and first studied architecture in the office of William Strickland. He designed the main building of Girard College in Philadelphia, a major Classical Revival structure, as well as other buildings there. In Washington, D. C., he did the interior of the Library of Congress and extensions to the Post Office, the Patent Office, and the Treasury. Walter's only building in Baltimore is the Eutaw Place Baptist Church [141].

White, Henry S. Taylor (1879-1943). White was born in Baltimore, studied architecture at the Maryland Institute of Design, and became a draftsman in the office of Baldwin and Pennington. In 1904 he formed a partnership with Howard M. Mottu. Over the next 50 years the firm of Mottu and White designed office buildings such as the Baltimore Life Insurance Company Building, now the Commercial Credit Company Annex [28], churches, schools and residences. White later was in practice with his son, Henry S. Taylor White, Jr.

White, Stanford (1853-1906). According to a contemporary critic, Stanford White was a bon vivant, a flamboyant architect, and a "brilliant and effortless designer." With his partners, Charles F. McKim and William R. Mead, he created sumptuous mansions, private clubs, and casinos for the rich as well as the more utilitarian churches, schools, and office buildings.

The son of a journalist and Shakespearean scholar, White was born and educated in New York City. At age 18 he joined the office of Henry Hobson Richardson, who at the time was developing his own style based on heavy, forceful Romanesque architecture. It was to influence not only White and McKim, a highly creative architect who worked for Richardson during the early stages of his career, but also John Wellborn Root and Louis Sullivan. White participated in the design of Trinity Church in Boston and in 1879 formed a partnership with McKim and Mead.

White's Newport Casino was the country's first major example of the Shingle style; several "cottages" for the members of "the 400," who summered at Newport, soon followed. In New York he designed the old Madison Square Garden, the Madison Square Presbyterian Church, the Washington Arch, and the Century and Metropolitan clubs. The Renaissance was the inspiration for many of these structures, and their interiors were enhanced by White's instinctive and graceful use of opulent materials and furnishings. He also produced jewelry, bases for statues, magazine and book covers, and a parlor car for the Pennsylvania Railroad. The results provided the backdrop for, and helped to define, an age of luxury for the country's new industrialists. The architect, a gentleman artist and man of the world, was himself a member of society frequently in demand at parties.

White's end was as dramatic as his life. While he was watching a revue on the roof of the Madison Square Garden, he was shot and killed by Harry K. Thaw who was jealous over the architect's purported affair with his wife, the former Evelyn Nesbit.

Stanford White's buildings in Baltimore are the Engineering Center [16] (with John Russell Pope) and Lovely Lane Methodist Church [149]. In addition there are three buildings designed by McKim, Mead, and White; they are the Winans House [124], Bennett Hall (see [150]), and the Goucher House [151].

Wilson, J. Appleton and William T. During the 1880s and 1890s the architectural team of J. A. and W. T. Wilson was extremely active in Baltimore. They designed churches and private clubs, but houses were their forte and they lined the developing blocks of Calvert and St. Paul streets between Mount Vernon Place and Mount Royal Avenue with examples of their work. Most were in the then-popular Victorian Gothic and Queen Anne styles, or the Wilsons' own occasionally startling variations thereon. Many of them, such as the east side of the 1000 block of North Calvert Street, known as Belvidere Terrace [126], still stand. J. A. Wilson was the secretary of the Fire Proof Building Company of Baltimore.

Wright, Frank Lloyd (1869-1959). America's most famous architect was born in Richland Center, Wisconsin, studied civil engineering at the University of Wisconsin, and worked for Dankmar Adler and Louis Sullivan in Chicago for seven years before designing his first building on his own, a residence, in 1893. Wright designed several other houses in the Chicago area in what came to be called the Prairie style. It was an indigenous, organic architecture consisting of intersecting planes, projecting eaves, and long, low horizontal lines symbolizing freedom and spaciousness. The culmination of the Prairie style was Wright's 1908 Robie House in Chicago.

By that time the architect had designed a highly original office building, the Larkin Building in Buffalo, and a church, Unity Temple, in Oak Park, Illinois. Both were monumental structures and had significant influence. Wright also pioneered in developing and applying new construction techniques. For Tokyo's Imperial Hotel in 1922, he devised a floating foundation that helped the building withstand the great Kanto earthquake the following year. "Falling Water," his 1937 house for the Kaufmanns at Bear Run, Pennsylvania, marked the first domestic use of indirect, fluorescent lighting and foam rubber cushions for furniture. Wright usually designed the furnishings for all of his buildings. His other well-known structures include the Johnson Wax headquarters in Racine, Wisconsin, and the Guggenheim Museum in New York.

Although some of his early designs show a Mayan influence, Wright belonged to no school of architecture other than his own. For many years he taught apprentices at "Taliesin," his residence-school at Spring Green, Wisconsin, and at "Taliesin West," in Scottsdale, Arizona. He had unique theories about architecture and cities and explained them in several books. The uncompromising architect-hero of Ayn Rand's *The Fountainhead* was based on Wright.

Some of Wright's most brilliant creations, such as the Larkin Building and the Imperial Hotel, have been destroyed. While his "Usonian" houses are quite small by comparison, they represent an important phase in Wright's architectural thinking. Only three of them were built including the one in Baltimore, the Euchtman-Macht House [200].

Wyatt, J. B. Noel (1847-1926). Wyatt was born in Baltimore, the son of a civil engineer. The family later moved to Cambridge, Massachusetts, and Wyatt attended Harvard University, graduating in 1870. He then spent a short period at the Massachusetts Institute of Technology and several years in Paris at the Ecole des Beaux Arts.

In 1880 he returned to Baltimore and established a partnership with Joseph E. Sperry. The firm of Wyatt and Sperry designed the Old Mercantile Safe Deposit and Trust Company Building [55], one of the city's outstanding Romanesque Revival structures, and Belvidere Terrace [126].

In 1887 the old firm was dissolved and Wyatt set up an office with William G. Nolting. The Baltimore Court House [51], the Old Patterson Park High School [89], and the Roland Park Shopping Center [183] were products of this partnership along with the Garrett Building at Redwood and South streets and the Keyser Building at Redwood and Calvert streets.

Wyatt wrote frequently about local buildings and municipal improvements for professional architectural magazines. In addition, he was secretary of the Baltimore Art Commission, a director of the Baltimore Municipal Art Society, and president of the local chapter of the American Institute of Architects.

apse the eastern (altar) end of a church, often semicircular and vaulted with a half dome.

arcade a row of columns and arches, sometimes supporting a roof, and forming a covered passageway, e.g., along the side of a building.

Art Deco a style of decoration appearing on buildings and other objects in the 1920s and 1930s; modernistic or futuristic effects were gained through the stylization of such motifs as fountains and sunbursts; in the 1930s, streamlining was popular.

Art Nouveau the style that began with William Morris and the English Arts and Crafts Movement of the 1880s and later spread to lamps and other furnishings. It is identifiable by the flowing, curved forms of flowers, waves, flames, and the female figure. The name itself came from a Paris shop that opened in 1895 to sell modern articles.

attic a low story above the cornice.

balustrade a handrail supported by small pillars; occasionally used as decoration along the roofline.

bargeboard a face board under the roof-edge of a gable, sometimes decorated by carving.

Baroque a style of architecture prevalent during the seventeenth and eighteenth centuries. It is characterized by elaborate decoration, curved forms, and subtle spatial effects.

basilica a church with aisles and a nave higher than the aisles.

battlement a parapet broken by vertical slots.

bay the portion of a building between two successive piers or columns.

Beaux Arts a form of classicism derived from the Ecole des Beaux Arts in Paris during the second half of the nineteenth century. Its features included symmetrical fronts broken into planes which advance and recede, doubled columns, and much ornamentation, especially including figure sculpture. Monumental flights of steps were also common.

bond the joints in successive courses in a masonry wall (see drawings). Some common ones are:

common bond courses of stretchers (bricks faced lengthwise) with each sixth course made of headers (bricks faced crosswise).

English bond alternate courses of stretchers and headers.

Flemish bond alternate stretchers and headers in each course and centered over each other vertically.

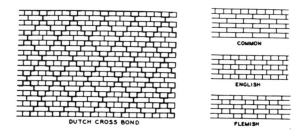

DUTCH CROSS BOND

COMMON

ENGLISH

FLEMISH

bracket support for a projecting floor or roof.

buttress a pier that strengthens a wall, sometimes absorbing the thrust of an inner arch.

casement a window hinged at the side.

cantilever a beam, or series of beams, projecting over an edge and supported by a downward force, such as a wall, behind the edge; the principle is that of the fulcrum. Also a type of bridge.

capital the top of a column, pier, or pilaster.

chancel the section of the east end of a church where the altar is located.

Classical Revival the revival of one of many possible classical styles. Much colonial architecture was based on English Georgian, in turn based on Palladio who used classical models. Jeffersonian classicism was more directly Palladian. There was a Greek Revival in the early nineteenth century, and in the late nineteenth and early twentieth centuries, a neo-Classical revival that was more Roman. Between these periods was Beaux Arts, also a form of classicism. Renaissance Revival was based at a certain remove on classical models.

clerestory upper part of a church nave, with windows above the roofline of the aisles.

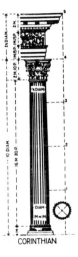

CORINTHIAN

Colonial a term that can encompass anything built in the United States during the colonial period. In this part of the country and farther south, colonial architecture followed English Georgian lines which were descended from sixteenth century Palladian models. The more important houses usually had a central hall, dormer windows in the top story, chimneys at the ends of the house, and often a one- or two-story pedimented portico. Country estate houses frequently had a five-part plan. In the early twentieth century, there was a Colonial Revival or neo-Colonial style especially popular for college buildings.

Commercial (Chicago) style high-rise, usually commercial, steel-frame structures with a great deal of glass. The Chicago window (a fixed central pane with smaller movable sashes on either side) and projecting bays are common. The style, which forms the basis of modern high-rise construction, enjoyed its greatest usage in Chicago between 1875 and 1915.

corbel a system of structural support, each of whose successive wood or masonry units extends slightly beyond the one below for example at the top of an exterior wall whose bricks gradually project outward to form a cornice. The principle is that of the cantilever. (see drawing page 306).

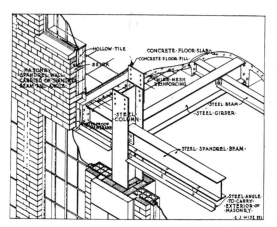

CUTAWAY DIAGRAM SHOWING THE CONSTRUCTIONAL ELEMENTS OF A TYPICAL STEEL SKELETON-FRAMED STRUCTURE. (Drawn by G. J. Wise.)

Corinthian one of the classical orders, with capitals decorated with acanthus leaves. (see drawing page 295).

cornice a decorative element consisting of the projecting molding at the top of a building.

course in masonry construction, a horizontal band (layer) of brick or stone forming part of a wall.

belt, or string course a narrow, slightly projecting plain band marking a horizontal division in the wall.

crenellation see battlement.

crocket a projecting leaf-shaped form used decoratively in Gothic architecture, particularly on pinnacles and spires.

crossing the intersection of nave and transepts in a church of cruciform (cross-like) plan.

cupola a small, often domed structure rising above a main roof.

curtain wall a wall, usually of metal or glass suspended from the framework of a building; most commonly seen on modern high-rise buildings of steel frame construction (cf. load-bearing wall); (see drawing page 296).

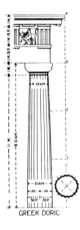

GREEK DORIC

dome a roof in the form of a hemisphere.

Doric one of the classic orders, with plain capitals (see drawing).

dormer a small gable in a pitched roof, usually containing a window.

drum a cylindrical wall supporting a dome, lantern, or cupola.

Eastlake named for an English architect and furniture designer whose books first became popular in America in the 1870s. The style features curved brackets along with porch posts and rows of spindles that often resemble table legs.

English basement half-basement in urban dwellings generally used for service functions.

entablature in classical architecture, the horizontal members above the column capitals, consisting of architrave, frieze, and cornice. (see drawing).

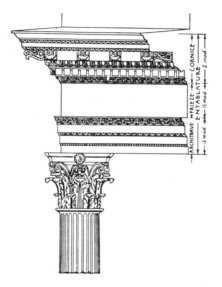

facade the face or front of a building.

fanlight a fan-shaped window over a doorway.

Federal an American classical revival style of architecture concurrent with the early days of the Republic.

fenestration the placement of windows in a facade.

frieze a horizontal band underneath the cornice, sometimes decorated with sculptural relief.

gable the portion of a wall under a pitched roof.

Georgian a style of classical revival architecture typically characterized by a central portion and two wings joined to the main building by hyphens. Popular in colonial America, it takes its name from England during the reign of the Georges.

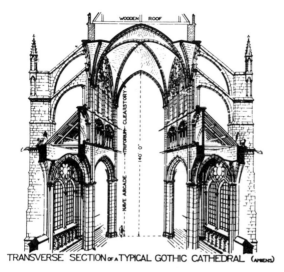

TRANSVERSE SECTION of a TYPICAL GOTHIC CATHEDRAL (AMIENS)

Gothic Revival probably the most common Victorian style, which began in this country at the beginning of the nineteenth century but flowered in the 1840s and later. There were many manifestations, from country parish Gothic to Tudor (see drawing St. John's College page 300); High Victorian Gothic (with much embellishment); the Stick style; and late Gothic when it was used for college buildings and churches in the early 1900s. Its features were the pointed arch, gables, window tracery, and steeples on churches and towers, turrets, and gingerbread on houses. Early Gothic revival was English in inspiration; High Victorian included Italian, German, and French elements and the use of polychrome materials; late Gothic revival was simpler, smoother, and more monochromatic. (see drawing).

header cross member in a series of beams or, in masonry construction, a stone or brick faced endwise rather than sideways in the surface of a wall.

half-timber a method of construction used in England and France in the 1500s and 1600s in which the spaces between heavy timber beams were filled with brick or plaster, leaving the wood exposed.

GATEWAY
S. JOHN'S COLLEGE : CAMBS

International a style of simplicity, angularity, and lack of ornamentation, featuring smooth surfaces and modern materials. It was developed in Germany in the 1920s by Walter Gropius and others and brought to America in the following decade. The buildings of Mies van der Rohe, while differing in some aspects from the early International style, are today thought to be this country's most characteristic examples of its purity and beauty achieved through careful attention to detail and proportion rather than embellishment.

Ionic one of the classical orders, with scrolled capitals. (see drawing).

Italianate the Italian Villa style, popular in the mid-nineteenth century, most often used for domestic buildings.

300

It is characterized by short, heavy towers, wide cornices, an asymmetrical plan, round-headed and sometimes hooded windows, bay windows, and usually a veranda or loggia.

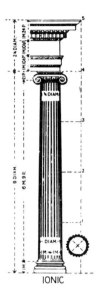

IONIC

lantern a small tower crowning a dome, usually with windows in its side walls.

lintel a horizontal beam resting on two posts for example, over a window. (see drawing page 306).

load-bearing wall an exterior wall into which the beams supporting the floors have been fixed, thereby bearing the load of the building. It is inefficient for high-rise structures, hence the development of the steel frame, which carries the floor load and the exterior curtain wall. (cf. curtain wall, see drawing page 296).

loggia a gallery.

Mannerist an architectural style that was an outgrowth of the Renaissance and forerunner of the Baroque, characterized by elaborate, highly individual, and even eccentric versions of classical styles.

mansard roof a roof with two planes, the lower being the steeper; named for Francois Mansart, a French architect (1598-1666).

modillion a small bracket, usually used in series to support a cornice.

molding a decorative band affecting a transition between two plane surfaces on the exterior of a building or between wall and ceiling inside.

mullion the vertical division between the panes of a window (the horizontal division is called a muntin).

narthex the entrance vestibule of a church.

nave the part of the church along its main axis (not including the transepts) where the worshippers gather.

Neo-classical see Classical Revival.

THE BASILICA : VICENZA

oriel a bay window on an upper floor.

order in classical architecture, the column and its entablature.

Palladian Motif an arched opening in a wall supported by columns and flanked by narrow, square-topped openings the same height as the columns. In series, pilasters or attached columns are used between the openings. (see drawing).

Palladio one of the greatest architects of all time, Andrea Palladio (1508-1580), lived and worked in Vicenza, Venice, and the area of northeastern Italy known as the Veneto. Beginning in the Mannerist period he made a careful study of classical models and developed a style that combined both Renaissance and classical inspiration in forms suited to the conditions of his time. His most influential form was the five-part country villa, with a central block flanked by straight or curving hyphens joining it to wings on either end. His buildings and his principles, delineated in his *Four Books of Architecture*, were introduced to England in the seventeenth century by Inigo Jones and became the basis for Georgian and later for much American colonial architecture.

parapet a low wall at the edge of a roof.

pediment the triangular face of a roof gable. In classical architecture, it was used over a portico; in classical revival styles, it is generally found over doorways or windows.

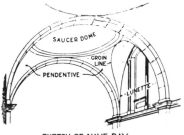

SKETCH OF NAVE BAY

pendentive a triangular segment of curved vaulting used to effect a structural transition from the corner of a square or polygonal room to a dome above (see drawing.)

Picturesque a style originating in northern Europe that incorporated classical elements into Gothic buildings.

pier a column of masonry.

pilaster an attached pier of shallow depth.

porte-cochere a sheltered area accommodating vehicles in front of the entrance to a building.

portico an entrance porch.

post tensioned concrete a method of reinforcing concrete, which has great compressive but little tensile strength,

303

by embedding steel rods and tightening them after the concrete has hardened.

pre stressed concrete concrete that has been strengthened by the use of steel rods under tension; one method is post tensioning.

N.E. PORTAL : BAMBERG.

Queen Anne a style popularized by the English architect Richard Norman Shaw. Its features are an irregular plan, a variety of surface materials, and large gables and turrets. It was enthusiastically embraced by American architects from about 1870 to 1890. Half-timbering effects and the four-centered arch were also commonly used.

quoins the stones at the corner of a wall given emphasis by special cutting, size, texture or joints.

Regency French and English architectural styles of the late eighteenth and early nineteenth centuries characterized by a refined classicism.

Renaissance a style of architecture representing a rebirth of classical forms and a revolt against medieval ones. It originated in Italy in the fifteenth century. Renaissance architecture is a generic term covering widely different styles found throughout Europe and the Americas up to the nineteenth century.

Richardsonian Romanesque referring to H. H. Richardson, generally regarded as the first American architect who endeavored to create a truly American style. His buildings, drawing on Romanesque and other models, had great mass and strength, with deep windows, huge arches (often called Syrian), frequently rough-cut stone, and a general feeling of simplicity and weight.

Romanesque various styles of pre-Gothic European architecture, based on Roman forms. A thick stone doorway formed by a series of receding arches is typical of the style. (see drawing).

rustication pronounced masonry bands that form a pattern. (see drawing).

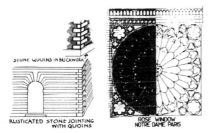

STONE QUOINS IN BRICKWORK

RUSTICATED STONE JOINTING
WITH QUOINS

ROSE WINDOW
NOTRE DAME, PARIS

Second Empire a style that came from the French Second Empire, 1852-1870, and was much in vogue in the United States between 1860 and 1890. The mansard roof is its most characteristic element; its silhouette is generally tall, with chimneys and dormers.

side-aisle the aisle of a church, parallel to the nave, between the supporting columns and the outside wall.

spandrel the wall panel between adjoining columns that separates the windows on one floor from those on the floor above; also the surface between two arches in an arcade or between the adjacent ribs of a vault.

Sullivanesque named for Louis Sullivan and popular around the turn of the century. Buildings in this style are highrises with vertical piers—separating the windows—that rise almost to the top where they are often linked by arches; strong, projecting cornices; and a profusion of the quasi-Art Nouveau decoration developed by Sullivan.

terra-cotta an ancient material consisting of cast and fired clay, used extensively in early high-rise construction in the United States. Its fireproof qualities made it valuable structurally, and since it could be molded and carved, it was often used decoratively as well.

tracery the curving mullions of a stone window, as in Gothic architecture. (see drawing page 305).

transept the lateral arms of a church with a cruciform plan.

truss an assembly of timber, iron, or steel beams that acts as a rigid unit and is generally used to support a bridge or roof.

    Bollman truss one of the earliest iron truss types in America (see [107]), named for Wendel Bollman, its inventor, an engineer with the Baltimore and Ohio Railroad.

    Vierendeel truss invented in 1896 by the Belgian engineer Arthur Vierendeel for short-span bridges.

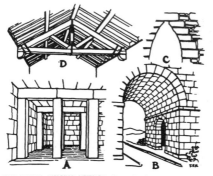

FOUR TYPICAL BUILDING METHODS. (Drawn by the author.) A. POST-AND-LINTEL. B. ARCH AND VAULT. C. CORBEL OR CANTILEVER. D. TRUSS.

vault a roof of arched masonry. (see drawings).

    barrel vault a semicircular vault that resembles a continuous arch.

    fan vault a feature of the English Perpendicular Gothic style in which a group of ribs spring from a shaft or corbel and then diverge.

    groined vault two vaults that intersect at a 90 degree angle.

FAN VAULT
CLOISTERS. GLOUCESTER CATHEDRAL

GROINED VAULT: CANTERBURY CRYPT

water table a projecting base course, sloping inward at the top, to prevent rain water from running straight down the wall.

Index of Structures

Note: The numbers in parentheses are building numbers; the others are page numbers. Only existing structures included on tours are listed in this index.

Index of Structures by Type

Note: Numbers included here are building numbers; to find page numbers, refer to index of structures (alphabetical). As closely as possible, buildings have been listed according to their original use; thus, Mount Royal Station is now part of a college, but is listed under commercial-industrial buildings, as it was originally a railroad station.

Residental

316

Bridges

Monuments

Education and Related Use

Miscellaneous

Index of Architects, Architectural Firms, Engineers, Planners

Note: In some cases an architect's name will appear only under the firm's name; that is because the name never appears in the text except in association with the firm. All numbers are page numbers.

323

Picture Credits

Archives of the Archdiocese of Baltimore: 37 (top)

B. & O. Transportation Museum: 162, 163

Bodine, A. Aubrey: 8, 27, 37 (bottom), 53, 54, 58 (top), 59, 102, 109, 113, 128, 137, 164, 179, 181, 205, 207, 211 (top), 213 (top & bottom), 215, 236 (top), 249, 261 (top)

Bodine, A. Aubrey Collection, the Peale Museum: 6, 19, 25, 35, 44, 74, 89, 105, 107, 112, 114, 122, 143, 150, 180, 194, 203, 214, 216, 225

Eaton, Jon-Eric: 13, 38, 45, 64, 69, 70, 73, 82, 83, 84 (bottom), 88, 90, 93, 94, 97, 100, 117, 126, 131, 136, 139, 140 (top), 147, 153, 154, 160 (top), 174 (top), 176, 191, 192, 212, 217, 221, 223 (top), 226, 240 (bottom), 241

Engineering Society, The: 24

First Presbyterian Church: XXXII

Fletcher, Sir Banister: 295, 297, 299, 300, 301, 302, 303, 304, 305 (right), 307

Franklin Street Presbyterian Church: XXIV, 34

Frederick, George A.: 87

George, Robert V.: 169 (top)

Grieves, James, Associates: 12

Hamilton, William C.: 170, 172

Hamlin, Talbot, "Architecture Through the Ages": 296, 306

Howland and Spencer, "The Architecture of Baltimore": 169 (bottom), 204 (bottom)

Hungerford, Edward: XXVII

Iglehart, Susan: 23, 29, 32 (bottom), 42, 65, 66, 67 (top & bottom), 75, 79, 81, 84 (top), 85, 98, 99, 110, 123 (bottom), 135, 144, 149, 152, 160 (bottom), 161, 178, 182, 188 (top & bottom), 190 (top & bottom), 201, 204 (top), 222, 223 (bottom), 227, 235, 242 (top), 244, 246, 247, 252, 266

Johansen, John M.: 60

Klender, William L.: The *Sun* Magazine; 185

Lautman, Robert: 61

McGrath, Norman: 251

Maryland Historical Society: XVIII

McElhinney, Susan T.: 9, 10, 11, 14, 16, 20, 26, 28, 32 (top), 36, 39, 41, 43, 46, 55 (top & bottom), 62, 76, 77, 78, 95, 96, 101, 106, 108, 115, 116, 121, 123 (top), 125, 138, 140 (bottom), 151, 174 (bottom), 177, 184, 206, 234 (bottom), 237, 238 (bottom), 242 (bottom), 243, 253, 254, 255, 257, 258, 264 (top & bottom), 267

Molitor, Joseph W.: 256

A Monograph of the Work of McKim, Mead & White: 171

Morrison, Hugh, "Early American Architecture": 294

Nes, Campbell & Partners (Blakeslee Lane): 173

The Peale Museum: 21, 250

Pennsylvania Historical Society: XXIII

Raedeke, Paul T.: 15, 17, 18, 22, 40, 120, 127, 130, 142, 156, 159 (top & bottom), 183, 186, 187, 189, 193, 195, 210, 211 (bottom), 228, 234 (top), 236 (bottom), 238 (top), 240 (top), 259

Saylor, Henry H.: "A Dictionary of Architecture": 298, 305 (left)

The Star-Spangled Banner Flag House: 111

Suter, Duane: 56, 175, 263

Unitarian Church (Peale Museum): 33

About The Authors

A lover of his native city, John Dorsey lives in its old Bolton Hill section. He graduated from Harvard in 1962 and since then has been writing feature articles on cultural subjects for *The Sunday Sun* where he is now an editor. In 1974 he won the first A. D. Emmart Memorial award for "journalism in the field of the humanities published in Maryland." A lecturer on history and architecture at Goucher College, the Walters Art Gallery, and the Baltimore Museum of Art, Mr. Dorsey periodically travels abroad to enjoy European art and architecture. An admirer and student of H. L. Mencken, Mr. Dorsey recently edited *On Mencken*, a volume of pieces about the former Baltimore newspaperman and literary critic, published by Alfred A. Knopf in 1980.

James D. Dilts, a free-lance journalist, is currently researching a history of the Baltimore and Ohio Railroad. A former prize-winning feature writer and urban affairs reporter for the Baltimore Sunpapers, and a jazz enthusiast, his articles and reviews have also appeared in *Downbeat, The Washington Monthly, Mass Transit,* and other magazines. A 1962 graduate of Northwestern University, he is the former editor of the official publication of the Baltimore chapter of the American Institute of Architects. Mr. Dilts has lectured at local colleges and universities on Baltimore's architecture and transportation development. He is the associate producer of "Jazz Hoofer," a recently-released, half-hour documentary film, funded by the Maryland Committee for the Humanities and the National Endowment for the Arts, on Baltimore tap dancer Baby Laurence.